mafioso

THE BLOODY AND COMPELLING HISTORY OF THE MAFIA
FROM ITS BIRTH IN ITALY TO ITS INVASION OF AMERICA
AND PRESENT-DAY GLOBAL INFILTRATION – TOLD BY
AN AUSTRALIAN UNDERCOVER INSIDER

mafioso
COLIN McLAREN

hachette
AUSTRALIA

hachette
AUSTRALIA

Published in Australia and New Zealand in 2022
by Hachette Australia
(an imprint of Hachette Australia Pty Limited)
Gadigal Country, Level 17, 207 Kent Street, Sydney, NSW 2000
www.hachette.com.au

Hachette Australia acknowledges and pays our respects to the past, present and future Traditional Owners and Custodians of Country throughout Australia and recognises the continuation of cultural, spiritual and educational practices of Aboriginal and Torres Strait Islander peoples. Our head office is located on the lands of the Gadigal people of the Eora Nation.

NATIONAL
LIBRARY
OF AUSTRALIA

A catalogue record for this book is available from the National Library of Australia

ISBN: 978 0 7336 4810 6 (paperback)

Cover design by Luke Causby/Blue Cork
Cover photograph of Lucky Luciano in Palermo, 1948, courtesy of Getty Images
Author photo: Craig Sillitoe
Map by MAPgraphics
Typeset in 11.2/14.8 pt Sabon LT Pro by Bookhouse, Sydney
Printed and bound in Australia by McPherson's Printing Group

MIX
Paper from
responsible sources
FSC
www.fsc.org   FSC® C001695

The paper this book is printed on is certified against the Forest Stewardship Council® Standards. McPherson's Printing Group holds FSC® chain of custody certification SA-COC-005379. FSC® promotes environmentally responsible, socially beneficial and economically viable management of the world's forests.

CONTENTS

For Elena Stella,
my head translator and researcher, who
worked tirelessly for three long years

Tu sei una grande Palermitana

'. . . the Mafiosi is by no means unbeatable. It's
a human act, and as with all human acts it has a
beginning, an evolution and it will have its end . . .'

Investigative Judge Giovanni Falcone of
the Anti-Mafia Pool, Palermo, 1989

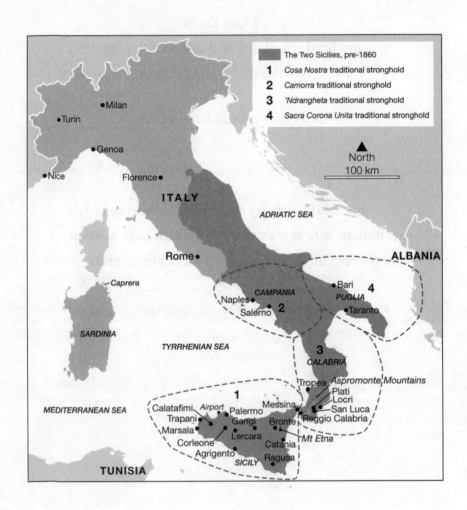

The Two Sicilies, pre-1860

1 *Cosa Nostra* traditional stronghold
2 *Camorra* traditional stronghold
3 *'Ndrangheta* traditional stronghold
4 *Sacra Corona Unita* traditional stronghold

North
100 km

Milan
Turin
Genoa
Nice
Florence

ITALY

ADRIATIC SEA

Rome

ALBANIA

Caprera

Bari
CAMPANIA
Naples
Salerno
2
PUGLIA
Taranto
4

SARDINIA

TYRRHENIAN SEA

3
CALABRIA

MEDITERRANEAN SEA

Tropea
Aspromonte Mountains
Plati
Locri
San Luca
Reggio Calabria

Calatafimi Airport
Trapani
Marsala
Corleone
Agrigento
Palermo
Gangi
Lercara
Catania
Ragusa
Bronte
Messina
1

SICILY

TUNISIA

PREFACE

As Jean Cocteau, poet and playwright, once said, 'What is history after all? History is made of events that end up becoming legends and legends, lies and falsities end up becoming history.' Educated Italians know that their history harbours secrets. Just how many, a lot of people don't actually care to know. However, Colin McLaren aches to find out, as sometimes foreign eyes end up seeing more clearly. It's what he finds that is the power of his book.

In the history of the unification of Italy there are indeed legends, and many stories revolve around Sicily, the beautiful and cursed land that has given birth to writers, politicians, thinkers and also the Mafia. The birth of the Mafia phenomenon is also wrapped up in legends and truths lost in time and historical interpretations. Garibaldi too paid the *pizzo* through 'mafia' *picciotti* as the author consolidates the historical revisionism that has Garibaldi – Italy's revolutionary hero – and his 'thousand men' conquering Sicily. And explains how history is tainted with the seeds of a young and embryonic Mafia phenomenon, something that Italians struggle to accept.

Historical critical revisions lead to questioning a lot about Sicily and its earlier inner workings, including the Mafia. But what is the Mafia? And how, when and why was it born? This book starts precisely from these questions. One of the fascinations about McLaren's book is his long journey: a fearless undercover agent in Australia who embedded himself into the Mafia with a view to not only stop them but also understand them. His journey takes him beyond Australia to get an even deeper understanding. Chasing the myth of what the Mafia is takes him far away – further even than Calabria, the region where most *mafiosi* in Australia come from – directly to the seat of the myth, Sicily. McLaren encounters the unification's half-baked truths and lies and brings them to his reader unapologetically.

McLaren confirms some of the academic thinking on the Mafia, such as the Americanisation of the phenomenon and the creation of the legend around the words Godfather and Mafia. He adds to it with archival research and his 'cop intellect'. His narrative is compelling, with stories that few Italians know, and many mob-watchers would not like. Eventually, in between Sicilian trips and real gems found in archives for the first time, this book asks the reader to reexamine the very core of its own initial question.

Does it matter what the Mafia is? Does it matter to know when and how it originated? Now that the myth is fully formed and enduring, what matters is that we take away its power. It's not the Mafia as much as it is the Mafia method, of intimidation, fear, violence, usurpation. It's not Sicily or Calabria, nor New York, as much as it can be the entire world.

Through McLaren's text we find the real value of grounded research: to go far beyond it and find new purpose and definition in knowledge itself.

Dr Anna Sergi
Associate Professor
Senior Lecturer, Criminology & Mafia Studies
University of Essex, England

MY JOURNEY BEGINS

SICILIAN SAYING:

A moddu cu tutti li robbi
In the water with all the clothes

Meaning, you are in trouble, in deep water,
with all your clothes on

It was the opposite of a joy flight. For the past three days, I'd been in the air dodging radar from one end of Australia – Melbourne, in the south – to the northern tip of Cape York and the mosquito-infested jungles of Queensland, a bee's-dick away from the equator. This remote peninsula is all about sweltering heat, crocodiles, and dingoes hunting wild buffalo in swamps. The company I was in and the humidity had me nauseous. The locals think this is God's country. Let me correct that nonsense, it's the country-for-no-men; it felt like I was in deep water with my clothes on, swimming with the Mafia.

I looked down, 5000 feet below, and saw the last of Australia's territory. White-capped, vivid blue waves crashed against sand dunes the size of a block of flats; it was so divine my breath was lost for the second time that day. I was in the back seat of a rented Piper Navajo Chieftain airplane, whose engines had been running too long. It flew like a bullet, and I knew there were a few real ones on board. Some of them were inside my tiny .32 calibre pistol, stashed away among the foam innards of the seat, just in case I needed to reach for the weapon quick. I guessed there were another three weapons nearby.

I'd left my home town of Melbourne three sleeps back to get this far: nowhere. We call it the never-never, which means you should never go there as you may never come back; it's where the Mafia grow their massive cannabis crops, undetected.

At the start of my plane trip it was just me and the pilot, as we leapfrogged up the eastern seaboard to outback towns, chasing fuel and keeping out of the way of prying air-traffic controllers. We cut over the Great Barrier Reef to spend the night with cane toads the size of Volkswagens. Then it was on to Cairns, the capital of the tropics, where lobster is served in buckets by uber-rich fishermen who can't look you in the eye.

The next day I met the owners of the other three guns, my Mafia friends. We'd been in business for nearly two years. They jumped aboard as we refuelled, before the pilot recommenced the flight north. That was daybreak, and there'd been some serious body odour since.

What was I doing on this tiny plane, in one of the most remote locations on the planet? I'd been asking myself this question since we'd collected these non-smiling, always-smoking dudes. Since I'd felt the weight of their weaponry in their carry-ons. I was an undercover cop who'd infiltrated the Mafia and was now fat in the middle of a massive drug-importation sting – millions of dollars of skunk-weed cannabis grown in New Guinea, so potent it causes hallucinations and makes the Mafia filthy rich.

Two years earlier, I'd been asked by my police commissioner to attempt a long-term undercover infiltration of the Sergi–Trimboli–Perre clan of the Australian Mafia. I was a detective assigned to the National Crime Authority, which was the premier law enforcement agency, and I'd stumbled on to an informer, an associate of the Mafia, who wanted to cut a deal. So, I got myself an introduction to the Mob and slowly climbed their treacherous ladder until I found myself in this aircraft, conspiring to import millions of dollars of drugs. I'd convinced my Mafia dudes that I was a dodgy art dealer, able to launder money and sell vast amounts of cocaine and skunk weed to my rich and famous clients. A watertight cover story that my crew of covert detectives worked months on developing. The litmus test of my acceptance into the scourge after a year of working my way up the ladder was having dinner with the Godfather, then cocktails after, and, as if a reward for my perseverance, we shared a hot tub with a couple of beauties who wanted to be movie stars. From there, it was all crime, conspiracies and – unbeknown to my targets – covert tapes, around-the-clock surveillance, satellite eavesdropping, phone taps and evidence-gathering for the biggest sting in our history. Equal to anything attempted worldwide.

My no-expenses-spared flight to the tropics was close to the home run of this nerve-racking gig where, for anyone who knew me, I disappeared off the face of the earth, to see no one until I got the job done.

I'll never forget the day the Godfather embraced me. Antonio invited me for a stroll through his orange grove on his farm property, far from any big city or law enforcement office. The sun warmed our backs and I allowed Antonio to play host. My tape was on and the satellite picked up our every word. Antonio walked with confidence, giving an occasional glance towards his fruit trees. He was wearing Italian jeans, soft calf-leather shoes, and a brilliant white Versace shirt, pressed to impress. He had the classic Italian style, as well as the charm. We were the same age, nudging forty.

Antonio had recently been anointed top dog: head of the Mafia in Australia. He was on a path of growth, willing to embrace new ideas and discover innovative ways of making money, fast. His 'family' was assessing his every move, as was the now-retired patriarch who'd been at the helm for more than twenty cunning, murderous years. The baton had changed hands.

'You like our ways, Cole,' Antonio said, handing me an orange as he peeled his own.

'Always have, since I was a boy.'

'You know the Italian life well.'

'It's the family ways that work for me,' I replied, enjoying my fruit.

'Why do you feel for family so much?'

Antonio stopped walking. Throwing his peel onto the ground and taking a bite of his juicy orange, he waited for my answer. He looked neither at me nor his fruit. The sun hit his face and he squinted.

'My road has been different from yours, Antonio. I have always wanted this.'

'Your road has been hard?' he asked.

'You could say that.' I thought of the frustrations of law enforcement.

'Don't ever make our road hard, Cole ... ever,' Antonio said, as he shifted his penetrating gaze to me. He finished his orange before wiping his hands on a clean white handkerchief. As we strolled back to the crowd, all Mafia, he placed his hand on my shoulder and spoke his final word on the subject: '*Ever.*'

I accepted his words as we wandered back, smiling, to the collection of rich Italian men, women and children mingling in a special day of sausage-making and barbecue. Antonio moved between his guests, all family except me, the lone, white Australian, a long way from home. They spoke their Italian dialect often that afternoon, the perfect way for them to converse without me understanding. I sensed the occasional sideways glance from the bewhiskered men; Antonio was seeking comment from his clan. I felt like I was back in school, being assessed for an exam. I had studied my subject well and wanted desperately to pass.

As I mingled, I saw that each glance I caught was accompanied by the faintest smile. More like a grimace, as each Italian gave me some thought. I liked that, then realised as I filled the wine glasses of many outreached hands that my invitation to their sausage-making day was merely a ruse. Of course it was. Really in play was my membership of the Australian Mafia. Or not. I was useful to them; they needed to launder money, and to sell pure cocaine, and I fitted as one piece in their global puzzle.

At the end of our day, Antonio made sure I left the farm laden with wine, trays of sausages and boxes of oranges. As I walked to my car, fresh-faced kids with peppermint smiles held my hand. Antonio opened the car door for me, whispering, 'Welcome to our family, Cole Goodwin. Let's do business.'

It was the 1990s, a time when it was commonplace for the Mafia, globally, to blow up police stations, judges and witnesses who got in their way. Murder was their mantra. In Australia, I watched the killings, and thought time and again it would never happen to me. Then, all of a sudden, my life changed.

I was flying through the tropics with my three mobster friends when I got the news that caused me to lose my breath for the first time that day: my NCA headquarters had just exploded, the result of a Mafia bomb, killing and maiming as the office was blown to smithereens. It made world news and completely rattled me, just moments before I opened the door to the fuselage and welcomed the Mafia on board, feeling the weight in their carry-ons.

I recalled the deepest sense of horror, as I came to terms with the fact that the Australian version of the crime scourge was just as ruth-less and dangerous as the Sicilian and the American. And here I was, about to climb into the clouds with men who blow up law enforcement buildings. I was trapped. My passengers were linked to the bastards who had sent the bomb, and they were smiling, showing me the front page of their newspapers: a newsflash of how the parcel bomb exploded covering bodies in red phosphorus, the stuff of match heads, burning and spitting flames in an act of carnage rarely seen anywhere. As the law enforcement world fell into shock, so did I.

But I was supposed to be a gangster, so all I could do was return the smile, masquerading as a death wish as I imagined phosphorus over my own body, burning me alive. Then I did what my training demanded, deflected my horror and got on with business. I had to; there were dozens of surveillance eyes on me in satellites, watching, sweating my every move, and secret lenses and microphones hidden everywhere.

In my one thousand days undercover it had been a constant play of strategies, each one designed to get me a step further, a few inches closer to my goal. Like moving pawns around a chessboard, I would try to be a move ahead of the king or rooks in the game, the Godfather, or the *capi* – the management who ran the day-to-day affairs. I was acutely aware that I was the only white Australian in the game, and should the proverbial shit hit the fan, I was the first person who would be looked at as the odd one out. The Skippy. The Aussie. The one with art brochures, not guns.

My Mafia contacts were no fools. Initially, as they entertained me, they were careful never to get too close to me. Later, after the walk in the orange grove with Antonio, all that changed. They saw great promise in me, with my willingness to launder dirty money. However, they took their time. Nothing comes quick in the Mafia, not even death. Most of the big decisions needed to be discussed, over and over. Talk is everything in the Mafia, so much so it can drive a task force crazy with the endless chatter in various dialects. Luckily, there was one man I owed my life to: my carefully chosen translator, Enzo, assigned to me by the anti-Mafia office in Rome. He spoke many Italian dialects and was an expert at pulling translations together quickly. Each time I was in the field, talking about drugs, murders and conspiracies, Enzo would listen in live. Should the Mafia make a comment in dialect about me or against me, he would hear it instantly and relay it back to me by cellphone codes. He was truly my ears with the Mafia, whenever I was not privy to their secrets. He was the one who listened to my targets' phone calls and ascertained that my hotel room was bugged, so my 'friends' could secretly assess me. He listened to them snooping into my bank accounts, and, in the early days, breaking into my apartment when I was out of town to check me out. Enzo worked around the clock, often sleeping at his desk so he could hear every word in order to keep me safe.

Within months I was buying ninety-six per cent pure cocaine in compressed rocks the size of footballs, worth a million dollars on the street. The business opportunities rolled on. One day the Mafia men drove into Melbourne, a city of five million people, and asked to meet me on the outskirts. They had a truckload of cannabis they wanted me to sell, worth millions. It was all mine! Another time they met me down a dark laneway and handed over ten huge garbage bags filled with drugs, which I purchased with unmarked bills straight out of the reserve holdings of the police department bank account. Another time they spotted me a kilo of cocaine on credit, to splash around my contacts and generate bigger orders. Then there was a conspiracy to import a hundred-kilo shipment of cocaine from Colombia. And on it went. Meetings loaded with numbers: $4000 a pound, $185000 a kilo, 200 kilos of this, ten-pound lots, a tonne of that, kilos of coke, three weeks before it lands, twenty hours before delivery ... on and on. Then there were the names to recall, as many as nine *mafiosi* in the room at a time: Pasquale, Antonio, Rosario, Dominic, Sergio, Rocco, Giovanni ... blah, blah, blah. In the end, my mind was a mess of numbers and names, and my body was like a used dishrag, exhausted; it was the perfect weight loss program. Then, one sleepless morning, I woke up in a sweat and realised I was a *mafioso*.

A few months after my joy flight to the tropics, as if an alarm went off to remind me it was time to come home, come back to normality, my covert house of cards came crumbling down, and my career as an art dealer ended. It was time to claim our targets, lock up our Mafia friends. With my life and sanity still intact, every police department in Australia was gathered to implement over a hundred raids across the country, ending the criminal careers of dozens of *mafiosi* and filling high-security prisons to the brim in three states. My targets and (now) ex-'friends' were all gifted an unwanted holiday in prison.

Such was my life in the Mafia ...

PART ONE

Writing history

CHAPTER 1
RUST BUCKET

SICILIAN SAYING:
Cu ti ci porta?
Who takes you there?

Used when you wonder why a person does such a silly thing

I was perched on a rust-bucket passenger ferry that chugs back and forth between the poverty-stricken port of Villa San Giovanni, Calabria, and the port of Messina on the island of Sicily. Relics from a slower era, these vessels work the murky waters, connecting the deep south to the long, svelte leg of Italy. They all look the same, painted deep ocean-blue and white, and wafting diesel fumes. I had found the ideal vantage point on the uppermost deck and was making short work of an *arancino*, a sticky Arborio rice ball.

The ferry made headway under a glorious heat haze from a scorching Mediterranean sun. Across Messina Strait, I could see the enigmatic island of Sicily. Sitting under a cloudless blue sky, it enticed me, like the backdrop to a snow-dome scene, teasing me to step ashore.

I pondered its majesty and imagined fragments of history that have shaped this land and its island people. Strategically located, it has witnessed the changing fortunes of a great many kingdoms. My mind's eye visualised the regimented Norman era with its impressive, circular stone forts that still dominate the coastline. I spared a thought for the bloodthirsty Greeks, scrambling off timber-hulled boats 3000 years earlier, planting grapevines and erecting their imposing temples to make their mark. So much history!

Located just off the 'toe' of Italy's 'boot', Sicily is the second-largest island in the Mediterranean archipelago. After twenty-one invasions, it stands defiant, even in the face of more treachery than the Elizabethan court. It has more dialects than the rest of Italy combined. What you see, however, is a withered land of granite mountains that seem to reach, painfully, for the heavens. The scrappy terrain is dotted with villages and Baroque cities, presided over by a volcano that won't sleep. Like its inhabitants, Mount Etna spits its anger often. Encircling this picture postcard are turquoise beaches, edging onto sunburnt soils carpeted in olives, with an Australian influence: eucalypt trees, imported a hundred years earlier in a failed attempt to stop soil erosion. In time, everything erodes in Sicily. I had arrived from my homeland to step into the sun and soak up some much-needed warmth. But I was also on a mission.

For years, since I left the life of a cop, I have been drawn to Sicily. I put aside what I'd experienced as an undercover cop and went in search of *casalinga* cooking, lime-washed villas, world-class wines and a rich sense of community.

For me, eating in Sicily is one of life's most idyllic experiences. Walking into your favourite *gelateria*, for example, and slurping down a massive dollop of gelato *fior di latte* smacked into a freshly broken brioche is unforgettable. Culinary utopia comes in many forms in Sicily. But, on this day, I just wanted to get off this rust bucket, back onto terra firma, and go on with my journey.

Messina is a big, brash, sometimes dark city, with never-to-be-spoken-about memories of the crime wars of the 1970s. Like so many others, it is just another town hiding its scars. Having suffered a devastating earthquake in 1908 that ruined ninety per cent of the city, the rebuilding program was waylaid due to the Mafia fleecing the repair money. But Messina is not alone when it comes to the Mafia: a disease, a plague, a criminal revolution and a way of life that encapsulates, violates and rapes all that is good in Italy, before stretching its slimy, suckered tentacles all over Europe. Then, without resistance, it embarked on an Atlantic crossing, surfacing, bigger and nastier than ever, to capture the Americas and the world.

The scourge has left an indelible mark, like a tattoo; its influence on Sicily will, it seems, never be erased. The Mafia's staple diet of standover tactics has flattened the enthusiasm of local businesses and their workers. I could only imagine the hurt that many have suffered, the losses that will never be recouped, and the fear of speaking out. Not forgetting the sideways glances locals get from affluent tourists. Everyone in Sicily has been looked upon, at least once in their lives, as a potential Mafia member, a relative or acquaintance of, a next-door neighbour to, or someone employed in a business that might be. The tough reality of living in the south of Italy.

The clanging of metal chains and idling motors below deck told me Messina was upon us. Within minutes our ferry kissed the tired wharf, jolting the metal beast to a stop. The ferry staff, an unshaven, swollen-bellied lot, all chewing pistachio nuts, lassoed the gigantic ropes to the pier joists. The drawbridge dropped, a signal for my real journey to commence. The purpose of which was more earnest on this occasion. This time I had come to Sicily chasing a far tastier morsel. I'd come to understand how the Mafia found its way onto the cultural table. *La Cosa Nostra*. And how it got to America and everywhere else.

As both a practitioner and student of the Mafia, and having jailed thugs who were a part of it, I had a long-held desire to answer one question: When was the Mafia born? My years undercover gave me an insatiable itch to know the origins of this gang of bad men. Though I had read avidly about the Mafia, from books that mostly sent me to sleep, I was always dissatisfied with the story of its creation and growth. Usually written by historians, academics or authors taking a stab at telling their tale, the books were often repetitious and rarely went back further than the Prohibition days. The origins, I thought, must go deeper than that. Surely, Al Capone didn't just wake up one day in 1925 and open a speakeasy with a gang of Mafia mobsters!

While undercover, I learnt about their tenacity in getting ordinary people to do extraordinarily bad things. I knew them to blow the leg off a suspected snitch (informer), by holding him down like a lamb to the slaughter, and placing a shotgun behind a kneecap before pulling the trigger, then leaving him to bleed out. Also, to shoot dead thugs they believed had ratted them out. And dumping their bodies to become fly blown in the outback. I met a hitman, imported from Italy to find a rodent in the organisation, trying to locate a weakness within the ranks (he never suspected it was me). The Mafia hate snitches more than anything else; they call such a person a *pentito*, a *mafioso* who is a police informer. I once tried to gain verbal evidence from my 'friends' after they had murdered a brave anti-drugs campaigner; just snatched him off the street, shot him dead, never to be seen again. I learnt how they applied pressure to innocent Italian immigrants, conned them into having their migration sponsored by the Mafia. Once they were in Australia, the Mafia called in the dirty favours.

I was fortunate to be able to walk away in the end. I was amazed to have survived my infiltration – despite the death threats – and I could slip back into society. Yet, from that moment, I remained petrified they would cash in their vendetta on me. As I kept on the move, trusting only in my own instincts, from one flophouse to another, ultimately, what followed were the many court cases. Where my 'friends' sat in the dock and stared me down, giving me looks of utter hatred as they listened to my evidence. They watched me standing in the witness box, sweat dripping down the back of my shirt, day after day recalling my con job on them. In these painfully long hearings, I had to tell the truth, the whole truth and nothing but the truth, including how I and my 'friends' would go out on the town, wining and dining, the Italians with their mistresses, naive women attracted to the Mafia. My evidence humiliated the wives sitting in court enough for them to ultimately storm out. It was daunting watching tough men, encaged behind bulletproof glass, glaring at me, day after day. All I could do was fire more evidence at them, hoping they would desist. They never did.

Why didn't they destroy me? At times my 'freedom' would wear me down. Not knowing whether they would, eventually, come for me. Tap me on the shoulder as I walked home after a late-night drink. Detonate a bomb inside my letterbox. Come at me in a crowd. But no. Instead, I would think the worst, every day, every night, for years. Until, one day, ten years after my Mafia 'friends' went to prison, the Godfather at the time, Antonio – the boss I befriended in his orange grove – was released from prison on early parole and travelled back to his home town to reacquaint himself with his mobsters. Trouble was, by then, a new broom had cleaned everything up, and all that was waiting for him was a sniper with a long-range scope. Antonio, the handsome Godfather figure, the man who had shared my dinner table dozens of times, was executed in his orange grove.

That was when it dawned on me. They had been waiting for the release of Antonio. His death was a stronger message to send, internally and globally, than killing an undercover cop. The family was sweeping up the errors of a past decade. From that day, I got it: there was no value in killing an undercover cop and having the might of every police department in the land come crashing down on them, when it was far neater to eliminate the cause of the problem, Antonio. Once I understood their strategy, I would learn to sleep again. Learn to stop seeing my pillow as the enemy. But I would never lose the itch to know more about this gang of men, how this hell came to be. The answer, I thought, might well be a seed hidden deep in the soil of Italy, roots buried far into the culture, and I wanted to try and find it. As I drove my rented Fiat Punto across the drawbridge and entered the streets of Messina, all I could think of was my mission: to find the earliest Mafia.

I headed south, towards Agrigento, which played a major role in the Mafia wars of the 1970s. My idea was to snoop around, ask a few people if they had any insights into when the Mafia started. To keep from exposing my real identity, I told people I was a researcher enquiring into the immigration of Sicilians to Australia. An uncontroversial cover story that no one questioned. I quickly came to see the lack of knowledge among locals about the old Mafia; no one seemed to know. Although I suspect they really did know. There was one reaction I won't forget: the stony, blank stare. This usually came from aged men. I soon learnt it was a look that said they don't want to answer, don't want to offer any information. Not even a smile, just a polite stretch of dry lips. I translated this stare as 'Fuck off'.

I sucked it up as I looked at these angry unshaven men; I had seen the same faces from my Mafia infiltration years earlier looking back at me. Hard Italians. Full of spit and low on compassion. I needed a better plan. Any plan, in fact. I was staying in an old villa, perched on a hill overlooking the Mediterranean coastline on about thirty acres of harsh land. The owner had decided to subsidise his income from his struggling olive plantation by creating a four-roomed bed and breakfast hotel. It had an inground swimming pool, and a kitchen that offered a range of tasty dishes, cooked by his mother, an elegant old lady who had the most personality in her family.

I spent five nights at this sun-bleached hideaway, catching up on my vitamin D and enjoying the *nonna*'s home-style cooking. On the last night, I discovered the *nonna* was a published author and local historian. She told a story that would change the direction of my search. She went into detail about the time of unification, the taking of Sicily by General Garibaldi and how it was ushered into the federation of mainland Italy around 1860. The great Garibaldi sailed into Sicily with a band of followers and marched on Palermo. Her great-great-grandfather, she said, took part in the unification march. He and his brothers downed their farming tools and walked to Marsala to join the Garibaldi volunteers. She went on to explain that her long-dead forebear was promised a slice of land for his trouble, if he stood behind Garibaldi. He did. And, she said, apart from farmers, some of those who gathered with Garibaldi were hardened rural men, tough guys. I realised I was hearing a historical narrative, peppered with facts passed down her family line. I was on the edge of my chair, the antipasto ignored.

I asked if her grandparent received his slice of land. The lady and her son drew smiles then said words at the exact same time, gesturing with their hands towards the floor, 'This is it; you are sitting on it.' I had goose bumps. The villa, I learnt, in which we were seated, the *casa* I was relaxing in, was built on the promised land, gifted by the administrators of Sicily to her great patriarch for his assistance with the unification efforts. On the wall was a framed certificate of the land subdivision and allotment, stamped c. 1862 and in the family name.

While the story of Garibaldi was ideal dinner-table conversation, I wasn't in Sicily to research the ways and victories of a red-shirted general. My interest lay in the black-shirted Mafia, so the next day I tossed my bags into my Fiat and readied to leave. As I fussed over my car, I explained my mission to the *nonna* historian. She whispered in my ear that the only place to find out about the Mafia would be Palermo, the capital of Sicily. However, she doubted I would be successful as the subject is almost never discussed.

A challenge, I thought! And with that I turned my Fiat Punto west towards Palermo with the view of knocking on as many doors as I could, to prove to the old historian that answers could be found in matters of secrecy. I felt a surge of enthusiasm the closer I got to Palermo, buoyed by the story I had been told the night before. The framed land title mounted on the dining room wall had convinced me that the truth in history could still be found.

CHAPTER 2
PALERMO

SICILIAN SAYING (REFERRING TO PALERMO):
La vecchia imbellettata
The embellished old lady

Meaning, the old lady who wears inappropriate clothes for
her age and way too much make-up

(by Luigi Pirandello, Sicilian winner of the Nobel Prize for Literature, 1934)

The first thing you notice about one of the most cultured cities in Europe is the basin-shaped stone mountains that stand guard around its million or so inhabitants. While I had been to Palermo before, I had not really studied it, or looked behind its eighteenth-century facades in the context of a city that might hold secrets. On my first day, I walked the streets of the old lady, noting her finery. She houses, for example, one of the world's great opera houses, the Teatro Massimo, and there's the famed Piazza Politeama, where, like clockwork, *Palermitani* stroll each evening as the sun goes down along the upmarket stores of Via della Libertà.

If Palermo, as suggested by the *nonna* historian, was the keeper of the Mafia secrets, then I needed to immerse myself within her. I needed a quintessential Palermo experience. For that reason, I sought out accommodation in the *centro storico*, historic town centre, where

I could set myself up and not have to imagine what old Palermo might have looked like in the days when the Mafia started.

Even though my relationship with this city – my touch, walk, feel for it – was Palermo in the twenty-first century, I wanted to sense the old town. Though, in reality, the city has not changed much in a hundred years. The horse and cart has been taken over by the Fiat 500, gilded carriages by Maseratis; and dusty streets and city alleyways have given way to cracked concrete highways and footpaths, and so it goes. The places for *passeggiata*, a nightly stroll, were largely unchanged. The street pavements of granite cut from nearby mountains remain and have held their own under the daily foot traffic of locals and a growing army of tourists. Now shiny, almost mirror-slippery, the stone pavements are a talisman of old Palermo.

The pavements also host the stalls of the day-to-day vendors of this always-trading city. Some stalls boast five and six generations at the trestles. Vendors holler their prices in an effort to sell their daily allotment of the ripest tomatoes or juiciest grapes. Bagging fistfuls of produce for the hordes of peasants, working class, and the occasional gentrified folk, all mingling over sun-kissed fruit and vegetables. Then there is the range of meats hanging in the midday sun, from cow to lamb, from goat to who-knows-what, garnished with enough offal to make me turn vegetarian. Well-attired ladies, who a hundred years ago might have swayed through the crowds in an elegant *bella figura* stroll (to be seen), wearing the finest satin and silk fabrics and stitched lace, have been replaced by working mums, just as beautiful, in tight jeans and designer tops. While the elegance may have gone, the sensuality has remained; *donne Palermitane* are as stunning as the *dolci* on offer in their pastry shop windows.

The most recognisable connections between old and new Palermo are the lime-washed facades of the city's apartment buildings, showcasing a rich offering of faded glory and distinctive Sicilian architecture. Within days, I realised this grand city still hummed with the rhythms of a bygone era.

I soon discovered that Villa Lampedusa, setting of Giuseppe Tomasi di Lampedusa's novel *The Leopard*, was taking guests. The barns that featured in the book had been converted into twelve rooms centred around a courtyard. It proved to be the ideal place to park my bones, set up my laptop and blow the dust off my keyboard. Being in this historic villa sparked my writing cylinders and stirred my investigative juices. I recalled reading *The Leopard* when I was a schoolboy; it was a book of swashbuckling adventure, full of pomp and hedonism, with the unification of Sicily as its backdrop. Once my room was secured, the first thing I did was to head to Feltrinelli's bookstore and purchase a fresh copy of the iconic novel. I read it at night, beneath the 600-metre-high rock face of Mount Pellegrino, for many a symbol of Palermo and her defiance.

I scoured the bookstores, hoping for inspiration. There were dozens of titles on the Mafia; however, almost every book was about contemporary *mafiosi*. Few of them would help me. With a day of disappointment behind me, I next hit the antiquarian bookstores. Their offerings were more to my liking: dusty tomes on back shelves, most published decades ago.

By the end of my first week I had a good bed, shocking wi-fi, a knowledge of the transport options in a city that pays no attention to timetables, and way too many books proffering the story of the Mafia. Yet none of those books focused on how and when the scourge began. I came to realise that the reasons behind the inception of the Mafia were probably lost in the collective consciousness of a people who simply did not want to recall. That I could understand, just as for a natural disaster, the horror of recollection can be as bad as the event itself.

I already figured my real source of history could only be in the printed form. Filmmakers over the generations have tended to stick to the Hollywood bullshit-take on the Mafia, stylised films like *The Godfather* trilogy that blur fact and fiction to the point that it is impossible to know what is accurate. Case in point, Michael Corleone – portrayed by Al Pacino – had roots in the town of Corleone, seventy kilometres south of Palermo, and when the law went chasing him for a double murder, he went there and hid. I've been to Corleone and they have no such family there, nor do they identify with Hollywood's take on their so-called favourite son. Indeed, the town of Corleone houses the Anti-Mafia Museum, boasting the real story of the 'contemporary' Mafia, and they scoff at the *Godfather* series. (Anti-Mafia is a commonly used name for those who take a political or social position against the Mafia.) The museum offered a pleasant day away from the toil of sifting through old books. I got to know the staff, who were mostly undergraduate students.

The museum is also home to the whopping prosecution brief of evidence, volumes of paperwork, that was used in the court case against many Mafia thugs, known locally as the Maxi Trial, considered the single greatest victory against *mafiosi*. The museum, however, lacked any depth of information on the organisation. There are no files or records that date back to the start of the scourge.

The museum's story of the Mafia is told through a series of photographs, almost all of them from the Mafia wars of the 1970s through to the early 1990s – large-format pictures of bodies in the street, cars bombed, pitifully poor people standing by. Most had been taken by an extraordinary woman, now in her eighth decade, Letizia Battaglia. She is adored in her homeland, mostly for her life's work of capturing the horror that is the Mafia.

The students conduct tours, giving the story behind each image, as if trying to explain the reason for Letizia taking the shot. The reasons, however, are obvious: documenting shock, horror, sadness and urban decay. And carnage.

I wandered behind the tour groups, of mostly overseas visitors, and listened. At times the information passed on was wrong. I wanted to correct the errors, but it wasn't my place.

One day, I challenged the manager of the museum and explained that the facts offered were, on occasions, incorrect and that, with respect to the many innocent people killed by the scourge, the museum might consider drawing up a script, a narrative, the students could use. That way the stories told would be factually correct. The manager stepped back and gave me that classic Sicilian blank stare, the 'fuck off' look they have perfected. I offered to write the narrative as a goodwill gesture. Still nothing; the guy was as tough as a walnut. I glanced at the exit door behind me and realised it was probably best to retreat.

If I gained anything from visiting the Anti-Mafia Museum it was a burning desire to find out the complete story of the Mafia and to allow that story to be told.

Among my daily delving, I often passed by a cute little shop off the Piazza Politeama called Libera Terra, which means 'free land'. The shop, like the museum, is staffed by students who support a Mafia-free Sicily. It's an expo of produce grown by young Sicilians who have been gifted land once owned by the Mafia. When Mafia gangs get investigated and the police find investments in rural land by their criminal targets, the prosecutor applies for forfeiture of said land by way of the legislation that permits confiscation of profits from crime. Once forfeited, the land is offered by the state to young Sicilians to better themselves through a variety of horticultural projects, such as vineyards, olive groves or beekeeping. Thousands of hectares have been seized and dozens of small farming projects are yielding extraordinary results across Sicily.

One day, browsing the shelves, I started chatting with a woman behind the counter, Gabriella, who, she told me, had a doctorate in Italian history and philosophy. We discussed the struggle Palermo faced, labelled as the global HQ of the Mafia. I told her I was in the early stages of researching my next book and needed information, to which she said, 'We will have the pleasure to help you, please sit down.'

She wrote out a list of *biblioteche*, state-run archival libraries, that house all the documents, files, reports and history of Palermo and Sicily. Her words to me: 'Sicilians never throw out a single piece of paper.' She was convinced that if I applied myself and took the time – many months – I would find the answers I was looking for. She followed up her list with a series of calls to prioritise the best locations to start my search.

The next day I went to my priority-one archive and met the curator. Once I outlined what I was seeking, the woman gave me a faint smile and a chair to sit my weary self on. She would be pleased to help. My forty-four-month journey through the archives was about to begin.

CHAPTER 3
ARCHIVES

SICILIAN SAYING:

Ogni ficateddu di musca è sustanza
Every part of a fly's liver is food

Meaning, even the smallest things can be useful

Gabriella was right when she proclaimed that Italians never throw out a piece of paper. I would dive into my research and pore over hundreds of dusty old tomes, most dating back generations. I opened and appraised hundreds of documents from a collection of thousands, seeking the smallest gems. There were acres of shelf space. I was aghast at the age of some of the books offered. Some were so frail they dropped specks of paper on my reading desk. Often, I was required to wear soft, white cotton gloves to protect the book or document. I was in a constant state of awe at the knowledge filed away. It was detective heaven, wading through the dust and the centuries, among the wood-panel walls and bowed parquetry floors.

Five main *biblioteche* suited my purpose: Gancia Archivio di Palermo, Istituto Gramsci Siciliano, Archivio di Stato di Palermo, Biblioteca Comunale di Palermo and the Biblioteca Centrale della Regione Siciliana. (The Centro Impastato library was helpful too.) Each place welcomed me, and the staff were wonderful in accepting me and my project. To keep it simple, I just told them that I was interested in early Mafia history due to *mafiosi* migrating to Australia. I learnt the value of working with archival curators, and the importance they placed on research. A curator can make or break a project; a good rapport was essential.

Dealing with curators who spoke a language or dialect foreign to me was a constant challenge. Luckily there were some curators I was able to confide in, some who became treasured contacts I was able to engage with as I navigated the seemingly endless array of documents. To give an idea of the scope of material, four institutions were each about the size of an aircraft hangar. The walls in these old facilities sometimes reached six or seven metres high. The Archivio di Stato di Palermo was purpose-built in 1800, with a ceiling fourteen metres from the ground. Standing inside my selected archive each morning, notebook, pen and white gloves in hand, I felt dwarfed by the room and my task.

Another institute that welcomed me graciously was the Istituto Gramsci Siciliano on the edge of Palermo. The institute is housed in leftover military bunkers from World War II, massive concrete domes once filled with ammunition and firearms from when Benito Mussolini waged war. There are twelve such bunkers. Other bunkers were used by the Arts and Drama Faculty of the nearby university, from where the omnipresent smell of cannabis accompanied my walks in and out of the facility each night.

The archive was in the hands of Enza, a middle-aged curator who spoke little English. Enza and I would communicate by way of hand signals and pantomime for months. Initially sceptical of my project, she warmed up after a few days when she realised I was not going away. She was also a friend of Gabriella and felt committed to my obsession. They both enjoyed the gossip my work brought to their day. Sicilians adore gossip as much as they adore *dolci*.

The first thing Enza did was show me her collection of books on the Mafia, all 702 of them. I counted them. Despite the number of books, few dated from the nineteenth century, and a great many were locked into the twentieth. The few truly old books were written by professors who, in my view, concentrated too much on the social aspects and psychology of the Mafia, with lashing of politics and economics, instead of telling me when and how the organisation started. I also believe university-published books sometimes don't allow all the facts to be flushed out because the research is often undertaken by time-poor students, as part of their required curriculum. With only a small window for research it was no wonder that the questions I sought answers to were not available, whereas I planned to allow myself years.

At Gramsci, many titles dated from the period after Mussolini came to power, when the shadow of Fascism dominated. Historical research and writing, I learnt, suffered a pregnant pause in Italy from around World War I until after World War II. Mussolini, who ruled with Fascist ideology and dictatorial powers from 1922 till 1943, was no friend of the Mafia. In fact, he declared war on them. The subject was taboo during the Fascist period, and therefore research on the Mafia was placed on the back burner for most of the first half of the twentieth century.

It was evident by the dates of the first publications in Gramsci that freedoms were restored in Italy by the 1950s. Writers, academics and researchers could speak their minds again and document the twists and turns of their country, albeit the subject was World War II rather than the Mafia. That is not to say the 702 titles in this institute were worthless; far from it, many offered gold nuggets I could use. I just needed to find them, one book at a time.

Each night, I returned to my room in Villa Lampedusa, tired and with sore eyes, but pleased. Financially able to support myself for as long as the task took, I was more worried about eating well than of running out of time. One evening, I strolled around the corner to a fantastic local trattoria, specialising in the many flavours of *salsicce* – Italian sausage – barbecued and served with the ripest local tomatoes, olive oil and red onions from Tropea in Calabria. This was food for a man, researcher's food, detective food. The smiling owner would have the coldest beer on my table before I even sat down, and in between an antipasto of spring onions rolled with *pancetta* and grilled to perfection, I'd tell him about my day. He only ever knew me as a researcher of immigration. It wasn't long before he allowed me to take over his music selection. I linked him into my Spotify collection, which allowed me to listen to my Italian favourites like

Pino Daniele and Fabio Concato. Life was good, the food delicious, and the people who worked and lived around my villa were kind to the Aussie from Melbourne.

As time marched on and pages turned, the local postgraduate students and professors who used the facility started to warm to my presence. Enza took a while longer, until I came to understand that she had a sweet tooth. Her colleague, Daniele, whispered to me one day to give Enza a *biscotto* and see what happened. The next day, on my way to work, I dropped into my favourite *pasticceria*, and, after two mandatory cups of *espresso macchiato* and a *cornetto* (croissant), I put together a tray of mixed *biscotti*. The tray won Enza over from the moment she untied the pretty ribbon from the wrapping paper, revealing twelve delicious *biscotti*. Each day, as a morning ritual, I walked into the archive with a tray of temptations, and each day Enza and I busied ourselves looking through the hundreds of shelves in search of secrets, dropping crumbs as we worked.

We toiled daily through the complex index system that only a Sicilian could understand: book titles, librarian numbers, codes, dates of publication, and the location of each book, which was invariably wrong. Then, Enza would march off through her maze of shelves and return ten, sometimes twenty, minutes later or more, book in hand and a smile on her face. Sicilian curating is a unique form of archival work. A bit like pin the tail on the donkey, it is largely based on guesswork and memory, a system that may not be accepted in other countries, but it works wonderfully in Palermo.

Before long, Enza introduced me to the photocopier and, after a quick look to her left and right, she played with a few buttons and allocated a hefty credit on to the machine, enough to keep me copying for ages, without cost. She was a real darling, a woman, it appeared to me, in need of a cause. Enza later confided that the Mafia had always scared her as a young woman, and for her to be able to help with such a worthwhile research project made up for her past fears. But she always put a finger to her lips as a gesture of silence should she supply a report or do something out of the ordinary, like the photocopy credit. Sometimes she would hand over a document and, with a half grin on her deeply suntanned face, she would place a pointer finger to her cheek and make the motion of a corkscrew accompanied by a wink – a well-known Sicilian gesture that meant whatever she was handing over was either important or genuine.

Most of what she discovered came about through memory, which got better by the day: a report or a few pages that she recalled filing away years earlier, or something that I might enjoy perusing, often dog-eared or on faded corn-coloured pages. Everything we uncovered seemed to suggest the Mafia was active from the late 1880s onwards; however, we could not find anything to take the subject back any further. We all felt there must be more hidden away, but where?

In among these endeavours and blissfully silent activity, I decided to take a three-day break, quit Palermo and visit nearby Trapani – a seaside town with a few hundred workers who toil in the local salt farms, or work on the many ferries that crisscross the Mediterranean to some of the lesser-known but more intriguing islands. I took a room in a hotel in the centre of town and spent three glorious days in the sun and eateries dotted along the thousand-year-old streets that make up the skinny-finger peninsula on which the old town sits.

Checking out, I struck up a conversation with an obliging older woman who had run the hotel since she was a young woman. The *signora* asked what I was doing in Sicily. I felt safe offering a slim overview of my real cause, the early Mafia. I explained my dilemma that very little had been written before the start of the twentieth century. What she said next made me sit up and take notice; it was something I suspected she rarely told any locals – that her great-great-grandfather was a *bandito*, a bad man, who had helped Garibaldi invade Sicily.

I had heard something similar from the *signora* at the quaint bed and breakfast when I first came to Sicily. Now, here was another woman whose long-dead relative had stood alongside the heroic General Garibaldi. At last, valuable snippets were falling from the lips of locals.

I had just finished *The Leopard* and discovered that the book is set in the time of the Garibaldi expedition to Sicily. The author inserts his fictional characters into the story of Italian unification and Garibaldi's invasion, based on historical fact – to tell the story of a heroic family dodging gangsters, highwaymen prone to theft and murder. Listening to the hotel-keeper's story, all I could think of was Garibaldi.

What was this woman telling me? Folklore? A fascinating slant on history? An old wives' tale? Or perhaps that the great Giuseppe Garibaldi had more help than was written in history books? If what I was hearing was true, who were these hardened rural men? Or, as the hotelier called them, *banditi*?

The next day, back in the Gramsci archive, as Enza was going out of her way to keep me busy, I posed a question to her: Have you ever heard or seen anything that suggested bandits were marching alongside Garibaldi? Enza gave it a moment's thought then gave me the infamous Sicilian blank stare; you know the one. This time, I believed, she truly had no information to pass on, and so we forgot about it.

While my greatest assets were the kindly curators like Enza who never let up, what I needed now was a translator or two. That way, once I found a document that might be a gem I could pass it on for translation to see if my hunch was correct. Enza offered me a list of accredited translators, academics who, for a fee, were willing to wade through my material. Two translators stood out, both hugely supportive and incredibly patient. Agata, a focused 28-year-old with a master's degree in translation, was multilingual and taught English and Italian as well as assisting professors with their research. Six feet tall and blonde, Agata rode a rattly old bicycle everywhere, often with her pooch sitting on the back parcel shelf. The two were a fixture on the streets of Palermo. She was everything a Millennial was meant to be – checking her cellphone every five minutes in case her jealous boyfriend called; stopping and starting her work way too often as she had trouble sitting still; and constantly feeding her dog biscuits as we worked. I found her refreshing, great fun, and tall!

Then there was Elena, somewhat older, and bursting with enthusiasm. Elena was as interested in documenting my search for the Mafia as I was. A local historian, she was teaching pre-university students and taking American academics around the ancient sights of her home city. She constantly amazed me with her knowledge and thirst for more. I spent my days, weeks, months going from one *biblioteca* to another, depending on what I was seeking, and with either Agata or, more often, Elena beside me. The latter was hugely respected everywhere she went; doors would open for her and, consequently, for me.

Often, we would head off to our chosen *biblioteca*, but not before stopping just around the corner in what became our favourite *pasticceria*, Bar Santoro, a fabulous 1950s cafe that baked the finest *dolci* in Palermo. We made a habit of having an Iris, a delectable pastry filled with ricotta cheese and sometimes Nutella. These tasty morsels were made famous after they featured in the brilliant film *The Mafia Kills Only in Summer*.

Like many such projects, too much came at me too quickly. Before long I was swamped, near buried in books. On one occasion, Enza was unable to see me behind a tall pile of books. In time, I slowed down and set a daily schedule of around four hours in a *biblioteca*, before going home and making notes.

One day, I was in the moment, turning pages, highlighting, riddling my notepad with ink, when I heard someone in the aisles of the bookshelves. The sound of rustling pages seemed to become louder before it stopped and Enza appeared. She had been on one of her seek-and-find missions. She then went back into the shelves, rummaging away. As if trying to annoy me, she stepped out of her maze once more and looked at me, exhausted. Her hair was ruffled. I said, 'Have another *biscotto*, Enza, slow down.' She shook her head, and replied, '*Io c'ho qualcosa di ancora piu dolce*' – I have something sweeter. She was smiling broadly as she walked towards me holding a three-page document.

Apparently, the question I had asked her about whether she had ever filed anything away that suggested bandits were marching alongside Garibaldi had stayed in her mind. It transpired that she had thought it over many times and recalled seeing a document, years earlier – the treasured document now in her hands.

She handed it to me knowing I'd be pleased. I looked at the first page, then the second, the third. An article written by a journalist from *L'Unità d'Italia*, a newspaper with an originally working-class readership with communist leanings. Dated 20 June 2010, the article was about the Presidente della Repubblica Italiana, Giorgio Napolitano, and his visit to Marsala, a trading port on the west side of Sicily, just down from Trapani, which I'd visited weeks earlier, the same place where the hotelier had told me about her relative, the *bandito*.

Elena, working alongside me, translated the article, which was headed 'Together with a thousand in Sicily were battling 1000's of *Picciotti*'.[1] What did *picciotti* mean? The article offered a quote from a speech by President Napolitano for the 150th anniversary of the arrival of Garibaldi in Marsala, where the President had given a rousing address to the gathered crowd. There was a picture showing a band playing with nationalistic pomp and ceremony, accompanied by school children and locals in their Sunday best clothing. The President mentioned the extraordinary involvement of Sicilians in the unification of Italy, recalling the departure of Garibaldi and his volunteers in 1860 from Marsala en route to Palermo to take on the ruling Bourbon royal house.

He spoke proudly of the thousand volunteers who helped Garibaldi, and said that without Sicily and the contribution of the Sicilians, it would never have been possible to achieve this victory and give birth to the union of Italy. What contribution? I thought. What Sicilians? Garibaldi was meant to be at the head of a thousand volunteers from the mainland. I read on. The invasion had been prepped by a gathering of Sicilians in late 1859, when the idea of taking the island by force from the Bourbons had first been mooted. Upon arrival at Marsala, Garibaldi and his volunteers were welcomed by locals.

The next part of the President's speech fleshed out the story. Once the battle started, the involvement of a band of *picciotti* – who fought to the end of the battle against the Bourbons, and on until the fall of Palermo – became, in the President's words, 'more than consistent'.

I was fascinated by the President's choice of language, especially that the *picciotti* were 'more than consistent' as they battled the Bourbons. The President seemed to allude to the *picciotti* being attuned or accustomed to fighting or killing. I was confused.

I needed to understand what a *picciotto* was, and I needed to ascertain why they were alongside Garibaldi when the history books stated there were only a thousand volunteers from northern Italy. What was the President saying?

I didn't wonder for long. I had a room full of students, two professors, a head curator and a senior translator all eager to explain the definition of *picciotto*. Definitions were tossed at me in their exuberance to explain. 'A young thug,' said one of the students. 'A young man of poor character,' said another. 'A *mafioso*,' said a professor. As the comments flew, I searched the definition online using Enza's Gramsci archive reference computer, and was able to define the word and find copious references. The *picciotto* was the 'lowest form of Mafia hierarchy' or, 'a young *mafioso*'. Another description was that of 'a low-level Mafia man with little respect', or 'a low-level thug of the Mafia'. The President was making references to thugs helping Garibaldi.

I would learn that the two lowest ranks of any Mafia family are called the *picciotti di liscio* and the *picciotti di sgarro*. Both are ground-floor-level thugs who answer to the organisation's *capi* (captains; singular, *capo*), thugs with experience in inflicting violence. Before attaining *capo* rank, *picciotti* need to prove themselves, do as they are told. Every *mafioso* starts as a *picciotto* and, if any good, he can rise to the upper levels of the family.

I understood the definitions, because that is the way of any club, band of thugs, bikie group, or criminal gang, and because during my time within the Mafia, I saw many *picciotti*. I just didn't call them by that name, nor did I know this Italian word. In Australia, we called them underlings; they were the shopfront of the Mafia, the brutes who doled out shocking violence, even murder. I had seen their violence many times over.

Respected Mafia historian Michele Pantaleone says the *picciotti* try to impress the head of the clan, and among their many roles they are killers, determined to show their boldness to climb the Mafia hierarchal ladder.[2] He explains that should someone commit a crime against the clan, the perpetrator may run or try to hide, but they know that they will eventually be found and killed by the *picciotti*. It all has to do with honour and the balance of power. It was the same with the Mafia I infiltrated in Australia. There was always the tough guy, the *picciotto*, walking in front of the crowd or watching from behind as Antonio and Rosario, the two head *mafiosi*, and myself, went out for the evening or strolled into a hotel to start a business meeting.

So, what on earth was the President saying in his anniversary speech about Garibaldi's unification of Sicily? The three-page newspaper article was undeniable; Garibaldi fought alongside *picciotti* – thugs – when he advanced on Sicily. For me, this was wonderful news as there seemed to be a strand in the history books as far back as 1860 showing the Mafia existed. Then it dawned on me, perhaps this revelation was also extraordinary news for Italians, who seemed to have been told something different about unification: that it came about because of the bravery of (only) a thousand goodly citizens.

Suddenly, the task ahead of me became a hell of a lot bigger, in effort and in importance. Elena suggested that I look at what the common teachings were about that time by consulting a school history book. To see what ten-year-olds were being taught. A smart idea, I thought, for a starting point.

Enza disappeared again down one of her dusty aisles and was back in no time to slam a copy of *I Grandi della Storia Garibaldi* on my desk. Printed in 1971 and used throughout Italy, it offered Italian kids the complete story of Garibaldi with a focus on the unification of Italy. According to the inside sleeve, the book had been in print since the 1960s; an up-to-date version is still used in schools today. As far as Garibaldi was concerned, the abridged schoolbook narrative went as follows.

In 1860, Italy was made up of several separately ruled states. General Garibaldi's name was put forward to Prime Minister Camillo Benso, Count di Cavour of the Kingdom of Piedmont-Sardinia (which I will shorten to Piedmont) to unite Italy, and take Sicily from its rulers, the Bourbons. The idea gathered momentum, and a Sicilian by the name of Francesco Crispi offered to gather volunteers to assist Garibaldi, should he set off on such an expedition. However, Cavour was uncertain, so Garibaldi sought the assistance of Piedmont's monarch, King Vittorio Emanuele II. News spread in middle-class circles, which influenced men to volunteer. Many of them came from Genoa, others from Milan, some from Turin, the capital of Piedmont. Very few had a military background.

The resultant expedition of the thousand volunteers who had gathered around Garibaldi, the *Garibaldini*, was an adventure funded by a mix of sources, some foreign, many of them donations. The poorly armed force set sail from Genoa on 9 May 1860, arriving at the Sicilian port of Marsala on the 11th. Soon after, the general and his *Garibaldini* took on 3000 Bourbon troops near the town of Calatafimi, to the east of Marsala, on the road to the capital, Palermo. Despite being outnumbered and having no artillery, in a three-hour battle the *Garibaldini* succeeded in forcing the Bourbon troops to surrender. Garibaldi declared himself dictator, shouting, 'Here we create Italy, or we die!', and marched his volunteers for three days to Palermo, alongside Sicilians. The *Garibaldini* ranks swelled and they managed to overpower their opponents. On 29 May, the Bourbons surrendered Palermo.

A truly fantastic story taught to tens of millions of children across Italy for more than fifty years. But how was it possible that such a powerful army like that of the Bourbons fell to a thousand volunteers, and where is the mention of the *picciotti*? I couldn't help thinking I was reading a fairytale.

CHAPTER 4
GARIBALDI

SICILIAN SAYING:

È a cucchiara i tutti i pignati

The spoon used to stir many pots of food

Meaning, the person is involved in lots of business

While history has had its fair share of revolutionaries – men driven by ideology or a thirst for power, or, in the case of Che Guevara, a confused sense of nationalism – none forced themselves upon struggling nations quite like Giuseppe Garibaldi. Certainly, none had a red beard, burning red hair, or wore red shirts as fighting wear as did Garibaldi.

Garibaldi stood out as a brilliant military strategist. He could read the play like no other general of his time, commanding respect and discipline among the peasantry.

Dozens of biographers claim he was the most beloved man of his century and the hero of two worlds, the Americas and Europe. Abraham Lincoln tried to tempt him with an officer's commission to fight for the North in the American Civil War. The US Consul in Belgium, James Quiggle,[1] wrote a series of letters to entice the freedom fighter to lend his ways to the Civil War.[2] Italians, at the time of his unification march, spoke of him as the brother of the Redeemer.[3] Any way one looks at it, Giuseppe Garibaldi was an extraordinary soldier in extraordinary times.

Born in Nice in 1807 to a family of sailors, Giuseppe spent his youth as a sailor on ships around the Mediterranean. At this time, Nice and much of northern Italy were part of the kingdom of Piedmont, ruled by the kings of the House of Savoy from Turin.

By the time Garibaldi was in his twenties, a mood of revolt had begun to pervade Europe; the old order was increasingly questioned. Garibaldi attended a meeting that would change his life. He became a member of the Young Italy group, a nationalist political movement led by Giuseppe Mazzini, who would play a key role in the future of Italy. The group's members included some of the brightest and most politically savvy minds of Italian politics, and in this milieu Garibaldi learnt to think in innovative ways.[4] The two Giuseppes became united in their belief that nations should be devoid of ruling monarchs, and that Italy should be united.

Mazzini and Garibaldi both tried their hand at politics in the city of Genoa – a key port in the Savoy kingdom – calling for change. Labelled conspirators against the government, pressure was applied to cease promoting their anti-monarchist views. They persevered, however, landing themselves in scalding water. Both fled before they could be arrested – Mazzini to central Europe and Garibaldi to South America. So started the life of the revolutionary.

Garibaldi, now in his mid-twenties, surfaced across the Atlantic in Brazil, convinced he could help other rebel causes. In South America, it seemed that anti-monarchists were everywhere, and Giuseppe cut his teeth on a relatively new style of warfare.[5] Guerrilla, as it became known, was an anything-goes style of fighting, ideal for undisciplined rebel groups.

Guerrilla warfare can involve such tactics as using hand bombs to cause maximum damage, engaging in close-quarter battle with knives, and falling behind enemy lines to sabotage infrastructure. The goal is to kill and move on to the next target.

In Brazil, Garibaldi moved fast and fought dirty. He soon became highly skilled at killing. So good at it that it was not long before he was welcomed amongst the toughest of all rebels, the Ragamuffins, who fought for the formation of Riograndense, an independent cluster of nine regions that had broken away from the Empire of Brazil, which had a powerful army. Garibaldi was given command of his own ship, along with a band of hand-picked mercenaries, high on bravery but low on strategic thinking. Garibaldi filled that strategic void perfectly. He cut the charismatic figure of a freedom fighter, with his red hair and ginger beard, knee-high boots and a belt full of side arms.

By 1838, his deeds led him to being made commander of the entire Riograndense naval fleet and his victories mounted up, much to the wonderment of the South American newspaper editors, who followed his exploits closely. His escapades found page three and four on most newspapers around the world. A legend was born, and the world had its first broadsheet hero since Napoleon.

In the Brazilian capital, Rio de Janeiro, parliament placed a death sentence on him. His only option was to flee to Uruguay. He relinquished his rebel shingle, but not before falling in love and marrying his female equivalent, Anita Maria da Silva, a beautiful and brave horsewoman. Together they had fought side by side on the decks of his ships against the Brazilian navy. But it was time to move on, to take his love and fight elsewhere. They moved to Montevideo, capital of Uruguay, and attempted normality. Garibaldi took a nine-to-five job as a mathematics teacher and fathered four children with Anita in blissful domesticity.

Anita was always the better horse handler of the two, her whole life having been spent on horseback. She made use of Garibaldi's downtime, teaching him her culture, and the life of a *gaucho*, a term given to fighting men or women on horseback, who could mount a charge, shoot while at a gallop, and slash their way through advancing forces. The *gaucho* fighters wore horse blankets or ponchos, often along with brightly coloured neckerchiefs and Indian beads.

While family life had its rewards, war was in Garibaldi's bones and he ached for a cause. In 1842, he chose his target: the Argentinean dictator Juan Manuel de Rosas, who was trying to extend his influence into Uruguay. In arguably his toughest role, Garibaldi teamed up with a troop of Italian expatriates and misfit adventurers to fight against de Rosas.

It was while leading these vagabonds that Garibaldi first wore what came to be his trademark – the red shirt, which he adopted to make his troops stand out among the other rabble in skirmishes. The shirts had been intended for use by slaughtermen in the nearby abattoirs of Buenos Aires but were 'liberated' by Garibaldi. In time, the Redshirts became a feared fighting force. Writers from around the world, such as Victor Hugo and Alexandre Dumas, penned glowing stories of the heroic general and his red-shirted revolutionaries. Garibaldi became famous, both in political circles and in the global press.

Despite an Italian death sentence hanging over his head, from his earlier capers with Mazzini, after thirteen years as a soldier of fortune in South America he ached to return home. In 1848, the year of revolutions in Europe, he set sail for Italy, his wife and children following soon after. On the announcement of his return, journalists worldwide wrote about him as an internationally recognised symbol of freedom.

Garibaldi now positioned himself on the right side of the King of Piedmont, before getting up to his red collar in intense, anti-government politics and military campaigns. His fight would take him to battles in northern Italy, Rome and Venice, often against the Austrians, who became his arch enemies.[6] It was his fight on behalf of the Milanese government that earned him the rank of general, although he never actually went through the usual levels of army promotion to earn the rank. This quasi-title stayed with him for the rest of his life.

His victories during this period could be summed up as magnificent; however, he often went against the wishes of his superiors, much to the delight of the press. It could be said that by this period he had become the world's first superhero, such was his following. For all his heroism, however, he fell into a deep sadness in 1849: while he was fighting near Venice, his wife died of an illness. Anita was only twenty-seven. She was buried near Ravenna but soon after her remains were exhumed. Distraught, Garibaldi buried her again, moving her from one grave site to another, as if to keep her near. He finally settled her corpse in Nice until, eighty years later, the State moved her remains to Rome.

The death of Anita and the years following were a time of constant change, and Garibaldi seemed confused, lacking in direction. His politics were becoming uncertain, as was his thinking. His passion for republicanism seemed to conflict with his now close association with the King of Piedmont. Was he seeking an easier road, after many personal losses? Was he happy to take the coin of a king, instead of fighting battles for the underprivileged? The soldier of misfortune soon became the hunted, as anti-revolutionaries tried to put a stop to his influence.

Sensing the end was near, Garibaldi made another exit from certain incarceration. He fled, first to London, and then to New York City, arriving there in the summer of 1850. What became of his children during this time is anyone's guess – such was the life of a revolutionary.

In America he took up residence on Staten Island, preferring this relatively quiet place to nearby Manhattan, yet the press still hounded him for stories; he was a gold-plated hero to them. The *New York Tribune* hailed him with the front-page banner: 'The World-Renowned Garibaldi'. Yet, the human headline just craved normalcy. In an attempt to lower his profile, he tried a small-business venture making Italian sausages, but it failed.

His presence created tension with the local Catholic hierarchy, which was dominated by conservative clergy of Irish descent. He clashed often with Archbishop John Hughes, head of the Catholic Church in New York, attracting media attention. The archbishop, known locally as Dagger John,[7] kept a close eye on the Italian; he had an intense dislike of Garibaldi's revolutionary ideas.[8]

After working as a labourer in a candle factory, Garibaldi realised he needed to move on. He missed the thrill of action. In 1851, he headed for Peru and joined their navy. His sea route would take him to China, Manila, and eventually to a wild land that suited his personality, Australia. His criss-crossing of oceans on fruitless adventures continued until Garibaldi felt it safe to return to Italy, which he did in 1854. By then, his alliance with Mazzini had soured. The republican fire in Garibaldi's belly had been extinguished, and monarchists had grabbed his attention.

Garibaldi formed an alliance with the new King of Piedmont, Vittorio Emanuele II, who would become King of Italy in 1861. This alliance had many, like Mazzini, suspect that Garibaldi had been courting the monarchists all along. Some also believed that Garibaldi had become a product of his own revolutionary life, a war dog who would side with anyone to gain a hold on what he really wanted: power.

Regardless, he was the right man at the right time, and Vittorio Emanuele sent Garibaldi into battle to destabilise Austria. Garibaldi would show Europe how cunning he could be.[9]

By 1859 he had shown his smarts and the King was sensing Garibaldi's worth. The stage was set to welcome the Two Sicilies into the fray.[10] As well as the island of Sicily, the kingdom included the southern Italian land mass stretching from the tippy toes of Calabria to the Royal Palazzo in Caserta, near Naples. The Two Sicilies were still controlled tightly by the Bourbons, a ruling family of French and Spanish origin, which had held sovereignty over the southern half of Italy since 1731. The Bourbon King, Ferdinand II, did not want anything to do with this wild dream of a new Italy, as promoted by discontents in Sicily. King Vittorio Emanuele, by contrast, saw that the movement would expand his kingdom.[11] The potential for conflict was ripe by mid-1859. Then, as if by an act of fate, the hard-nosed Ferdinand died, along with resistance to change. His timid, politically unsavvy son, King Francesco II, preferred dancing in the grand halls of his palace to fighting, which encouraged the kingdom's dissidents to step up their campaign to take Sicily.

All eyes turned to the red-headed general from Nice. They needed Garibaldi to get his red shirt out of his closet and prepare for politics, the press, and what he did best: battle. Trouble was, Garibaldi was distracted.

The general adored his home city. It was Nice where he finally rested the corpse of his wife in 1859, after ten years on the move. This sunbathed city was part of Piedmont, and bordered France. In return for French assistance in the war against Austria, the King and Prime Minster Cavour offloaded Nice to the French.[12]

Garibaldi heard of the sell-out of his hometown like everyone else – in the newspapers. No consultation, no warning. Outraged, he stormed into the Piedmont parliament in Turin, hurling his opinions at all. The loss of Nice from the Italian map wounded Garibaldi so severely that he started to loathe Cavour for promoting such an unpatriotic move.

Once the reverberations settled, heads turned in all directions to witness the fallout. There was none. The King was not a man to defy; his decision on Nice was final. It was said that Garibaldi never forgave the King for his political removal of Nice, yet they stayed close. The King needed the red-shirted general and the general needed a fight. Again, he was lost, and made odd decisions, while ignoring his four children, who were scattered across Italy. He swallowed his pride and fell under the spell of the piper, King Vittorio Emanuele.

Around this time – the end of 1859 and into the start of 1860 – Garibaldi suffered yet another blow to his pride. A public, if not global, humiliation that would close in on him and cost his reputation dearly. Over the New Year period, he was taken romantically by an eighteen-year-old girl who ran dispatches from the front line of the Austrian skirmish to Garibaldi as he planned his army manoeuvres. The daughter of Count Raimondi of Como, a lakeside city in northern Italy, Giuseppina too was lost to a cause, wanting to involve herself in the war. The 53-year-old Garibaldi was overcome by her beauty.[13]

Within days of meeting, he proposed marriage and days later, on 24 January 1860, Garibaldi married Giuseppina. The age difference had tongues wagging. The couple exchanged vows with the blessing of the bride's father, who was younger than the groom. Behind the scenes the same question was whispered over and over, 'What has he done?' As news hounds rushed to consider their take on Garibaldi's unusual choice of marital partner, editors around the world readied themselves for the whole story. Garibaldi, meanwhile, was contemplating his role in the taking of Sicily, and wrote a letter to his colleague, the esteemed politician Agostino Bertani. In part he stated, 'you can assure your friends of Southern Italy that I am always at their disposition when they are willing, ready to act . . .'[14]

Was he being over-exuberant, offering an act of romantic bravado? Did he make his first commitment to fight for the dissidents of Sicily as a boastful gesture in the company of his soon-to-be bride and father-in-law?

On the same day as their wedding, Garibaldi discovered a letter written by his young bride declaring her love for another man. Garibaldi confronted her; she confessed.[15] Then came the bombshell: his bride of only a few hours was five months pregnant to her secret lover. She had, in fact, two lovers floating around claiming rights over the unborn baby. Instantly, the general was looking foolish. A man who could conquer all, confront the worst horrors of combat and implement the cleverest of strategies, had to accept his image was now in tatters. To the middle classes, he was a laughing-stock. To others, he was an old fool who had lost himself to a ridiculous choice of companion.

Garibaldi walked away from the marriage that same day, failing to consummate the union. He made a rare retreat and went into hiding. Newspapers claimed he was mortified. He ended up on the island of Caprera, his country home, as newspapers labelled him 'lovesore', and splashed damning headlines about his 'violent love story' on their front pages. The humiliation simply would not stop.[16]

The next month he came up for air and headed to Turin, where he was lost for weeks on a project that distracted him from his misery: planning to take back Nice from the French government.[17] Yet he never consulted a now-frowning Vittorio Emanuele. As he tinkered with his plan and gathered rifles and supplies, he was constantly pestered by Sicilians to lead their fight for freedom, yet he stayed shy of any commitment.

Then, at a meeting of minds in Genoa in early April 1860, the general met a man as mysterious as himself, Laurence Oliphant. After many conversations, Garibaldi made a decision that would change his life forever and that of six million southern Italians. The South African–born Oliphant, sometime author, other times world traveller, who meddled in political squabbles, was also a high-level spy for Britain sent to win over Garibaldi.[18] The British government had commissioned him to embrace Garibaldi and convince him to abandon his plans to re-take Nice and to lead a raid on Sicily.[19] The British had had a strong commercial presence in the Two Sicilies (mostly Sicily) since late in the previous century, particularly in the fortified wine and salt town of Marsala. Now, with the coming of the Suez Canal, they wanted more, and were willing to offer weaponry and a naval escort to assist.[20]

The general and the British spy would meet once more, seated on a train together. Oliphant watched the general open hundreds of letters professing loyalty and adoration, mostly from admiring men, some of whom wanted to join a cause with Garibaldi. Oliphant slowly shifted the conversation to the matter of Sicily, so that by the time the two men parted company, General Garibaldi had dropped his plans for Nice and stepped away from the train with a clear vision to cross the Tyrrhenian Sea all the way to Sicily.

The King breathed a sigh of relief, and, by mid-April, all eyes, except those of Cavour – as we shall see – were firmly on Sicily.[21] The war dog announced to the world's press his change of plans, just as some thought his tumultuous life might have become a tad unhinged.

Did these two shocks – the loss of Nice and the debacle of his young, pregnant bride – have an impact on Garibaldi's thinking, given they happened just months before his assault on Sicily? Was his public humiliation a reason to create a distraction, and listen to the merits of taking Sicily? Whatever was on his mind, his decision was perfectly timed, at least by the newspapers in Sicily, which proclaimed: 'Garibaldi is coming!'

The next three weeks were a frenzy of organisation as rifles and ammunition were gathered. By April 1860, Genoa was full of republican hotheads, who stood to reap the benefit of the revolutionary initiative.[22] And the man up front was Francesco Crispi, now head of the dissidents.

Newspaper houses were on double shifts to keep up with the public demand for the story that pushed Garibaldi's marriage off the pages. From that point onwards, the story of how Sicily was taken, invaded, stolen, persuaded or enticed into becoming part – in effect – of northern Italy has various interpretations. There are hundreds of accounts of Garibaldi and his arrival in Sicily: books by scholars, historians, media luminaries, and varying biographical works. What appears to be a commonality throughout is that the purpose of Garibaldi's presence in Marsala, Sicily, was to unite Italy.

Garibaldi and his men, with the acquiescence of Vittorio Emanuele, set sail from Genoa on 9 May aboard two steamers. Somehow in those frantic days before sailing, the general had gathered enough volunteers to accompany him on his voyage. From an original list of 400, he managed to round up just over a thousand men, as well as a small number of British weapons and a miserable amount of ammunition. Their Enfield rifles were best suited for farmers trying to curtail rabbits and foxes, not to shoot the trained soldiers of the Bourbon army.

At the eleventh hour, the volunteers had become the biggest problem in this coup. As volunteers – simple folk, churchmen, lawyers, doctors, professors, journalists, students, pharmacists – most had never held a weapon. They were ambitious men, 'all of talent, learning and integrity, men of theory',[23] who shared Garibaldi's goals and stood on the ships' decks facing southwards.

Both ships were horribly inadequate for the task of docking a troop of a thousand men at the port of Marsala; however, the landscape was changing daily and the man with the red shirt was moving fast. No one seemed to complain too loudly; it was a case of take or gather what you could, as the expedition was on!

If we take the viewpoint of the phenomenally popular book *Garibaldi e la Sicilia Collezione Romeo*, featured in archives all over Italy, then the story goes like this:

> A confidential letter was sent by Garibaldi – but also leaked to the press and to the capital of the Two Sicilies to give notice of the intended expedition, however there was no response. King Vittorio Emanuele and Garibaldi had the view that inhabitants of the island of Sicily were anti-Bourbon government and there was great unrest among the people. They told of a land that was awash with violence and that landowners were at odds with farmers. The Savoy government leaders of Northern Italy sat, sweating on word from Garibaldi, apparently Vittorio Emanuele was anxious that no excessive violence be used during the expedition. He saw great promise in the taking of Sicily, a move that would accelerate him to King of the whole shooting match, but bad politics was not to hinder his agenda, at least not bad press . . .[24]

The rest is history. But is it set in stone?

Most history books portray the great General Garibaldi as the hero of the nineteenth century. But was he? And what does the inception of the Mafia have to do with a soldier prone to wearing red shirts? I, along with my Italian researchers, got to work. The first thing I learnt was that Camillo di Cavour was not uncertain about the invasion of Sicily, as the history books suggested. He was dead against it. Indeed, as I would discover, Cavour tried to halt the general, to put an end to invading a sovereign nation. As Garibaldi and his volunteers sailed towards Sicily, Cavour wrote to his most trusted confidant, Costantino Nigra, 'I regret the Garibaldi expedition as much as anyone. I could not stop him going for force would have been necessary.'[25]

Then came a re-think: Cavour needed to put an end to the nonsense of Garibaldi's invasion of the Kingdom of the Two Sicilies.[26] He ordered Count Persano, head of the military in Sardinia, which was part of Piedmont[27] and strategically located halfway between Genoa and Sicily, that should Garibaldi's ships dock in Sardinia (for food and fuel) Persano was to 'arrest the expedition. I authorise you to employ the squadron command.' Indeed, Cavour took it one step further, stating that Garibaldi should be arrested anywhere he could be found.[28]

These riveting telegrams made it clear that Garibaldi and his band were now wanted men, acting without authority, on two stolen vessels on the high seas, armed with intent. Let's not forget, Cavour was the Prime Minister. A flurry of telegrams between Cavour and the Count raced through the wires for the rest of the day, reiterating Cavour's demand to arrest Garibaldi. The issue came up as to whether they had power to arrest the expedition should it stay on the seas. It was understood they had no such power; any arrest would need to be on northern Italian soil. The tension mounted.

Count Persano ended the chain of instructions confirming his intent to arrest on Savoy soil: 'I have understood and resolve to let the daring soldier of fortune proceed to his destiny [Sicily].'[29]

So, what was the status of Garibaldi and his loose band of men at that point? Revolutionaries? Pirates on the open seas? Fugitives? Or all three? And, on arriving in Sicily, what would Garibaldi do with the nation, should he succeed? He was not a diplomat, so what diplomacy could he offer? At this moment in history Giuseppe Garibaldi could best be described as a soldier of fortune, who was a fugitive from his own country for the third time in his life. The world's press, a frustrated Prime Minister Cavour, and an anxious King Vittorio Emanuele waited on every word from an island that was about to suffer its twenty-second invasion.

CHAPTER 5
THE *PICCIOTTI*

To help better understand the sentiment on the island, Francesco Crispi visited Sicily in the months prior to the invasion and contacted dissidents from across the harsh land. He discovered the mood was mixed: some wanted to see a revolt, others not; some were concerned about the likely military backlash. Certainly, hard men of the land up against aristocrats from the city, who demanded too high a rent for their dirt blocks, had grounds for conflict. There had been years of impasse between both sides, a deadlock of mistrust, leading to violence. The tough-guy farmers – who would sooner fight than waste time sitting around a table of suited moustaches – discovered violence was their only tool in negotiations. They turned to the assistance of a band of tougher men for whom violence was their stock in trade: the *picciotti*, men capable of dispensing the worst aggression, including murder.

The Urban Dictionary defines *picciotto* (phonetic: PE-CHOT-O) as 'a low-level thug for the Mafia; a low-level Mafia member with little respect; a person at the bottom of a Mafia hierarchy; a rank of Mafia associate; a young *mafioso*; the lowest form of affiliation of Mafia type criminals'. The word *picciotto* can be found in many history books. Some of the definitions link weapons and macabre ways of harming or killing in the name of the *picciotti* (the plural form), with reference to their being a Sicilian band of thugs spread wider than Italy alone.[1]

As an interesting aside, one day while walking to the archive I was researching in, I came across a massive street march along Via Maqueda, the main street of Palermo that leads to the Teatro Massimo opera house. Hundreds of university students were protesting, waving flags and white cotton bedsheets painted with words in splashes of red and black. They stopped in front of the opera house to hear a series of speeches. The word PICCIOTTI stood out, bolder than the other words. Curious, I asked the banner carriers about the word. They explained the protest was an anti-Mafia march. They were there to make it known to the Mafia that Palermo rejects any attempts by the Mafia to influence younger Sicilians into lives of crime. They highlighted that the Mafia had a history of damaging locals through encouraging them to commit crimes in the name of the Mafia. The ranks of the Mafia had many *picciotti*, young Sicilians doing the dirty work. The protest was designed to send a strong message of 'no more!'

Apart from spending time in conversation with an extraordinary group of twenty-somethings and taking way too many pictures, I felt immense pride in their united rejection of the Mafia. I stood alongside a young woman who was very anti-Mafia in her views and soon to graduate from law school. We talked a while. I asked her what the university teaches about the scourge, to which she replied, 'There is a growing feeling in all of Sicily that our elders have not done enough about Mafia. We must show the rest of Italy that the Mafia has no place here or anywhere.' She looked awfully earnest in her tie-dyed T-shirt and knee-high boots.

•

Long ago, back when I was a student, the corruption of young adults was far easier than it is now. I recall my formative years, growing up in the big city of Melbourne. I was born into poverty, to a violent, thieving father who beat my darling mother daily and had myself and three siblings in fear. We were always on the move, evicted from house after house, for unpaid rent. My father rarely worked, preferring to stand over people, stand over us. He made his living stealing and occasionally tossed a few coins towards my mother. As a kid, I never had a hero; I instead had a heroine: my mother. By the time I was sixteen we had lived in fifty-three houses and I had attended thirteen schools. Yet, all along, I ached for normalcy, prayed that the violence would end and a better life would be delivered. I felt kinship with many in Sicily – those unable to effect change, those who live in fear – I understood their plight. Their dreams. To be free of Mafia. In time, my own life changed. But first, I needed to stand up to my father and toss him out of our house and our lives – a daunting task for a teenager.

•

In Sicily today there are eyes all over the Mafia. What I witnessed in this protest was Sicilians standing up against the Mafia through education, a key factor in bringing about change. Different to only a few generations back, when a young woman could only expect to marry and bear an apartment full of needy children. Heading to the archive, I was buoyed by this experience.

In the early nineteenth century, decades of differences between the man on the land and the man who owns the land had seen the ranks of the *picciotti* swell to become a force to be reckoned with. Wild, dangerous men without care. But, importantly, none were organised. Back then, the aggressive manner of the *picciotti* – overseen by elders from each village who acted as patriarchs, or bosses (Hollywood calls them Godfathers, yet Italians use no such word. I allow this word in my book only to help readers understand the pecking order, otherwise it's a word that should be shunned) – was rarely challenged by local police, and the Bourbon military refused to involve themselves in domestic issues. Hence, the aggressors became a law unto themselves. A pre-Mafia scourge was growing. The *picciotti* were the soldiers of that pre-Mafia. The law school student I spoke to wanted, along with her fellow students, to stop them from ever returning to Sicily.

As a native Sicilian, Francesco Crispi was born into the squabbles that led up to unification, where one side worked the land with calloused hands, and the other side had the soft hands of a rent collector. Crispi knew that the *picciotti* might be a force, if united; a useful asset. On 4 April 1860, weeks before Garibaldi set sail, a group of insurgents protested in the streets of Palermo against the Bourbons. They met outside La Gancia, a church in The Kalsa, the historic part of Palermo.

The church was sacred ground, where those less in favour of Bourbon rule met and discussed their attempts to disrupt the government; it wasn't a place for thugs, *picciotti*. Crispi tapped into the insurgents. The intended protest was strategic: to check the Bourbon response, how quick or lazy they were, bearing in mind the unrest on the island. As a tease, the protestors set about waving the tri-coloured flag of northern Italy: red, white and green. Crispi sat back to see the outcome.

The response was shocking. The church at Gancia became a blood bath, total carnage, as protestors, armed or not, were cut down, killed where they stood. The response became known as the Gancia massacre. From Gancia, the police chief moved his men on to the hill town of Carini; he had word there were *picciotti* mustered, waiting. The *picciotti* didn't have to wait long. They were soon surrounded by military, their weapons confiscated, and many beaten badly, suffocating their militancy.

Newspapers wrote of paving stones covered in blood, as those who were not taken prisoner faced a brutal death at the hands of the waiting Bourbons. What Crispi and Garibaldi did not know was that the Bourbon King had sent another 10 000 trained troops to Sicily in reaction to the protests, to support the existing 21 000 troops on the ground. By early May, a week before the expedition arrived, Palermo and Sicily were overrun by military – a force that could be, as shown at Gancia and Carini, as murderous as required.

Meanwhile, Garibaldi and his thousand volunteers were on the seas and heading south, into a zone that was twitching for action.[2] En route, it was reported that the *Mille* – the sentimental name given to the thousand volunteers – were also twitchy, getting nervous. Unrest among them was constant, a natural reaction for any military force, especially among cleanskins, most never having held a weapon.

Garibaldi pulled his mini fleet into Messina harbour on the east of the island, the opposite coastline to Palermo, for the night. Trepidation filled the hulls of both ships. The roll call for the thousand volunteers actually numbered 1089. They mostly consisted of professors, lawyers, doctors, medics, students, pharmacists, artisans, priests, salesmen, students, as well as a farmer, a lone woman, a boy and one old man!

Peppered through these ranks were a handful of Carabinieri, police from northern Italy, though they were too few to make a difference. The vast majority on board were from across the roof of Italy, with fifty Sicilians in the mix. Only one-third of the men were of the ideal fighting age: eighteen to thirty-five years, and almost an entire company (a unit of up to 150 men) were fresh-faced students from Pavia University. In the opinion of observers who witnessed the *Mille*, they believed they were absolutely not the type of men needed for this expedition. Incidentally, contemporary oil paintings of the unification march and battle are almost biblical in style, showing the general, centre frame, with his back straight, firearm or sword out, ready to save the people. Many of the paintings and written accounts depict the *Mille* wearing flaming red shirts, yet there is no mention in the inventory for the ships of any such garments. The lack of mention of red shirts in the dusty old books from the nineteenth century is telling. There are no references to red shirts in any of the dispatches between Garibaldi and his hierarchy, or in personal correspondence. Where the general would acquire such a vast number of red shirts is anyone's guess. Bear in mind that it was only in mid-April, three weeks previous, that Garibaldi had committed to the voyage.

On 11 May, as the ships approached Marsala harbour, some political manoeuvring took place. The waiting Bourbon ships would be unwise to fire upon Garibaldi's two vessels, mainly because a misfire could have hit a nearby British ship or stevedoring office, causing death or injury. The British had licence over the harbour for commercial reasons. The British navy was also the most powerful globally, and an error of judgement by the Bourbons might be seen as an act of aggression. Instead, the British – who knew the play between Garibaldi and the Bourbons – allowed Garibaldi's ships unhindered access to the port, and watched the drama unfold.

Once the famed *Mille* and Garibaldi marched onto British-occupied soil and took safe haven, the Bourbons snatched Garibaldi's steamer ships, taking them out of the arena of war, all the way to the Bay of Naples, never to be seen again. But Garibaldi had other matters to attend to.

On 14 May, the march was on. Waiting ahead of the *Mille* – by way of a day-long walk – were 3000 battle-savvy Bourbon military men, armed to the teeth. These were soldiers blooded from the riot at the Gancia church weeks earlier. A formidable battalion backed by tens of thousands of troops secreted across the island. A battle was inevitable; it was what the troops were there for, and for the newspaper-adored Garibaldi, a must.

At about the halfway mark between Marsala and Palermo sits a stunning landscape known as Calatafimi-Segesta, shortened in time to Calatafimi. A dot on the map really, but an important one. It is home to the remains of an ancient Greek village, built 3000 years earlier, which stands complete with its own acropolis. Having visited it many times, I can attest to its magnificence. With its sweeping views across a series of undulating valleys, out to the speckled islands of the Tyrrhenian Sea and Mount Erice, the site rivals the majesty of the Acropolis of Athens. Erice, the highest peak in southern Italy, provided front-row seats for the march from Marsala of Giuseppe Garibaldi and his nervous swarm of *Mille*. It truly was an ideal setting for a picnic, or a battle.

Someone must have yelled charge, and the long-awaited battle began with fighters from both sides clambering up the tranquil rolling hills. The uniformed Bourbon soldiers faced their enemy, but they weren't just the *Mille*. Coming at them were a different – unknown – breed: 900 hill men, wild, screaming, savage bushmen hurling murderous abuse, and animating the pastoral land with muskets, rifles, handguns, long-blade knives, bombs, horses, uniforms and blood. Nine hundred rural gangsters, toughs, Sicily's worst criminals and killers, were suddenly in the game, in the fight, in front of the volunteers: the *picciotti* had arrived. And the Bourbons were magnificently caught by surprise.

Reading of the extent of *picciotti* involvement caused a feverish search in the archive as my team looked for credible mentions of the Calatafimi battle. What stirred me was how many history books paid scant attention to the involvement of the *picciotti*. The few that mention other fighters brushed this fact aside. This was a constant of the Garibaldi and *Mille* narrative, printed ad nauseam.

After reading about this battle, in varying accounts, I started to wonder if this was the story some wanted others to believe. It felt rehearsed. Yet, every now and again a snippet presented itself to test the veracity of the commonly accepted version of the battle for unification. Such as how Garibaldi was joined by 1000 men from the towns of Alcamo and Mount San Giuliano, wild men wearing sheepskins, all armed – '*picciotti*' – who had no sense of drill or discipline, and who came like a mob behind their ex-feudal chiefs.[3]

As those who sit in archives can testify, the more one digs into history, the more one finds. Like discovering that Garibaldi ordered the prison doors in Marsala be thrown open upon arrival, to let the criminals join forces with those already gathered, find a weapon and do what was ordered. The more I read, the more the gold nuggets became visible. Such as how once Garibaldi arrived in Marsala he went to the banks and looted them empty (more about that later).

There are varying mentions of the *picciotti* in respected texts, often of numbers well above 900. To understand the numbers that fought, it is important to know what a squadron is: an army term used to denote numbers of men in a battle.[4] A squadron can be 300 or more soldiers. The number of squadrons in play alongside Garibaldi is difficult to say, as the propaganda of the day has blurred the facts, yet there are witness accounts and stories that give some indication. The word 'squadron' is often used alongside the word '*picciotti*'.

One account mentions a squadron of 421 *picciotti*, bad men armed and fuelled by anger, in the one cluster.[5] Garibaldi's discontented allies had promised help and gave it, but the bands of *picciotti* stepped forward to join Garibaldi only after he showed that his own volunteers could stand up to the royalist troops.[6] The *picciotti* came from the rural area of Lercara, a small town in the interior of Sicily, forty-five kilometres from Palermo. The town of Corleone – on the other side of the mountain to Lercara – might be Hollywood's home of the Mafia, but Lercara has a genuine historic connection to the Mafia. When tracing the prominent fathers of the Mafia, Lercara stands out as one of the founding towns. It is, for instance, the birthplace of Charles Luciano, who went by the nickname of 'Lucky', and is rightfully considered by some to be the father of the contemporary American Mafia. I'll tell you much more about him in chapter 17.

Sicily was full of 'bad' towns back in the days of unification, and there were many squadrons in battle. It can only be assumed these towns sent their most desperate men. In 1901, author Giuseppe Fazio mentioned there were many *picciotti* involved from towns all over Sicily, including a squadron from Sant'Anna, another rough-and-tough dot in the interior. Sant'Anna would play a significant part in the unification. It was home to the Triolo brothers, Giuseppe, Stefano and Benedetto, wealthy farmers who knew the region of Alcamo and Calatafimi well and were Garibaldi patriots. These prominent men were able to gather hundreds of *picciotti* together.

On invading Sicily, it was well known that the red-shirted general was a political bedfellow of Francesco Crispi. Their shared ideology went as far back as 1854, and the Triolo brothers were involved with every step of Francesco Crispi's plan for unification. Only a week before the intended invasion, they flew several tricolour flags of Italy from the town flagpoles to alert locals and *picciotti* alike that Garibaldi was on his way, and those willing should clean their weapons and gather their ammunition. The ever-vigilant Bourbons got a whiff of the Triolos' plans and seized their guns before the brothers fled to continue rounding up men. It was widely reported that the Triolo brothers met with Garibaldi and Crispi when the *Mille* ships docked at the port of Marsala, along with 500 armed men, many of whom were *picciotti*.

Then there were an additional 700 armed men, some farmers and hard-done-by locals, from the hilltop town of Monte Erice and the sea-salt town of Trapani, who came under the leadership of Giuseppe Coppola.[7] This region was alive with criminals. Trapani was considered to be a major centre of criminal activity; robbery and murder were rife. It was so murderous one magistrate spoke out publicly in an effort to quash violence in his corner of the island. A cynic might say that the battle of Calatafimi at least gave the criminals something to do, and that a few might also have been got rid of.

An observer at the time estimated some 3500 thugs, locals and *picciotti* fought on the side of Garibaldi.[8] This same historian goes on to describe the *picciotti* as being Sicily's 'delinquents', a word used to describe violent thugs in the 1850s and found throughout the prefecture reports on the security of cities in Sicily. ('Prefect' is the title given to the most important law officer of a city; the Prefect oversees it all and reports to government.)

To the eyes of the unwitting Bourbons, the *picciotti* had come crawling over the bald hills in the midday sun wearing sheepskin jackets. One contemporary account, not repeated in later, official history books, states: 'The *picciotti* came from all directions screaming, with weapons, like mad men with faces like gun barrels, full of rage, killing everything. The Bourbons were over-run, constantly attacked by gangs of bandits.'[9]

One volunteer on the ground, respected journalist and poet Ippolito Nievo – a brave man from Padua who landed at Marsala – wrote a letter home stating: 'We have been helped by auxiliary squads of volunteers made up of the most part of emeritus brigands who are ready to fight against the Bourbons, just as an excuse to make war on the landowners.'[10]

For three hours the bullets landed, and guns were reloaded. For three hours men fell, injured or dead, and those who could walk staggered away to save their lives, until the front of the attack was weakened, and the Bourbons dropped their rifles and ran. Still, the hard men of Sicily did not give up. The squads of locally recruited *picciotti* had a dubious military manner, yet they contributed powerfully to the cause.[11]

The great disappointment with the rifles doled out to the revolutionaries was their settings. The English-supplied Enfield rifles were pre-set – sighted – at 300 yards, and therefore frequently missed or overshot their targets, and there was a scarcity of ammunition. Some volunteers only had ten rounds each.[12] Still, by this point, all fighters on Garibaldi's side were blended as one, fighting to the death.

One volunteer wrote home after surviving his experience at Calatafimi: 'There we came under a perfect hail of bullets, which from the smoke wreathed mountain two guns began a furious cannonade against us . . . our men were falling all around him [Garibaldi] it was terrible to see the dead and wounded.'13

The outcome – the taking of Sicily – could not have been anticipated, except by those who had heard the whisper that the *picciotti* would come into the game, and deliver the red-shirted general his expected victory. A win of disproportionate slaughter relative to the thousand naive volunteers from Genoa.

On discovering these accounts, I thought back to when Enza found the three-page report of the President's speech, in which he let slip that the *picciotti* played a major role in the taking of Sicily, the liberation of a land. Then I stopped for a moment and thought of the value of a tray of *biscotti*!

Once the Bourbons were in retreat, in a defiant act of victory, surrounded by *Mille*, *picciotti* and brave locals, a beaming Garibaldi raised the tricoloured green, red and white flag in the name of Vittorio Emanuele. Quoted globally, he then yelled across the bloodstained fields: '*Qui si fa l'Italia o si muore!*' – Here we create Italy, or we die!14 I wonder if the general spared a thought for his lost Nice and poor choice of bride, even as he was on top again.

A book I was studying had a beautiful representation of the battle scene at Calatafimi. The original painting, considered a masterpiece, sits in the National Gallery in Perugia, as do many similar artworks of nationalist pride. In this painting, the *Mille* are depicted wearing red shirts, their swords aloft and rifles hot with plumes of smoke, overpowering the equally gallant Bourbons, as General Garibaldi stands centre field, victorious. Yet there is not a single representation of a *picciotto*, a bandit thug, a criminal, driving the Bourbons into defeat.

From Calatafimi, it was a two-day march to Palermo. Time to lick whatever wounds the *Garibaldini* had before the killing and conquering continued. The ranks of Garibaldi's *Mille* swelled with 'four thousand more *picciotti*'.15 As the news spread, the gangsters kept coming, all the way to the centre of Palermo. On 27 May, Garibaldi, prior to his charge on Palermo later that day, did a side tour to the town of Gibilrossa to meet Crispi's ally, Giuseppe La Masa, and stir up the waiting fighters. The town was now swarming with *picciotti*. The death toll is difficult to assess. The history books I read either failed to offer a number or seemed to ignore it.

Although some books dared to mention casualties, the figures were almost always on the low side, ranging from a mere 68 dead and 292 shot, stabbed and injured, to many times that number. Braver authors put the figure at as many as 2500 killed and countless injured. Regardless, a death toll anywhere between these numbers is a massacre, enough to fatten ravens for years and leave a valley of dry bones for historians to ponder.

Once in Palermo, more *picciotti* linked with brave local Sicilians stepping out of the laneways and into the bloodbath. It must be understood that not all fighters on Garibaldi's side were gangsters or *picciotti*. Among the heroic 'scoundrels' were, for example, local businesspeople, citizens who saw merit in a revolt.

As the fighting intensified, the reaction of those in power in Palermo was predictable. They closed ranks and told locals working in the administrative offices nothing of the military defeat at Calatafimi; nothing about the bloodthirsty attack on the Bourbons; nothing that might scare a population into vacating the jewel in the war. A prince, domiciled in Palermo – and clearly in fear of his life – wrote on 13 May an urgent dispatch to his King, Francesco II, in Naples, stating that:

> Sicily is deeply agitated. Palermo, whose spirit is hostile against
> the government, shows a desire to revolt, and the fear of the
> revolutionary vendetta makes also honest men become reckless.
> It is being predicted at the gates of Palermo that not only will
> the fate of Sicily be decided, but also the fate of the monarchy.[16]

With the fall of Palermo on 29 May, the march continued. Garibaldi's army now numbered over 6000 blooded fighters. And still their ranks grew. With every kilometre, every victory, more men and more guns joined the angry flock. As they marched across Sicily there was an ongoing call to action to bandits, to anyone with a gun. When Garibaldi's army stopped to await a ferry crossing from Messina to Reggio Calabria, the number of bandits and goodly citizens had reached 18 000, and the body count they left behind was forgotten.[17]

The question begs, it screams: What of the story of the *Mille* red shirts?

Most history books agree on the rest of the story. The now god-like figure of General Garibaldi kept his aggression on the road, throughout Sicily, across the Messina Strait, over the mountains of Calabria, into Basilicata, and on to Naples to the steps of the stupendously large *palazzo* of King Francesco II. For most of the invasion, the King hid inside one of his palace's 400 rooms, ready to surrender to the 20 000-plus *Garibaldini* 'soldiers'.

Did the success of this bloody invasion of a sovereign state depend on the thugs at the general's disposal? The annihilation of the Bourbons was assured because of the general's instinctive military savvy. Cavour's predecessor as Prime Minister, Massimo d'Azeglio, tucked away safely in Sardinia, said of the victory, '. . . but when you defeat an army of 60,000 men, conquer a kingdom of 6 million people and 8 casualties, one ought to think that something out of the ordinary is going on'.[18] 'Out of the ordinary' flies in the face of the *Mille* story.

D'Azeglio's scepticism falls in line with a comment that was proffered to me by Louis Mendola, a New York–born and educated historian who lives in Palermo. He draws a comparison of the *Mille* with the Allied invasion of Sicily in World War II. He told me, 'It took an Allied force of many hundreds of thousand soldiers and support personnel one year to take Sicily and work its way to Rome, yet the Italian history books say 1000 *Mille* did the same task alone and in a fraction of the time.'[19] Mendola's scepticism is better understood when you realise the Garibaldi contingent used single-shot rifles, whereas the Allied troops had modern armour, air support, amphibious craft and endless firepower.

While the number of casualties stated by d'Azeglio is wrong, his suspicions were astute. Something else must have come into play: subterfuge. In this case, Garibaldi letting his enemy think that he was either weaker or less able to match the Bourbons. After employing a range of clever subterfuges, he allows surprise to enter the game, and unleashes his stronger assets to win the battle. Hence, the *picciotti* were hidden away until the fight started. It was the perfect sucker punch!

By all accounts, the Bourbons were a powerhouse, capable of countering anything that came at them. As foot soldiers, they were a force unequalled – by sheer numbers – at that time in Europe. Yet mainstream Italian history insists on offering an illogical version of events, and the question remains: How on earth could a thousand students, doctors, pharmacists, an old man, a boy and a woman over-power such formidable strength? Yes, subterfuge played its part.

As historian Denis Mack Smith states:

> Garibaldi only had a thousand soldiers of his own (volunteers) and an inadequate supple of arms, yet three weeks later a large army surrendered to him and almost all the island had been won . . . this astonishing result has always been hard to explain because it was not accomplished by a grass-roots movement of mass patriotic idealism.[20]

He acknowledges, however, that 'the lawless bands [of *picciotti*] did more than anyone to bring the Bourbon government to a halt. Once the initial indispensable service of these bands was complete, it was the first object of Garibaldi to create a regular militia which would relieve his revolution of the embarrassments of their support.'[21]

In his memoir, Francesco Crispi states that the formation of such a militia was indeed the subject of the First Decree, which followed the assumption of dictatorship by Garibaldi, dated 14 May 1860.[22]

Having spent two decades in a large police department fighting crime, I know that force, savvy and numbers are the only ways to combat adversity. The Bourbons' control over the common people and their killing expertise were well known in Europe. However, it is the subterfuge of Garibaldi that interests me most. I employed subterfuge every day for three years against *mafiosi* when they thought I was a money-laundering art dealer. Being part of a task force up against the Mafia, I used the strategic tools of covert policing: subterfuge, cunning, smarts, research, planning and insight. They all go together.

General Garibaldi won his victory using subterfuge. In hindsight it is easy to see. He used a methodology that other generals learnt to use: disinformation and misinformation. Undercover cops use it, spies use it, and, yes, army generals and high-level crime cartels use it. Information deliberately placed in the game to either confuse the target or cause them to think something different. In the case of Garibaldi, his use of this tactic came from his many campaigns against dictators and despots in South America.

Garibaldi's subterfuge started in Genoa in early May 1860, once he had committed to the invasion, and agreed to what the dissidents had conspired to create. He was astute enough to call it an 'expedition', which is a softer word to use in the public arena than 'invasion'. A brilliant move. Journalists back then were no Bob Woodward or Carl Bernstein; they tended to write what they were told, happy enough to get the story and create heroes. No one questioned authority. Ruling monarchs and despots ensured the masses were fed the stories they wanted. The general cashed in on this, informing the eager press of his planned detour to Sicily, via Tuscany (nowhere near Sicily). A ploy to throw the boyish King Francesco and his head-scratching generals off the trail, when all along he was sneaking his way down the peninsula to Marsala. He even put word out that he was going to land in Palermo. But that was never an option. As it was the most heavily fortified port city in Europe, he would have been sunk within minutes. Instead, he aligned himself with his Masonic contacts in London and after his secret meeting with the spy Oliphant he was granted clear passage to the British-controlled port of Marsala.

Getting the jump on the Bourbons at Marsala, however, gave no certainty of ultimate victory. Once on Sicilian soil, the real disinformation came into play. Garibaldi's stroke of absolute genius was to publicly roll out his sole arsenal: volunteers. He let it be known weeks ahead that a thousand squareheads were to take on the Bourbons: naive physicians, shopkeepers and academics. Men, a lone boy and a woman brimming with national pride that they were going to be part of the birth of a wonderful new nation. The newspapers took the bait, telegraphing Garibaldi's plan that the Bourbons would be overcome by volunteers, and that is exactly what is in the history books.

Only a fool would believe the David-size northern Italians were ever going to pull down the might of the Bourbon Goliaths, a fact observed by the past Prime Minister, Massimo d'Azeglio. Yet this magnificent subterfuge rolled out, for all to see, as the ships docked in Marsala. They got away with it mostly because there were no journalists there; no one to correct what would go into the history books. No objectivity.

The response from the opposition? Three thousand soldiers to battle a bunch of academics. The Bourbons were fooled. But all along Garibaldi had the early makings of the Mafia up his sleeve. Briefed, armed, juggling bombs and belts of ammunition, waiting on the other side of the hills. It's quite brilliant if you dissect it: the ultimate military strategy – a manoeuvre that would change history, and nobody saw the Mafia coming!

Trouble is, more than 160 years later, the subterfuge has been unpacked, unpicked, and exposed thanks to what Gabriella from Libera Terra once said to me: 'Sicilians never throw out a single piece of paper.' It's all in the archives, for someone to come along and find, read and translate.

In keeping it secret, the subterfuge had to be maintained, and this required 'fantasy' – old-fashioned bullshit – to be written into history books. Sold not only to the masses, but editors, foreign correspondents, historians and the families of those taking part. How to do this? Easy, the general was an expert at creating legends. He had done enough of it in his time with his use of red shirts on Uruguayan vagabonds.

With Cavour now livid at Garibaldi and a reluctant supporter of unification – since the taking of Sicily – Garibaldi got to work, shoring up his legend, and creating co-fathers of unification: Cavour, King Vittorio Emanuele and Giuseppe Mazzini. All they needed to do was make heroes of the *Mille*, who fought behind and alongside the *picciotti*. All brave folk, no doubt, but puppets on a bigger stage.

Garibaldi's greatest victory was selling the legend – the heroics – of the *Mille*. It was the perfect script. The many artworks of the time hanging in national galleries, particularly in the south of Italy, testify to the success of this strategy. Splashed with red shirts, they focus on the general and the *Mille*, with no sign of a *picciotto*. Indeed, the total absence of *picciotti* in the unification story falls into the category of evidence by way of omission, a maxim known to detectives.

During the propaganda phase after unification, key phrases were promoted in the name of the thousand volunteers, with the constant use of the term *Mille*. Commemorative plaques were erected in most cities to honour the *Mille*. Almost every major town or city in Italy has a street called *Via dei Mille*. An oft-used phrase in Italian is *grazie*

Mille, which translates, 'Thank you to the thousand', or 'a thousand thank-yous', any way you say it.

Garibaldini is a direct reference to the 1089 non-soldiers and the term given to the 'expedition of the thousand'. Additionally, one street in every village, town, or city across Italy is named after the gallant Garibaldi and victorious King Vittorio Emanuele, yet there is not a word of the *picciotti* who caused the victory.

This concerted effort went a long way to promote nationalism and snuff out, or deflect, any suggestion of the *picciotti*, the filth of Sicily, being the saviours of an invasion. While everyone knows victors write their own history, the Italian unification story has become the greatest snow job of nineteenth-century European politics.

•

After six months in Palermo's archives, I wanted more – more facts, more books and more reports that could help uncover the starting point of the Mafia and who these men were. More importantly, I wanted to know which individual rallied them for their finest moment in history.

Another issue was troubling me. Garibaldi's first objective as dictator was to issue a decree that would relieve his revolution of the embarrassment of using bandits and criminals to overrun the Bourbons. Why was he embarrassed? He was no doubt proud of his brave volunteers from up north and the local patriots, but with the *picciotti* it was a different story: he used murderers to murder his way to Naples.

With his reputation shot to pieces in the few months leading up to invading Marsala – his unruly outbursts over Nice and marrying a pregnant eighteen-year-old – I can understand how he would desire to stave off further embarrassment. But surely there were far more pressing social reforms to be tackled than to waste his first decree on the use of bandits. Not so. It appears the great man wanted to expunge any record of his choice of 'soldier' in his victory. A classic example of dissolving the means to an end. In this case, though, the means were extraordinarily violent. And not prudent.

But, as Garibaldi came to know in 1860, there is no prudence in love or war.

What had Garibaldi promised his bandits in return for their dirty work? One thing I knew from my past career as a detective, bad men don't come cheap. I went back into the Sicilian archival vaults and put on my white cotton gloves. I was in search of the architect of the invasion of Sicily, and what money was promised to these extraordinary thugs.

CHAPTER 6
THE SPY

SICILIAN SAYING:

Cu mancia fa muddichi

Who eats makes crumbs

Meaning, it is impossible to do something secretly

Over many years I had a fascinating career within the Covert Investigation Unit (CIU), an elite undercover squad in Australia. It is like many other famous spy agencies around the globe, such as the French DGSE, British MI5, the CIA, Mossad, etc., which pride themselves on having the best trained, most effective operatives in a dangerous world where stealth and cunning are everything, and death is not rare. In this regard, the CIU was truly impressive, with a training budget equal to its tasks. Spies cannot be trained on a wing and a prayer but, rather, need intensive tutorials, the best lecturers, finest training facilities, and state-of-the-art equipment. Even then, despite the best intentions, some fail to deliver the goods, surrender to pressure, or walk away due to fear or a lack of mental toughness. Failures must be tolerated. An operative who cannot comply with the harsh standards must find another career path before they get someone shot or an operation burnt.

In time, I would be promoted within the CIU to the role of Controller, a key position. The Controller designs the strategies used by the undercover operatives as they infiltrate their targets. It was incumbent on me to know the laws related to covert work inside out, as I carefully selected each operative and guided them through each phase of their training. Later, if trouble loomed and an operative was harmed or (worse) killed, the eyes of scrutiny would always fall on the Controller. Luckily, I never suffered there as I went to extraordinary lengths, making sure whoever I sent into the dark world of a Hells Angels bikie clubhouse, or a gang of violent armed robbers, or the Mafia, were the ultimate, the very best trained operatives. The lucky one per cent of one per cent of the police force. Or, as some might say, the unluckiest!

Spy agencies of today have learnt from past experience, going back to the Great War and Mata Hari, one of the first spies of note. It was therefore surprising to uncover, in the archives of Palermo, records of a spy operating 160 years earlier during the unification of Italy, and I don't refer to the British spy Laurence Oliphant. Rather, I refer to a spy who had received no training, no intensive tutorials, and no one to cry out to for help should he become exposed. Indeed, all he had was a wing and a prayer, a few false documents and disguises, and spades of cunning. I came to admire him greatly.

Born in 1819, on the southern side of Sicily in the Greek-influenced city of Agrigento, Francesco Crispi would rub shoulders with all factions of Sicilian life. Agrigento was known as a tough city as far back as the Middle Ages. It was the first port of call for those fleeing north from Africa, for Arabs invading from the East, and indigenous Sicilians wanting to distance themselves from the authorities in Palermo or Catania.

Agrigento was not enough for the law graduate Crispi. He abandoned his home for Naples, where he hung out his shingle to practise law. His case history is best described as unremarkable: a total of 132 civil and criminal cases. Still, he did what he knew best, made contacts and kept a notebook of useful names. The little man with the huge moustache knew they would come in handy one day. What he did not know was that, despite his ordinariness, he would go on to serve his country as prime minister, twice. Before then, he had much turmoil to face, such as the swelling sentiment that Sicily and Naples should be integrated within a new, united Italy.

During this time, Francesco Crispi discovered that, like Garibaldi, he too was a man with a passion for republicanism. Upon his return to Sicily during the European revolutionary year of 1848, he, alongside others, found themselves in hot water with the Bourbons, as farmers, workers and militants took to the streets to protest poor wages and ruthless landowners.[1] Blood was spilt, voices cried out for an end to Bourbon sovereignty and Crispi headed for Piedmont.

As we have seen, Piedmont, part of the Savoy kingdom, was ruled by King Vittorio Emanuele, so Crispi had to walk at a slower pace than he did when in radical Sicily. During this time of reflection on all things Italian, he shared his thoughts with Giuseppe Mazzini. They would remain close. Despite Crispi's subdued nature, he was soon writing separatist articles in newspapers and even attempting to publish his own newspaper.[2] His activist politics displeased the King, whose tolerance ran out in 1853. Crispi fled to London to avoid prosecution and went country-hopping, searching for somewhere to hide until the temperature cooled.[3] It was then that he aligned himself with the Masons.

In 1858, he entered France to take a swipe at Emperor Napoleon III and joined a band of French anarchists, who attempted to assassinate the French leader. Their weapons of choice were a cache of home-made bombs, small enough to be thrown on the move. The day arrived and a nervous Crispi and his four fearful accomplices set upon the passing Emperor, tossing bombs at their target. However, unlike Garibaldi, Crispi was no urban guerrilla. The assassination attempt was just that, an attempt, and Napoleon III survived. Eight innocents lay dead on the streets and more than a hundred passers-by suffered horrific injuries. Crispi went for cover, doing what he knew best, avoiding detection.

Paris was outraged, and the hunt was on. Three of the scoundrels were caught. Once convicted, two were publicly guillotined, while the ringleader, Carlo Di Rudio, was banished for life to France's worst prison, Devil's Island.[4] He escaped within months and travelled to the United States. Years later, the escapee confessed from the sanctuary of his home in New York City that Crispi was the other bomb carrier, the missing pawn in a botched attempt to overthrow the government.[5]

Apparently, as Di Rudio told it, Crispi dropped a bomb in the middle of the ruckus and injured himself in the explosion, though not badly enough to stop his run or his politics. Like a bad penny, the ex-lawyer soon bounced back to take another swipe at another monarchy.

He sprang up again in 1859 in Piedmont, when the talk of an invasion of the Two Sicilies was first mooted by the island's discontents. He immediately joined the alliance. Now a revolutionary, Crispi lost himself in planning and scheming, believing his day in politics had finally arrived, albeit with a mix of odd bedfellows. The only drawback he could see was the dissidents' lack of military power; to achieve such an audacious task he needed General Garibaldi, if he could be persuaded. The Savoy military under the control of King Vittorio Emanuele could not be used, as the moment troops were mustered it would send a signal of a military coup. Crispi and his Sicilian supporters were at a loss. It all depended on Garibaldi, but the general's rage was focused on Nice.

Crispi had a more clandestine idea. As a Sicilian, he had contacts across the island – all listed in his notebook – and, unlike his co-conspirators in the alliance, he had no trouble making his way in the many directions open to him. Plus, as a native of Agrigento, he was aware that the area was full of hard men. He also knew that men with a criminal past often respond to big ideas, especially from a man with a moustache, so Crispi put his plans on the table.

He set sail for Sicily, in an attempt to shore up support and test the waters as to the possibility of an armed coup on the island. In August 1859, Crispi entered the port of Messina, jumping off his ship with enthusiasm. As his stride hastened, he became aware of a growing alliance within Sicily to overturn Bourbon rule. He also knew that none of his northern Italian co-conspirators were up to the task, so he assumed a false identity and went looking.[6] He took on the persona of an Argentinean tourist, Manuel Pareda, turned up the collar of his shirt, flicked both sides of his moustache and got to work.[7] One of the world's first ever spies was on a mission.

His extraordinary act of cunning was to broker support: manpower, firearms and funds for a coup. With his smooth talk, he started knocking on doors. And whispering.

Crispi spent weeks going from *palazzi* to grand villas, meeting, dining and speaking to non-Bourbon aristocrats, wealthy men who desired a national identity. Farmers, in particular, had tired of the arrogance of the Bourbon landlords, who denied the workers a decent return for their efforts. Some turned to crime and robbery to better themselves.

As he moved, Crispi soaked up the discontent, then set about forging a path of solidarity. On his travels he met a unique breed of rural native: the *picciotti*, tough guys a younger Crispi had grown up with and stayed shy of. His visit also allowed him to see firsthand how the south had become awash with low-level thugs who took to easier pursuits, to a life of crime. A life of violence, theft and robbery was a more tempting vocation than working for a pittance on a farm.

He tapped into this mood for change.[8] He envisaged a time of great lawlessness if the social climate never altered. As a republican, a revolutionary and a Sicilian, Francesco Crispi ached to be the agent of change.

Crispi called in his closest republican friends, such as the Triolo brothers, who had enormous support and access to vast numbers of *picciotti* in western Sicily. Crispi visited Stefano and Giuseppe Triolo at their home in Alcamo, close to Calatafimi – the location of the key battle for unification the following year – and they formed an alliance with *picciotti* manpower.

Another ally, Giuseppe La Masa, rallied his connections in response to the call from Crispi. They had shared a voice for change during the unsuccessful 1848 revolution, and eleven years later the fire was just as fierce in their bellies. La Masa wrote a tell-all memoir years later, after unification, disclosing that he advised Garibaldi and Crispi on guerrilla warfare concepts for an invasion of Sicily. A man of great strength, in both body and mind, he gave his ideas to Crispi to pass back to General Garibaldi, should he be persuaded to join the coup.[9] La Masa's ability to convince teams of *picciotti* to join the coming battle was fundamental to the shifting strategies of Crispi. He was confident of gathering many men, up to 3000 in all.

A famous oil painting hangs in the Regional Gallery of Art in Sicily depicting a battle-weary La Masa standing, surrounded by six tall, never-say-quit, rifle-bearing *picciotti* with the look of killers. In a surviving La Masa manuscript, there is a tiny handwritten note to Garibaldi that found its way to the general via Crispi. It is a reference to the *picciotti* and disheartened men he had gathered for the invasion, men who were waiting for orders. It reads, '[I am] surrounded by sad people at whose head is Crispi.'[10] An undeniable reference to the work of Francesco Crispi, who travelled the island in search of fighters.

Days before the 1860 invasion, La Masa addressed a group and was heard to say, in part, 'Don't you see the clouds that gather on the horizon? We protect the storm and we act promptly and boldly before the . . . Bourbon coalition try to crush us . . .'.[11] It is clear La Masa wielded great authority over the *picciotti*, he was key to the eventual outcome that Crispi initiated.

Each night, Crispi, the once lawyer, now spy, spoke and socialised in his clever disguise, in a different town. He kept on the move, ensuring he stayed clear of the parasitic informers who fed snippets of information to the island's police. Often, he dropped the name Garibaldi into the conversation, a strategy that stirred enthusiasm. One night he slept at the Trinacria Hotel in Palermo, under the name of Signor Freeman, and set up meetings with fellow conspirators to plot the overthrow of the Bourbons.[12] He learnt that most people cared little for unification, just for their own liberty and the downfall of the ruling monarchy. Names like La Russa, Inzerillo and Losquiglio, tough-guy leaders of large bands of *picciotti*, offered help and waited for the word. Biding their time, they started amassing guns and ammunition, stashing them in warehouses.[13] With preparations in full swing, Crispi got word from the republican Giuseppe Mazzini, playing politics in London, to 'hurry to act', that King Vittorio Emanuele was getting anxious.

As Crispi travelled about, pressing his hand into the palms of those wanting to help, a secret society was galvanised. Sicily, in Crispi's mind, was ripe for change, and there was one thing that made change possible: the hard-nosed king of the Bourbons, Ferdinand II, was now dead.[14] He had died in May 1859, and his son and heir was as soft as *burrata* cheese.

Crispi took the smell of revolution one major step forward: he organised the making of bombs – weapons he had experience with from his failed brush with guerrilla warfare twelve months earlier in Paris.

In his thinking, the bomb was still the ideal tool for armed combat. Large enough to cause havoc, they were made in their hundreds, thousands, in farmhouses and sheds, and stored in secret locations to be used when the time was right.

Before he left the island in September 1859, an agreement was locked in for an all-out attack on the Bourbons in six weeks' time, in October.[15] Once all the handshakes were made, Crispi stole away from the heat of the conspiracy and returned to Savoy knowing he had shored up support from some of the hardest men in Sicily, the *picciotti* and their patriarchs. Then he set about trying to convince Garibaldi of the plan, leaving the bomb-making to angry farm men – until the time for battle.[16]

No sooner had Crispi announced his devilish plan than the fruits of his sojourn to the south started to sour. Vital snippets of information seeped out from the villas and farmhouses into the ears of police snitches; the coup was whispered about to the Bourbon police chief, the dogged Captain Salvatore Maniscalco.[17] Not a man to be underestimated, Maniscalco worked his way through the rumours and concluded that an invasion was indeed imminent, and, like mice to a larder, Sicily was soon swarming with military, placing any thought of a political coup in the too-hard basket.

Crispi took the news hard. However, he had another bigger, better idea brewing away. He would head to London and negotiate the use of a Sicilian port to allow Garibaldi – should he come on board – to dock his invading ships there at the start of his invasion. Unhindered passage onto Sicilian soil would aid an invasion and, in Crispi's thinking, it was prudent to find a port where the Bourbons did not have a dominant presence.

On this clandestine journey, Crispi pulled out another disguise and another covert identity. His alias was Tobia Glivaie, a Maltese-born British subject. He gathered the most convincing travel documents, issued in London, dyed his hair black, and grew a short-cut beard to match his trademark moustache. Complete with a briefcase of supportive papers, the 'Brit' importer and exporter with a strange accent made his way to the stevedoring offices in London to meet with his Masonic contacts. The British had a long and lucrative trade history with Sicily.[18] They had docked their ships at Marsala for decades. Trade was so good to the economy of both nations, that the British took to upgrading the port and docking facilities in return for exclusive licence to the harbour.

Such unhindered passage could only escalate the success of an intended invasion. Once clear passage was achieved, and a contact established in the respected British export company of Hopps, Ingham, Whitaker and Woodhouse, Crispi returned to Sicily before Christmas to test the reaction to Maniscalco's investigation, and to see if the Bourbon government was putting any additional security measures in place.[19]

The fly in the ointment was the police chief Maniscalco. He hated Sicilian patriots and had a track record of torturing anyone suspected of plotting an uprising. The prison cells of Palermo were awash with would-be patriots who had failed in their poorly thought-out ways to liberate the island.[20] Known for crushing the thumbs of his prisoners, screwing their feet to the floor, or covering their heads in bags for lengthy periods of silence to extract information, Maniscalco was no layabout when it came to loyalty to his King.[21] He also employed a network of informers to bring him up-to-date information of any invasion.

While on the island, Crispi again met his team of heavyweights and, because of the increased pressure applied by the chief of police, it was decided that the notorious Salvatore Maniscalco must be disposed of, murdered. It was thought his death would cut the head from the information-gathering snake and shift attention to a major investigation (into who killed the police chief), thus allowing the real work of a coup to advance behind the deflection.

Crispi and his confederates needed a henchman to take on the task of killing a police chief, a job he knew wouldn't be difficult on an island teeming with *picciotti*.[22] He and his co-conspirators chose the murderous Vito Farinella. He was well known for his past slayings on behalf of the leaders of the *picciotti*. But when the day came – 27 November – and the police chief presented himself in public at the cathedral, the hitman stepped forward and lunged with his knife, only to fail dismally, slightly wounding his target.[23]

Farinella panicked and fled on foot through the crowd, and Crispi, waiting nearby, pulled together another disguise and escaped the island. But not before paying his would-be assassin 600 ducati in gold for his botched efforts.

When Crispi's ship was well clear of Sicily's coastline, Farinella was arrested with the cash still in his pocket and hauled to police head-quarters to enjoy a session of Maniscalco's interrogation methods. True to his *picciotti* upbringing, Farinella took whatever the police chief dished out. He maintained his silence about who his employer was, while Crispi took off to plan his next move.

Crispi's espionage escapades saw him described by those in the know as a 'secret agent', and member of a clandestine underground movement within British Freemasonry. By March 1860, after meetings with key British traders, he returned to Sicily under yet another alias, and became instrumental in pulling together a team of insurgents to stage a protest at the Gancia church. To test the waters. And to visit a dance hall.

Their back-room activities concealed by a glamorous dance party, the rebels set about making bombs and rifle cartridges, all designed for use against the military once Garibaldi arrived; when that was, no one knew.[24] In time, the rebels were called *squadre*, 'bands of Rebels and Peasantry from the mountains of the interior, all armed'.[25]

The interior of Sicily was now swelling with *squadre*, living an almost nomadic existence in and around the villages, *picciotti* hidden from Bourbon authorities by the massive stone mountain faces that surround the city of Palermo, awaiting orders. Weeks before the arrival of Garibaldi a 'few hundred such rebels, some criminal, lay in wait, well-armed' and with one single focus: to take on authority.[26]

Meanwhile, in Palermo, on 4 April, sixty insurgents tucked them-selves into the back of the Gancia church, where they braced themselves with weapons.[27] As described in chapter 5, the Bourbon authorities reacted brutally, massacring the rebels.

With hostile eyes now all over town, Crispi again made a beeline to Savoy. It was clearly apparent that the security forces within Palermo were large and furious. What Crispi knew, which the security forces struggled to appreciate, was that the equally furious *picciotti* and their leaders, along with key aristocrats and citizens, were also ready, hidden away like spiders.

On 7 April, the alliance for change committed to the intended invasion of Sicily and the plan for volunteers was readied. By then war was obvious, and Garibaldi had the perfect ace up his sleeve, a gift delivered to him by Crispi: an army of rural thugs. He just needed to commit, to take up the cause.

Crispi could only have been pleased with his spy work. There is little doubt of its brilliance. He was Garibaldi's capable forward scout. But Crispi was not alone in gathering support. The efforts of Rosolino Pilo, his close colleague and fellow Mazzini supporter, were of great importance, especially among the *picciotti*.[28]

Pilo had lived alongside Crispi in London for months, plotting and planning about freeing their beloved homeland from Bourbon rule. In fact, the great republican himself, Mazzini, wrote a note of encouragement to Pilo as he sailed to Sicily, urging him to find the men to aid victory: 'Garibaldi is bound to rush . . .'.[29]

Pilo arrived in Messina in April, travelling in secret with his closest friend, Giovanni Corrao. They were virtually the same age and both in sync with Crispi's revolutionary path.[30] Along with La Masa and Garibaldi, they were exponents of guerrilla warfare, which sat well with the cunning ways of Crispi.

Pilo and Corrao marched on, crossing the island in their quest for manpower. They were shown enormous respect by rural Sicilians, and by folk in the big cities of Palermo and Messina, as they gathered their 'troops' – more than 800 *picciotti* and other locals. Pilo also falsely claimed that Garibaldi was on his way, when in fact Garibaldi was still mulling over the idea. Pilo's misinformation had the desired effect; it stirred rebels to get involved, as well as the inmates locked away in Vicaria Prison in Palermo, who got themselves into a frenzy over the coming of the great saviour, General Garibaldi. A typical reaction by low-level thugs looking for leadership. Day and night, they chanted about the pending arrival of the red-shirted revolutionary.[31]

Pilo and Corrao lay in wait with their men on top of the mountains, surrounding Palermo. By late April, the northwest side of the island was alive with an increasing number of lurking criminal gangs.[32] At night, constant wayward shots could be heard in the hills as anxiety fuelled their anger.

There has long been a question mark over the quality of *picciotti* Corrao mustered. A few early historians suggested they were the first iteration of what became known as the Mafia. Brutal men. Certainly, there is no mention of him gathering academics or gentry for the task ahead – each mention is of the hardest of men. As criminals usually respect men harder than themselves – the way of the criminal jungle – it seems obvious that Corrao had a certain pull, a power over the *picciotti*.

Corrao himself was labelled by historians as their leader. Others merely saw him as a patriot. Regardless, for Garibaldi to commit, he needed Corrao. And it worked. Eventually, word came that the red-shirted general had taken up the cause; he would lead an expedition to Sicily.[33] The newspaper editors went wild with headlines, and Francesco Crispi sighed with relief.

Once the invasion was underway, Garibaldi gave Corrao the rank of colonel and sent him and his men into a diversionary battle outside Palermo. Pilo, equally revered, also took his *picciotti* into deadly battles, both on the streets and in the countryside. But within twenty-four hours of entering Palermo, Pilo was gunned down, shot in the head, and died where he fell. Corrao, shattered, pushed on and led one campaign after another, thrusting his *picciotti* deeper into the heat of battle in Palermo.

(Three years after the taking of Palermo, two undercover police were seen loitering near Corrao's home. Soon after, the legendary leader of the *picciotti* was murdered in his street. The three wise monkeys were out that day; no one saw anything, no one heard anything, and no one was prepared to say anything.)

In his post-unification report on the 1860 battles and those who took part in them, the Prefect of Palermo was open about the existence of a new scourge (the Mafia) spreading across the land. He suggested that Corrao may have been the first link to understanding the Mafia, the old *picciotti* and its early structure. The Prefect stated that Corrao was at the centre of it all, colluding with the *picciotti*. An intriguing viewpoint by the leading law enforcement officer, and an unusual opinion for its time.[34] An observation I support. Indeed, I would go one step further and suggest that Corrao was one of the very first structured leaders of what became – at the time of his murder – the *mafiosi*.

As I would discover in my research, that thinking, however, has opponents. Some believe Corrao was among the first to intuitively understand the relationship between the earliest Mafia and politics.[35] A political observer of the time preferred to say that Corrao acted merely as a conduit between the extreme left-wing opposition, the Bourbons and common criminality. In other words, using the resources he could muster, a means to justify the end. Since when does society condone using violent thugs and murderers to advance an ideology or political path? I find it hard to accept this 'means to an end' argument, preferring to call a spade a spade: Corrao used his earliest Mafia thugs for what he wanted to achieve.

Regardless, the Prefect was, at last, pinning a label on who these bandits really were (or became). The Prefect's reports are fascinating to read. He explained what these hard men were capable of. And how they were able to influence a country through their cunning leadership with people like Corrao, Pilo, the Triolo brothers. And ultimately Francesco Crispi and the hero to them all, Giuseppe Garibaldi.

The behaviour of the *picciotti* back then was identical to how the Mafia operates business today, using the tactics mentioned by the Prefect, including the infiltration and manipulation of society.[36] All Corrao did, in engaging the *picciotti* on behalf of Garibaldi, was to use radical offcuts of society to prop up urgently needed numbers to steal a country. It is a pity Corrao died so young, the same year the Prefect wrote his report. Whoever Corrao was, and whatever his real role with the island's *picciotti* was, Garibaldi and Crispi were certainly the beneficiaries.

Crispi was so supremely confident his intended *coup de grâce* in Calatafimi would succeed, that he even risked the life of his wife, Rosalia Montmasson, who was the lone woman in the famed 1089 volunteers who disembarked at the port of Marsala. She survived the battle, spared from death or injury in the mayhem of violence, and marched behind the bloodied *picciotti* and *Garibaldini* into Palermo.[37] Her husband, courageous Francesco, was nearby, in the company of the Triolo brothers on the other side of the hill, tapping his conductor's baton on his dais. The rest we know.

Why was Francesco Crispi's wife, a Frenchwoman from Marseilles, on the ship that arrived at Marsala to take part in the attack on the Bourbons? Why would any man risk the life of his beloved wife for such a potentially fatal folly? The records show he adored her.[38] Why put her in harm's way? Certainly, she offered no skills to assist Garibaldi's men, and was probably seen as an annoyance.

Crispi must have known victory for Garibaldi was assured, as he had the commitment of the *picciotti* and their leaders. If Garibaldi's *Mille* had acted alone, his wife would have most certainly been slaughtered. Another indicator of how confident Crispi was of success was his appointment of a Trapani lawyer, Giuseppe Maurici, a man who had represented hundreds of *picciotti* thugs over many years. Crispi had Maurici waiting at the port of Marsala the moment the ships docked to reassure those worried about legal representation.

One thing troubled me about the story that had seeped out of the archival documents: what benefit were the *picciotti* and their leaders hoping to gain for their crucial role in overturning the Bourbons? As a detective, I have known many criminals. Thugs and murderers have no goodwill in them, none! The *picciotti* must have wanted a payoff to throw themselves at the Bourbons' bullets. But what was it?

Crispi's payoff for his espionage was to take the highest office in the new Sicily – Minister of the Interior and Finance. But in true Crispi form, that did not last long. The King cut him loose within months. And Garibaldi was on the nose, but why? The press, who had been fed only propaganda up until this point, were starting to ask too many questions. Within a month of the invasion, stories were peppering the stuffy air in the corridors of power. Cavour wrote to his confidant, Costantino Nigra, 'We must therefore prevent Garibaldi from conquering Naples and we must try and annex Sicily as soon as possible.'[39]

This poignant letter shows the real sentiment of the Prime Minister towards Garibaldi. Also telling is a letter written by Cavour to his trusted colleague as Garibaldi marched towards Calatafimi: 'I did everything in my power to persuade Garibaldi not to go on this mad escapade. I sent La Farina [lawyer and administrator] to talk to him, who came back with an assurance that the whole idea was off ... I had given orders to Rear Admiral Persano to arrest Garibaldi.'[40]

Both King Vittorio Emanuele and Cavour were fearful that unless both warriors of freedom were removed from Sicily all hell might break loose, but they did not leave until they'd negotiated legal protection for Sicilian *picciotti* and their leaders. No criminal charges would ever be laid for their actions during the expedition.

The King and Garibaldi propagated, until their deaths, a marshmallow version of what happened on 11 May 1860: a courageous general with a red shirt and a thousand volunteers went to Sicily on an expedition to unite Italy. It is, however, a fairytale. Used to deflect attention from a seed sown at the time. A lone, hard, underground seed that would eventually grow to become the Mafia, the worst, most feared gang in the world.

CHAPTER 7

HAYSTACK NEEDLES

SICILIAN SAYING:

Cosi chi pàmpini

Things with leaves

Meaning, when something great bears fruit

In my world, the place I spent a couple of decades investigating, it was all about evidence, testimony, unravelling, and the search for the truth. Detectives the world over have a maxim: *Failure to search is failure to find.* In searching for how the Mafia came into existence, it was, at times, like looking for a needle in a haystack. After so long in the archives, my search for that elusive truth was knitting together a narrative, and what I saw surprised me.

As a detective, though, I had learnt that the truth is like the sun: you can shut it out for a time, but it does not go away. I have always wanted to be a detective, as far back as I can recall. I have such a vivid memory, as a fourteen-year-old, on the run from my father, as my mother found a tiny one-bedroom apartment for us to live in. All five of us, sleeping on top of each other, but we were always happy, once free of the violence. We kids would sit around playing Beatles records as Ma kept the kitchen full of delicious home-cooked meals. Then, shattering our tranquillity, late one dark night my drunken father came calling; he had found us, as he invariably did, smashing his way into our safe haven and setting upon us – his target was my mother. As we banded together and fended off his blows, all we could hope for was that a police siren might be heard among our screams. After what seemed like an achingly long time, the flashing blue lights of police cars strobed through our windows as the blue uniforms raced to our safety. And, in no time, the wolf was taken from our door. Yet again. It's that basic saviour role of police that embedded itself in me, over and over. There would be no other career for me than that of a detective. I loved every minute of it. Oddly, growing up with violence never did any lasting harm to me. Indeed, it helped me understand violent men and, in time, the Mafia.

Now, in my search for the origins of the Mafia, I had facts that challenged the very making of Italy, its sacred unification, the Risorgimento. Facts that brought to the surface carefully hidden shenanigans, which looked like Italy's dirty secret. I had no interest in the subject of the taking of Sicily, no desire to cause controversy. My dilemma was the year 1860, and I knew I would face the wrath of many unless I could find supportive materials to prosecute what I had discovered.

I understand that a population may struggle with the issue that their great day in history, the creation of a twenty-region Italy, may have been based on a lie, a carefully constructed one, in which they were served up a hero, a spy, a brave thousand and a massive victory. It sounds fantastic that the earliest form of Mafia was almost certainly the reason for the victory at Calatafimi. So, what to do? Easy, keep digging. If it happened as the hidden narrative suggests, then there must be more to learn. I went back into the dust, under the reading lamps, and put on my cotton gloves. I also rang Enza with the promise of more *biscotti*. And rang Elena and vowed that we would share more Iris *dolci* at Bar Santoro, then I contacted Agata and told her to put some oil on the squeaky wheels of her bicycle. We had work to do.

The word 'Mafia' first appeared in a dictionary in 1868. Antonio Traina put 'Mafia' in his Sicilian–Italian dictionary, with the following definition: 'new word meaning action, insolence, arrogance, boldness, haughtiness: collective noun meaning thugs, people who believe they are tough men because they use brute strength. On the contrary they are like beasts.'[1]

It usually takes at least five years for a new word to find a home within the pages of a dictionary. Scholars need to be sure that a word is not just a passing fad, so they wait and see if society holds on to that word. In the case of Traina, he must have waited long enough to realise the word 'Mafia', like the gang itself, was not going away.

Giuseppe Marino, a Professor of Contemporary History at Palermo University, has spent his adult life trying to unravel the Mafia mystery. His teachings on the subject are spoken of globally. Of the first dictionary mention of the word, his opinion is that it is also necessary to find out the origins of the social phenomenon of the Mafia. It is not enough to just register the appearance of the word in a dictionary. However, there is nothing Marino, I or anyone else can find, that one can hang a hat on to suggest the Mafia goes back to the seventeenth or eighteenth centuries. If there was, there would be a book about it.

More than a hundred years ago, an Italian professor of law, Gaetano Mosca, attempted to explain that in seventeenth-century Spain, villains absconded to Italy, to the Spanish-occupied territories, such as Sicily and parts of northern Italy. Once they took hold in their new land, they soon became 'the Mafia'. I heard this explanation many times during my research. Mosca's explanation, though, is too thin; he does not explain why the first Mafia in Sicily, from Spanish migration, did not (also) eventuate in northern Italy, or in other parts of the globe as the Spanish expanded their empire during this period. Simply put, there is nothing to support the theory.

Carlo Gemelli, a nineteenth-century historian and professor, when researching for his book on the Belgian Revolution, commented that (perhaps) the Mafia started in feudal times, a century before unification when land barons were forced to hire thugs to protect their properties.[2] Nice theory, one I have heard often, but Gemelli was unable to take it any further. What he did say, which makes sense, was that groups that later became the Mafia honed their tactics, their skills and their ways, around the time of the revolution in Sicily in 1848.

On a more humorous note, the popular writer Giuseppe Petrai, in his *Novel of a Bandit*, invented the beginnings of the Mafia with a precise date, June 1799, and a specific locality, Mazara del Vallo – a brightly painted, lime-washed town in the southwest corner of Sicily, now home to many African refugees. He claimed the founding members were known locally by the names Pig's Paw, Dog's Nose, Giacalone, Uncle Pascà and Iannone.[3] Nothing more has ever come of this work of fiction, and I place it in the same category as Mario Puzo's famed novel, *The Godfather*: a good read, written by an author with a wild imagination.

With greater credibility, Pasquale Villari, a nineteenth-century historian and professor of history, says the Mafia was born by spontaneous generation.[4] I tend to agree, in part; what happened in Calatafimi was, to some degree, spontaneous. The violent clash with the Bourbons was not years in the planning. It was a rushed campaign, pulled together by Crispi and *picciotti* leaders and kept secret. The only information an individual *picciotto* could have known were last-minute time and date details, and to get to Marsala quickly and bring your guns and bombs!

From digging through the shelves and finding fragments like these, it began to look as if the winning theory was that the Mafia came into existence about the time of Garibaldi. In the Prefect reports out of Palermo, the name 'Maffia' appears on 25 April 1865, after unification.[5]

Then I found something that made me sit up and have another *biscotto*: a paper drafted by magistrate Pietro Calà Ulloa from Trapani, on 3 August 1838. He wrote:

> There is no office worker in Sicily who does not prostrate himself to the order of a bully and who does not think to profit from his office. This general corruption has made the people resort to overly timid and dangerous remedies. There are in many towns brotherhoods, sort of sects that define themselves parties, without any political purpose, with no other bond than that of depending on a leader, who can be a landowner or an archpriest. The lack of the authorities has multiplied the number of crimes! People come to tacit agreement with the offenders. As thefts occur, the mediators offer transactions for the recovery of the stolen objects.

> The number of such agreements is infinite. Many senior officials
> cover them up with impenetrable strength.[6]

This comment was made ten years before the 1848 revolution and
twenty years before Garibaldi and Crispi conspired a coup. What the
magistrate – who would have dealt with thousands of criminals in his
time – makes clear is that there was a sect, a brotherhood, in existence
in Sicily before unification. We also know, as previously mentioned,
a gang of 700 fighters from the Monte Erice and Trapani regions
joined the battle at Calatafimi, so one expects many of them were
early incarnations of (what became) Mafia. The key I gleaned from
the magistrate's report is the word 'sect'. There is much to understand
about that four-letter word. While he did not call it 'Mafia' – for surely
the magistrate would have mentioned the word – he was, nonetheless,
on to it, on to the bubbling of a scourge. A chilling prediction from
an astute man. The magistrate lends weight to Professor Giuseppe
Marino's comment that it is important to consider the margins of
feasibility of the deeds accomplished by Garibaldi:

> A thousand men would not have been enough to put out an
> army and finally conquer a kingdom, without the decisive help
> of forces much more substantial, that in fact emerged numerous
> and fierce from the popular Sicilian reality, and were present
> following the 'hero' since the first battle of Calatafimi, the day
> after the landing of Marsala and the proclamation of the dictator-
> ship in the name of Vittorio Emanuele, king of Italy. There can
> be no doubt that these forces would never have come to light.
> The picturesque and anarchic phalanxes of the *picciotti* – who,
> from Calatafimi onwards, had become increasingly important
> in terms of quantity and military quality, constituted the irre-
> placeable mass of manpower, to conquer Palermo, to drive out
> the Bourbons.[7]

Marino adds that the powers behind the invasion of Sicily prevailed
because if they wanted to win, they had to follow the political line of
Francesco Crispi, who was the political mind behind the expedition.

I agree. Lord Brancaccio di Carpino, an aristocrat who favoured a revolt against the Bourbons, describes the events vividly:

> We went daily in the nearby countryside to enlist the animate peasants under the tricolour flag; by instinct the native peasants hated tyranny by conviction and principles as they hated the more educated classes. It was a hard necessity to recruit people of all ranks: we were unfortunately forced, not being able to avoid this choice, to welcome all those who said they were ready to fight. Regarding the activities of the *picciotti*, it is not true that the followers of the revolutionary squadrons were all criminals: sad men there were too, many, but the honest men were not less. Nor is it right to confuse with one another in a bundle, and judge them the same way.[8]

He is saying that he saw an equal number of criminals as there were good, wholesome volunteers.

In his work *Notarelle*, writer and staunch supporter of Garibaldi Giuseppe Cesare Abba states he was at the battle and saw 'heavily armed highlanders with certain rotten faces, and certain eyes that look like gun mouths'. He adds, 'all these people are led by men, to whom they dutifully obey'.[9] Abba did not have great sympathy for the Sicilians, who appeared to him as an incomprehensible mixture of nobility and barbarity; in effect, the same words or explanation as Lord Carpino. Of the *picciotti* teams, where Abba records their ferocity on various occasions, the Lord describes them as 'criminal representation'.[10] This description is close to another description of the time: 'that men, out of breath, bloodied and exhausted by three hours fighting pressed on like a bunch of demon-possessed creatures who seemed to have come out of the ground'. Clearly not a description of pharmacists, doctors and students![11]

I found more. The well-respected British historian G. M. Trevelyan recorded over a hundred years ago that Garibaldi was a leader endowed with a profound revolutionary instinct, who introduced into the movement the ingredients, or, rather, the socially subversive 'yeasts', that could operate quickly in opposition to the interests of the barons and the middle class. To call the *picciotti* 'the yeast in the recipe for unification' is an interesting description, but it arguably camouflages the role of the *picciotti*, which seems to have been vital to the taking of Sicily. To cite Occam's razor – the principle whereby the simplest explanation is usually the right one – the *picciotti* were used to fight alongside Garibaldi and the *Mille* to win Sicily. To exclude the bandits is to suggest that the success of the *Mille* was a divine miracle.

The historian Marino observes that the barons who supported the national revolution fed it with rebels and adventurers capable of making people obedient and faithful instruments of the so-called Sicilian interests.[12] They were joined by common criminals, escaped from prison when Garibaldi threw open the gates of the prison in Marsala the day he landed, whom he then rallied to fight alongside him. Garibaldi did not check criminal records or consider moral character; he just needed fighters, manpower (not doctors), to get the killing done.

This fits with comments by Diego Tajani, a magistrate and politician of the time, who said there were in many towns brotherhoods and sects that defined themselves without any political purpose and had no other bonds than their dependence on a leader: a simple overview of a Mafia clan.[13] Magistrate Tajani indicated that the public administration asked the Mafia for favours in exchange for protection and favours of their own. Later in the nineteenth century, the Minister of the Interior, Giovanni Giolitti – who would go on to be Prime Minister of Italy five times – suggested something similar: the Mafia knew who they could harass, and who they could not.[14]

Duke Colonna di Cesarò, a Sicilian noble, also said something quite compelling about the early Mafia. A statement he made to the Parliamentary Commission of Inquiry of 1875[15] is telling on matters post-unification, and the willingness of the earliest version of the Mafia, alongside peasants and city-dwelling Sicilians, to bear arms against the Bourbons:

> I think that the Mafia is a legacy of Sicilian Liberalism, because when Feudalism fell, or rather, when Feudalism consciously renounced its power (in 1812), at the same time the Bourbons broke the loyalty sworn to Sicily, and since then a continuous and implacable struggle between Sicily and the Bourbons began.

I say Sicily because all the Sicilian social classes were in agreement
in this fight.

He ends by saying that Garibaldi, during his invasion, made prompt
and efficient use of the population (*picciotti*) to inflict a mortal blow
on the Bourbons, by a class of person that was used to taking the law
into their own hands. Another astute man.

The admiral in charge of the British fleet, Sir George Rodney Mundy,
allowed Garibaldi into the port of Marsala, along with his *Mille*.
Once he saw them safely ashore, he took his battleship to position off
Palermo harbour and played a minor, yet politically pivotal, role in how
things unfolded over the coming weeks. In his diary, published in
1863, he recalls: 'the Government was overwhelmed as rebels flooded
in from the countryside'.[16]

Lucio Tasca, a post-Fascism period Mayor of Palermo,[17] held a
strong position on the invasion of Sicily under Garibaldi, believing
unification could not have happened without the help of the Mafia,
or the *picciotti*.

Historian and author Gaetano Falzone (1912–84) believed there
was a wide variety of different men who held the separatist banner
and loaned themselves to Garibaldi for the cause of unification.[18] On
one hand were students who abandoned their studies and middle-class
families for adventure. On the other hand were bandits and escaped
lifers, serious criminals, along with a gang from Niscemi, a small
village towards Agrigento, who took up the fight.[19]

Citing the diary of Admiral Mundy, investigative journalist Ignazio
Coppola writes in his article 'I Vespri Siciliani' that by the time
Garibaldi had reached the gates of Palermo, his *Mille* were buoyed
by 2000 *picciotti*, many of whom were led by famous *mafiosi* of the
time. Coppola goes on to describe the wholesale looting and mayhem
that ensued.[20]

Another early twentieth-century historian, Luigi Genuardi, wrote
that Garibaldi was met by '1500 *picciotti* members, undisciplined, and
armed to the fullest, all animated by the spirit and powerful voice of
their leaders'[21] in Marsala before setting off to fight the Bourbons.
On the evening of 26 May, at the gates of Palermo, after the historic

first battle at Calatafimi, Garibaldi addressed another 'four leaders of *picciotti*, each of them in charge of hundreds of wild men, each wanting to be amongst the first fighters to enter the city'. There is also mention of Garibaldi going for a late-night visit to the village of Gibilrosso to meet another 3000 *picciotti* to ready them for the attack.[22] From there the general went on to meet the Sant'Anna team of *picciotti*, led by Crispi's friend Signor Triolo and his brothers. He wore out his leather boots, cutting across to the town of Giacinte, to stir up yet more *picciotti*.

Another historian, Francesco Renda (1922–2013), in his book *History of the Mafia*, had a notion that the Mafia started around the time of unification and makes an interesting comment on how it evolved.[23] After 1860, he suggests, there was a 'steep change in the Mafia . . . primarily in its rapid and widespread diffusion'. He describes an evolution whereby the *picciotti* became violent brigands, who were more organised following unification in 1860. 'Brigand' is a word used regularly in the police reports of Sicily, describing perpetrators of violence and members of violent sects. Within a few years, no county in western Sicily remained immune. The gangs gained thousands of members, and organised groups covered a large part of the island, including eastern Sicily.

Renda does not underestimate the organic and profound link between the coming of the Mafia and the new politics of Sicily. It could be argued a unitary state was born in Sicily as a Mafia-like political sub-strategy. The leaders of the *picciotti* always had political savvy in their bloodstream. Sicily still had a way to go before politics really swam in the same dirty water as the *picciotti*, then on their way to becoming the Mafia. All that was missing was a name to be feared, a hundred meetings, and organisational skills.

The earliest use of the word 'Mafia' was in 1863 in the play *I Mafiusi de la Vicaria*, by Giuseppe Rizzotto and Gaspare Mosca. The title translates as *The Mafia of Vicaria*. Vicaria, sometimes spelt Vucciria, is an old part of Palermo, the Arab quarter, and home to the most feared prison in nineteenth-century Palermo, overfull with violent criminals. Were the writers suggesting the prison was full of the worst of the worst, villains considered Mafia members?

The three-act play centres around a protagonist who lords it over the criminal population of the prison.[24] Each day, the *mafioso* figure takes the only seat in the common room of the prison and spits his orders to his fellow inmates, issues jobs, and promotes the best-performing *picciotti* up the ladder.

Despite being a comedy, the play was hard-nosed about showing how the head of the prison inmates controlled the other prisoners. It would be reviewed as a profoundly harsh message about life and crime in 1860s Palermo. It is unclear if Rizzotto and Mosca used the name Mafia in their play after hearing it fall from the lips of hardened *picciotti* in the back streets of Palermo, or if the reverse was true: once the play became a hit the *picciotti* gangs adopted the word. From my law enforcement experience, knowing how criminals name themselves and their clans, the latter is highly feasible.

Regardless, with or without the name 'Mafia', the crime gang problem in 1863 Palermo was a big issue. The Mafia – by whatever name – had come to town: to Palermo, to Sicily and across Italy. Over the next decade, the play ran in theatres across Italy, all the way to Savoy.[25]

At the time, the Mayor of Palermo stated publicly that Vicaria Prison was a sort of government unto itself, where the Mafia issued orders, such was their influence behind stone walls. One of the original theatre programs has survived and is now part of Palermo's historical archive. Battered and torn, the word 'Mafiusi' is plain to see. Spelled differently than it is today, the word has been through its own journey, like the mobsters themselves. 'Mafiusi' was shortened, usually by journalists, to Mafia. (From here on I will use the common word, 'Mafia'.) Some academics offer an explanation, without evidence, that the word came from the 200-year period when Arabs ruled Sicily, before vacating the island, leaving the word '*mahyas*' behind, meaning blusterous, the noun being '*mahyasa*'. Another word from the Arabic period is '*mo'afiah*', which refers to one who is arrogant in manner and behaviour. There is also an Arabic word for rejection that is spelt *marfud*. All of them are fair to me. The point is no one person or authority has been able to offer irrefutable evidence of any use of the term earlier than Rizzotto and Mosca's play.

Pushing the word aside, possibly the most compelling documents on the earliest days of the Mafia lie in the Prefect reports. I've read many of the annual Prefect reports. They are hefty documents that would have taken many weeks to compile. Baron Turrisi Colonna was well considered by all and accepted the prestigious role of Prefect of Palermo from 1861. He was head of the National Guard and would serve twice as Mayor of Palermo. He wrote a comprehensive report each year about the state of the city and the security issues he faced.[26]

I pored over the dusty pages of his reports with Elena, cotton gloved and careful not to tear or harm the fragile paper. One of the first things Colonna mentions is that Sicily's young were attaching themselves to gangs. He used the word 'sects' to describe the thugs and gangs that were overtaking Sicily and Palermo. He had seen the sects developing as far back as the revolution of 1848, and feared that unless resources were thrown at them, the problem would worsen. He knew that the same sects had offered their services to the Garibaldi invasion.

Reading Colonna's reports confirms when the Mafia came into its name. He often mentions perpetrators as part of sects. The word 'Mafia' is then included in the dictionary compiled by Antonio Traina in 1868. These three key pieces of evidence – the Prefect report of Colonna, the jailhouse play and the dictionary inclusion – make it undeniable that 'Mafia', as a word, as a name for the violent gangs, came into existence in 1863. If the gangs were called 'Mafia' before Colonna wrote his report, then he would have called them that. He would have updated Rome and given the crime problem a name, not just called them sects.

Thankfully, to better understand the epidemic that became the Mafia, Colonna goes into detail, recalling the 1848 revolution, and how the fight for change ran across the island until it petered out. The most disgruntled fell into a life of crime, focusing on theft, muggings, robbery, and the movement and sale of contraband. Then came the formation of the sects. Crime became organised, and organised crime became the problem for Colonna. Gangs were able to run amok, get bolder, tougher, mostly because the Bourbons failed to throw resources at the scourge.

The ten years leading up to the unification, according to Colonna, were of great concern. The worst scourge, he observed, was evident in the rural areas, where law enforcement was minimal.[27] He called it, in his 1861 report, 'the bad seed of association'. With limited police manpower, the sects were shut down, only to pop up again, down the road, in the next village.

Colonna mentioned the days before the invasion of Sicily by Garibaldi; the Bourbon authorities, on alert due to the botched protest at Gancia, identified a sect of old-time gangsters living off contraband.[28] The sect had also stashed away a huge cache of weapons. What was the purpose of such dangerous booty, weeks before the *picciotti* ran wild alongside Garibaldi? The answer is obvious.

Throughout the sixty-three-page document, Colonna uses the word 'sect' fifty times, and by the time he sent his report to the government, the way to refer to *picciotti*, sects or bandits became 'the Mafia'. Colonna was the first to note that stringent rules were starting to emerge. For example, any sect member who talked to police would be killed immediately.[29] Times were tough, so were the rules. Colonna enlightened government that the sects were becoming well organised. While management of the sects was in its infancy at the time of the 1863 report, Colonna reported that the sects had locked in a standard operational procedure that, whenever possible, police must be killed on site, at random. Colonna ends his report with a plea for help, noting that the Sicilian provinces will never have public security until they obtain adequate security resources from the government.[30] To this day, the good people of Sicily are still waiting.

To verify my facts, I gained permission to read the same security report for the year earlier. That report says the political upheaval associated with the unification violence precipitated the emergence of crime gangs, and that if the situation did not improve, then what lay ahead would be 'deadly' for Sicily. Each page is a reiteration of atrocities, death and violence, and the writer places the blame fairly and squarely at the feet of the Sicilian government.

CHAPTER 8

THE PROMISED LAND

SICILIAN SAYING:

U pisci feti ra testa
A fish smells bad from the head

Meaning, the cause of bad behaviour depends on the boss

Francesco Crispi was the smartest man in the revolutionary room when he jumped off his ship at Messina in 1859 and ran around Sicily in his disguises to meet with leaders of the yet-to-be-called Mafia. He would be rewarded for his work, getting a firm handshake from men who would carry out the nasty work of violence. But surely these same men wanted something for themselves? No soldier of fortune, mercenary or paid killer jumps into a fight unless there is a payday. Under the criminal code there is no honour among thieves; they are the first to put their hands out for a 'whack' of the spoils and a slice of the action.

Growing up in Struggle Town, Australia, with a thief for a father and an uncle who worked on the wharves, stealing vast amounts of consumer goods from container ships, I saw firsthand the mindset of the criminal. Nothing is for nothing; there is always a payday.

Once Garibaldi and his fighters banished the Bourbon authorities, the revolutionary brains trust – Crispi and Garibaldi – rushed a legislative decree through the now 'in limbo' parliament. It was a law both men were keen to enact; they spoke of it on the battlefield after Calatafimi. Garibaldi wanted to reward those who killed and conquered, and most had backgrounds less than ideal for a revolutionary.

On 2 June 1860 – two weeks after taking Calatafimi, and only days after securing Palermo – the decree ordered the distribution of municipal property to the citizens, in favour of those who had fought for the homeland. This was in line with the decree to quickly install a militia and move on the rabble who fought for Garibaldi, who 'rose in arms'.[1]

The two laws went hand in hand. When the land decree was passed, Crispi was Secretary of State. He ordered five decrees in all, including a law enforcing harsh penalties for looting and murder.[2] Like a foul stench, word of land on offer to fighters spread far and wide. A slice of land seemed fair recompense for putting your life on the line and matched Garibaldi's whispered promise to any *picciotti* or peasants who took up arms against the Bourbons.[3] Their slice of Sicily, albeit tiny, was nonetheless a mound of self-esteem.

Crispi and Garibaldi's promise to give government-owned land was clever. It instilled discipline in their fighters, especially the *picciotti*, who were difficult to control, lawless, and without the usual respect of brave volunteers.[4]

It didn't work as well as intended. Reports of atrocities were common. Still, the mix of thugs and scared peasants kept up the fight, becoming heroes, knowing and believing that one day soil would be their salary. The promise of land also acted as motivation to turn good and bad men alike into killers. Garibaldi's letter to the people of Sicily, moments before the unification battle commenced, reads:

> Sicilians, I have brought you a body of brave men, who have hastened to reply to the heroic cry of Sicily . . . to arms, then! He who does not snatch up a weapon is a coward or a traitor to his country. We will get muskets, but for the present any weapon will do in the hands of a brave man. The municipalities shall provide for children, women, and old men deprived of their support. To arms, all of you![5]

The general's words suggest that the families of brave men would be looked after by the municipalities. There is no discrimination. Reading of this reward system, my mind drifted back to the wonderful dinner at the bed and breakfast house a year earlier, and the family story told by my host's historian mother about the land given to their ancestor, a fighter for Garibaldi. I could imagine the sentiment at hearing of Garibaldi's offer. At last, suppressed farmworkers, tormented local thugs, men on the land who broke their backs for Bourbon barons, and downtrodden wives could become landowners. Life could change.

A young Henry Adams, whose grandfather and great-grandfather had been Presidents of the United States, was in Naples at the time of the unification.[6]

Later to be a historian and Harvard professor, the 22-year-old wrote in his autobiography that he had just graduated from Harvard and was seeking adventure. On a hot day in southern Italy in 1860, he was given a handful of dispatches for the captain of a US ship anchored off Palermo. Adams jumped aboard the first boat out, arriving the next day. His name alone got him into the Senate House at this key time in history when land was being promised and government was (sort of) underway. He spent time with Garibaldi, who was full of nervous energy and had the manner of 'a wild animal'.[7] The general was in the company of his 'piratic' staff.

Adams was drawn to the soldier, now in the role of dictator. He recalled him as 'certainly the most serious of the doubtful energies in the world'.[8] Adams recalled the calm voice of the general wearing a red flannel shirt. The reason for the red shirt was not known to Adams; he saw it as an oddity, not the uniform so often mentioned in history books or paintings. He doesn't mention anyone else wearing red shirts, certainly not the *Mille*. Was the legend of the garment stitched into history from that day?

Adams records the tone of that meeting, Garibaldi acting as 'anarchist and banker'.[9] What did he mean by 'banker'? That word annoyed me like a nettle from a Sicilian thistle as I continued my research.

In his autobiography, Adams describes his newly acquired friend as both an Italian 'patriot and a pirate'.[10] 'Pirate' was another word that itched me; in any language 'pirate' means one thing. Adams later referred to Garibaldi's autobiography, when the general had trouble understanding his own actions, believing he'd been an instrument for a class he cared little for. Adams' lasting impression of the general was that of a simple-mannered, seafaring captain, leading Genovese adventurers and Sicilian crime gangs.

The legislative decree promising land, however, proved difficult to implement. The shock was, the land in question had already been allocated to others. Politics and greed interfered with the gesture. But the fighters were not to know this; at least not just yet.

Maybe it was best to keep it quiet, keep the fighting in full frenzy, as the promise boosted the fighters' appetite for war. The violence inflicted during the battle for unification was so bad at times it was considered the worst in centuries, akin to the horrors inflicted on innocent citizens back in medieval times. Garibaldi's troops committed terrible atrocities on unarmed citizens, hence the need for the decree to enact severe penalties for murderers and looters. Palermo had fallen to the misery that only humans can create. Church bells rang as bombs and bullets turned the cultured city into hell and ash, as houses burned, and people were massacred. *Picciotti* were swarming everywhere.[11]

Promising land for military service was not foreign to Italian politics. It goes as far back as the Roman Empire when centurions – the most battle-hardened army officers – after spearheading their army's way on behalf of their rulers through Britain, Europe and North Africa, promised land to mercenaries to recruit them to their cause.[12]

In the Mount Etna area, on the eastern side of Sicily, there was a revolt against the new order of unification and Garibaldism. Easterners had softer socialist views and less *picciotti* crime than their neighbours to the west. Cities like Catania and Syracuse were home to scholars, well-educated folk, idealists, visionaries, as well as families involved in shipping, trade and commerce. A village called Bronte, on the ashen black slopes of Etna, became a symbol of the latest wave of politics being forced upon them: explosive, swift and with casualties. At their protests, a general from Garibaldi's army decided he had no patience for the voice of democracy; he shot dead nine innocent people, and injured many others, ending any opposition.[13] Not satisfied, he went to another rally killing a further six, thus bringing utter mayhem to the island. He then returned to the expedition, ensuring the Sicilians got the message, gunshot-loud and clear: do not step in the way of the revolution.[14]

By the end of June, Cavour was fearful of the politicking of Garibaldi, the laws he was making on the run. By 13 November, there was chaos in the administration of Sicily, particularly in Palermo, as Crispi too was now on the outer. Though a good spy, he was proving to be a disastrous administrator. Protests started as malcontents drifted onto the streets, voices wanting to be heard, yelps of anger against what was happening or wasn't happening. The citizens, who had suffered immeasurably, were becoming embittered, and seeing the criminality before their eyes they screamed for common sense and civility.[15] The suggestion that all Sicily wanted this revolution was being seriously challenged.

Cavour stepped in and sent a team of diplomats from Piedmont to take control of Palermo. He installed Giuseppe La Farina as caretaker of the debacle, leaving Garibaldi to be the loose cannon in the war zone. La Farina had tried but failed to talk Garibaldi out of embarking on the invasion back in Genoa, his arguments delivered on behalf of Prime Minister Cavour.

The two chieftains behind unification, Garibaldi and Crispi, were losing popularity as quickly as they had gained it. The common Palermitan was starting to wonder what was happening in their part of the world. La Farina seemed their only hope, and would, at least, have Cavour's full support.[16]

During this time, the inevitable came to the *picciotti*. Before the surrender of the Two Sicilies at the steps of the Royal Palazzo outside Naples, whispers, rumours, then the truth permeated the ranks of the fight-weary warriors of Garibaldi: there would be no land after all, no slice of Sicily. The Promised Land became a broken promise.

Despite the legislative decree, the possibility of claiming the land in a way that was legal finally proved an impossibility.[17] Garibaldi was said to have been broken at the news.

It's this broken promise that laid the foundation stones of the Mafia, like nothing that came before.

It's very simple to understand if you know the mindset of criminals. You never promise what you can't deliver. As a cop, I saw the ramifications of ill-conceived promises, time and again. Countless numbers of murders within the criminal world were caused by bravado, bullshit and broken promises. Before I went undercover in the Mafia, I spent many years investigating homicides. The hardest to solve were those in which criminals had fallen out, over money, women or a broken promise.

The broken promise gave rise to a wave of peasant and *picciotti* revolts, particularly thunderous in the provinces of Palermo, Agrigento and Trapani, the foothold of the earliest form of Mafia.[18] For months into the new year, bitter disillusionment reigned. It was destined to last for decades. This blow to the wild men who gave their all to the revolutionary cause would have a devastating effect on Sicily. Having given up fighting for Garibaldi, the *picciotti* returned home and licked their wounds: no medals, no land, no recognition and no chance. Then, with their leaders and elders, they brooded, and, like a time bomb, they ticked. Stewing in their anger, they witnessed neighbouring municipalities honouring the gift of land, while others were not. It was becoming an inconsistent mess. Early release prisoners, promised the same land for their fight, also heard the confusing news. No one had the patience to wade through the bureaucratic confusion; self-ishness festered, and the rule of law was forgotten as riots erupted everywhere.[19] Dialogue gave way to mayhem as collective violence flooded the streets and officials went searching for an answer; some even started re-promising the land. Such administrative uncertainty only heightened the tension and caused more confusion.

Trapani was awash with homicides, kidnappings, looting, robberies and destruction. A fire of anger raced across Sicily.[20] Elena and I would be glued to prefecture reports, housed in the Gancia Archivio di Palermo, page after page of atrocities, blood splashed everywhere. The tricoloured flag of victory was replaced with three other colours: white, red and purple, the colours of flesh, blood and bruising as random innocents were killed where they cowered, murdered and bashed where they stood. A National Guard captain told of the violence, seeing thugs revolting against one another:

> like wolves driven by hunger from the mountains, [they] began breaking into houses. We witnessed an orgy of terror. One man was dragged through the streets by his feet after suffering the most-filthy indignities, all the time being pricked by knives and then burned half alive in front of the house of his son.[21]

Another outbreak claimed the lives of eighteen citizens as the village collapsed into violence. A 'bestial mob' ran riot, causing a 'complete state of anarchy' as houses were burned, even the home of the priest of the town. The only way to stop the wholesale killing was to employ summary executions.[22] Bad-tempered, bloodstained thuggery was met with a bullet to the head by police, who were operating in an atmosphere of total fear.

Then came the macabre, as is often the case with the lowest form of criminal: a respected legal notary was torn apart in the street and burned alive. They then cut out his liver and heart, and one of his killers ate it in front of a crowd that had degenerated into a pack of crazed savages.[23] The Sicilian calendar had raced back to the Middle Ages. Police reports of those times are full of similar wrongs, dozens of massacres, too many to place on these pages. If ever there was a set of bloodthirsty deeds to highlight the arrival of the Mafia – the birth of an underground festering nest of hatred – the broken-promise massacres are surely it.

Governor Paternostro di Corleone stated that 'the ability for everyone to steal and act in whatever manner they liked' was the largest problem in his town.[24]

If there was irony in the sheer horrors of what happened, it would be in the land itself. Remarkably, some municipalities did end up granting small slices of land to a few who fought with Garibaldi.[25] An example of the fog of war where chaos was now in bed with administrative blundering.

But with the emergence of violent gangs and mass killings, was it too little too late? Had the festering land issue become the ember to ignite a Sicilian underbelly? Smouldering, waiting for years, since the days of feudalism? For this author and ex-anti-Mafia detective, I believe the actions of the *picciotti*, the criminals – the same crazed men who had tasted blood months earlier on the killing fields of unification – was the arrival of the Mafia. It was the defining moment in history when bad men became evil men. Despite inexcusable atrocities, this moment in time is the Mafia's Gettysburg, their Normandy. A shocking, inexcusable baptism of fire, as they swarmed the land, killing and destroying in the name of soil, before they crawled under their rocks and thought about regrouping.

The year 1860 can be stamped as the inception of the Mafia.

By contrast, Garibaldi and his *Mille* had captured the headlines, and hearts and minds, of a new nation. News of their victory spread around the world, offering stories of bravado, not bloodshed, as everyone loves a smiling hero. Municipalities hurriedly built statues of a coiffured Garibaldi and a debonair King Vittorio Emanuele, erecting them in every park, piazza and city hall across the new land. A massive team of enamel painters created new signs for renamed streets, boulevards and piazzas in memory of the general and the King. No one wanted the news of bad men being refused land, preferring a brighter version of history. Stories of students, who, as a supreme act of sacrifice, dropped their chalk and dusted off their hands; doctors, leaving their stethoscopes and syringes; pharmacists who put aside their medicines and glass jars; and shopkeepers who bolted their shop doors tight – all jumping a steam ship to sunny Sicily to fight for King and country

As for the promised land, someone left the cake out in the rain, and most promises went unpaid. There would be no cigars for the *picciotti*. Nor for the poor and their grubby-faced offspring. All that was left was what the *picciotti* knew well. From then on, the poor, the *picciotti* – anyone with a gripe or a broken promise – took matters into their own hands and smashed their way through Sicily, thieving, bashing, raping and pillaging.

Landowners who had something to fear took on armed men as bodyguards. Ironically, the men who acted as bodyguards were more than likely gangsters themselves, carrying weaponry and lashing out, capable of anything. The Mafia became the violent expression of popular anger, united into a criminal network made up of men who believed they had been treated like dogs. These men never again trusted in justice, other than the type they could achieve with their own hands.

Who was responsible for this madness, this creation? Garibaldi? Francesco Crispi or King Vittorio Emanuele II? Or all three? The reports and books I read suggested a dangerous camaraderie had been birthed: bad men who helped one another, like brothers, till death, allowing each other to escape from the claws of justice, and silencing witnesses along the way. The wounds of unification convinced the Mafia that justice was only for the rich. Therefore, the Mafia became a law unto themselves, governed internally by their own code of conduct.

Once the name 'Mafia' took hold, the word 'picciotti' faded away. It was heard less often in the shadows of darkened laneways as a token of fear, replaced by the more troublesome 'Mafia'. Both Elena and Agata, my translators, mentioned that picciotti is now considered an old word, forgotten in day-to-day language. History has many examples of words losing their impact, such as 'cattle rustler' in nineteenth-century America – the worst bandit of the Wild West – and 'gunslinger', a word that would have struck fear into the hearts of timid farmers. Yet now these words have almost disappeared, lost their potency, and are even slightly humorous.

As the Mafia grew, and the community came under its spell, their leaders were not blind to the wisdom of having lords and gentry as partners in their pursuit, as well as politicians and police – any alliance that would help shape their structure in decades to come. They all become strategic threads in a tapestry, weaving the values and aims of the Mafia.

When Garibaldi flung open the prison doors, allowing the worst of the worst to rush out, they joined with the criminal sects, and Palermo became awash with gangsters.[26]

General Corone, part of Garibaldi's attack on Palermo, recalled to a parliamentary committee afterwards that the red-shirted general fast gained the loyalty of the Sicilian peasants, who became a mass movement. He recalled that, in his opinion, 10 000 criminals were released from prisons, and they went on a killing spree, some murdering whole families, as well as fighting.[27]

Law, order, civil obedience and wellbeing were all casualties of the unification process. The jails being emptied out coincided with Garibaldi passing his decree to supply a slice of land to any fighter for his cause. How many of the jailbirds were promised land? How many were motivated to kill on a promise of soil? There must have been more – by way of motive – to the massacres, the palaces being burned down, the raping and looting, than just violence for the sake of violence.

Palermo was reduced to a war zone, where one side had the might and the other side struggled to stay alive. The Prefect of Palermo, Baron Turrisi Colonna, observed the persecution and massacre of the old-guard policemen in the province of Palermo. Old Palermo was now on her knees at the mercy of criminals.

The new police department, which was hastily formed in an attempt to restore law and order, became a hotchpotch of petty criminals, murderers and individuals with the shadiest of characters. War was on, unification was alive, the march continued, and Garibaldi was doing press interviews on the run. As his army of *picciotti* ran ahead, slaughtering their way across the roof of the island, then onto Calabria, they left behind a Palermo that had not yet seen the blood dry on its smooth cobblestone streets. Anarchy bloomed, and Palermo was a city of corpses and bones. At one point, looting was so rampant that prefects from other regions were asked to enter the city and take charge. Fleeing old-guard police joined the many sects and clans that ran wild; a case, perhaps, of if you cannot beat them, join them.

There seems little doubt that the promise of land to a poor Sicilian would have been a tempting incentive to bear arms for a cause they might otherwise not have cared for. The same promise to a hardened criminal, a *picciotto* thug who only knew crime, would seem like a gift worth snatching, a generosity hard to imagine in dirt-poor rural Sicily. To have that promise taken away was enough to see angry men become crazed men, for the *picciotti* to become an organised Mafia. As for the handful of high-ranking invaders who had caused this social disaster, how could they ever have possibly prepared for something that was impossible to predict?

•

As a fascinating adjunct to the involvement of the *picciotti* with the great General Garibaldi, a year after the unification of Italy was ratified the general went back to Calabria, leading his volunteers and *picciotti* in a further battle. Little did he know he would face the greatest test of his life and greatest terror. Whilst fighting raged in the Aspromonte – an endless network of caves and tall timbers – Garibaldi advanced his men in what he described as a 'thirst for blood', only to face his enemy head on. He became surrounded. Shots rang out over and over, and the general lay wounded, his left thigh taking a bullet. His aides worked feverishly on their leader, but he was again shot 'seriously' in the right ankle. He was doomed, even by his own account, incapable of standing.

With his fight at an end he contemplated disarming his troops. Surrendering. His troops were fleeing in all directions, leaving the general vulnerable to execution. Miraculously, out of right field came a gang of *picciotti*, loaded with weapons and ammunition. They stood their ground for a full fifteen minutes, firing upon the enemy, protecting their supreme leader. The warfare of the *picciotti* would safeguard Garibaldi until the arrival of one of his colonels who – once the *picciotti* stepped aside – went about negotiating free passage of the badly wounded general whose red shirt was now blood-red.

This single act of courage by the rabble of Sicily is testament to their value in battle. If ever there was an action to prove that value, the saving of the life of General Garibaldi in the Aspromonte hills is surely it.

Yet that one undisciplined military sortie would receive (generally) no mention in newspapers nor heroic baubles, and almost no pages in history books to enrich the value of the *picciotti* gangs.[28]

CHAPTER 9

THE MUSKETEER

SICILIAN SAYING:

Mu vitti 'stu film
I have already seen this film

Used when you don't believe someone

Alexandre Dumas, author of *The Three Musketeers* and *The Count of Monte Cristo*, was fascinated by Garibaldi. He played a pivotal role in Garibaldi's expedition, recording the battle at Calatafimi and the general's march to Naples. Dumas also wrote *The Memoirs of Garibaldi* (1860), for which the unification hero offered him exclusivity.

It was a time of much secrecy; Sicily's new administration – the supremo Garibaldi, the reluctant Cavour and the overactive Crispi – had implemented a wall of silence; no one offered comment. Except for a few writers, such as Dumas, the newspaper editors of the day were constantly guessing what was happening. Garibaldi and Crispi, editors complained, were disrespecting the public's right to know.[1] The prominent Catholic press openly criticised the occupation of Sicily by Garibaldi, condemning the invasion.[2] Newspaper journalists asked hard questions about reports of violence and the methodology used by the invaders, yet King Vittorio Emanuele held firm; nothing would be released except through official channels, and then only to Dumas.

The man who spent his life writing fiction – books about extra-ordinary characters, tales of legend – found himself with the biggest character in the world, and the biggest scoop of his long life. A devotee of Garibaldi's cause, Dumas got so swept up in the unification effort that he donated arms and funds to Garibaldi.[3] He embedded himself inside the battle to write the most popular account of the taking of Sicily, claiming to have been with Garibaldi when the *Mille* first attacked the Bourbons. *The Memoirs of Garibaldi* offers a unique narrative to promote the legend of the red-shirted general. On its release, the book was eagerly bought by millions around the world. It has since found its way into public libraries and archives everywhere and has enjoyed an infinite number of reprints. In the marketing blurb, Dumas states the story is 'told by an eye witness', himself.[4]

The work is no doubt biased, due to Dumas' financial support and offer of arms to Garibaldi. The role of arms supplier and funder of the unification effort must have surely compromised his objectivity. However, no other writer was given such exclusive access to Calatafimi, Garibaldi, the volunteers, the hierarchy of the general or the *picciotti*.

The Memoirs of Garibaldi is high on accolades and low on details, and leaves the reader wondering if Dumas really was at Calatafimi, or anywhere near. I suspect he was in Palermo and Naples, once Garibaldi achieved the surrender of the King of the Two Sicilies. Certainly, some scholars of Garibaldi believe Dumas was not near any action at all. Historian Lucy Riall believes Dumas arrived in Palermo in June 1860[5] – three or more weeks after Garibaldi landed in Marsala. 'He was there', Riall writes, 'to edit and embellish Garibaldi's memoir . . . hence he became the self-appointed historian of the Thousand, who brought to the task the right blend of journalistic realism, poetic licence and narrative skill'.[6]

Was Dumas too close to Garibaldi? The reader must judge. Henry Adams makes a vague mention of Dumas as being with Garibaldi when they met surrounded by 'piratic' staff. Dumas' remarkably short account of the battle can be summed up as follows:

> After much politics in the north of Italy, Garibaldi set about
> preparing his mission hastily, as far as food supplies, livestock

and provisions were concerned. Likewise, he moved quickly on the gathering of the (now famous) *Mille*, the thousand men that sailed with the General from Genoa to Marsala. On May 12th, after arriving on Sicilian soil, and before leaving Marsala, one hundred and fifty Sicilians were given weapons and ammunition. The war effort was acting in the name of Vittorio Emanuele, the (now) King of Italy. Dumas was told by Garibaldi that there were three and a half thousand Bourbons waiting for battle. Garibaldi was in a hurry, he never wanted to waste time and started moving towards the direction of Palermo, in line with his volunteers. The General was hopeful that any confrontation would be held in the area of the north west of the island. On the way they were joined by two squadrons of armed men swelling the overall force. Once in place they waited a few hours further for the arrival of another two gangs of armed men. In time the Garibaldi army attacked the Bourbons, a battle raged. Eighteen Bourbons were killed, and one hundred and twenty-eight men wounded. The result being the Bourbons were overcome, they surrendered, and Garibaldi marched on to Palermo.[7]

This version of events is remarkable for its lack of factual detail. While the book fattens up once Garibaldi gets to Palermo, the story of the initial battle and retreat of the Bourbons is, to say the least, thin. Dumas' account, however, does make mention of the armed men who joined Garibaldi and the volunteers. If we take his narrative as correct, there could have been thousands of armed men unaccounted for in the fight. On page 141 he mentions 'bandits', then he mentions (over and above the *Mille*) two squadrons and two armed gangs, an extraordinary number of fighters, and this number dovetails with many other accounts. But why didn't Dumas give more attention to these fighters?

The inclusion of these armed men in the battle is worthy of a full chapter detailing who they were, what they did, and where they came from. This detail is what a writer searches for in developing their story arc to entice their readers. But the French writer skips around it and focuses his pen on Garibaldi, although, to be fair, he does call them *picciotti* many times over in his book, describing their fighting as guerrilla in style, and showcasing men capable of very bad deeds.

The book implies others spoke to Dumas after the battle at Calatafimi and (perhaps) away from the earshot of the general. Indeed, his whole book has a retrospective manner about it. I suspect that is because Alexandre Dumas did his best work, a blend of fiction and non-fiction, from afar. He was, more than likely, sitting on an easy chair in a hotel somewhere awaiting news from his recipient of funds and weapons. The *London Illustrated News* reviewed *The Memoirs of Garibaldi*, saying: 'His version of history would be a Sicilian romance with all the information gleaned right and left and from opposite sources crammed into it. No offence to our neighbours across the Channel [Dumas was French] but they have a most extraordinary fashion of relating actual occurrences.'[8]

Historians and professors alike have doubted Dumas' account, accusing the author of being subjective, and, given Garibaldi's role in creating the narrative, implicating the general himself. The book contains an acknowledgement by General Garibaldi, dated 14 May 1860, even though the battle at Calatafimi did not commence until 15 May. Alexandre Dumas, the man who could spin a story better than anyone else for his time, rushed his book out and turned Garibaldi into the greatest military leader in Italian history, and the *Mille* into folklore icons.

The battle at Calatafimi happened before the advent of reportage and investigative journalism.

Waterloo, in 1815, had been much the same. The story of the battle was told by General Wellington, the victor. Generals told newspapers what to print. In the case of the expedition to Sicily, who better to spread propaganda and disinformation than the world's best-selling fiction writer, Alexandre Dumas?

His version of Italy's unification became history's recollection of the events, and a reference point for academics and newspaper editors. Dumas' account cornered the market and championed the names of Garibaldi and King Vittorio Emanuele.

In 1861, once his book had been published, Dumas was given a lucrative posting as Minister for Museums in the unified Italy. Based in Naples for three years, it was a role he relished until public protests saw him asked to vacate the position. The people of Naples couldn't take the well-fed Frenchman and his wild stories any longer.

Another book, *The Campaign of Garibaldi in the Two Sicilies* (1861), claiming to be a historical account of the unification of Italy, was written by Charles Stuart Forbes, a non-fiction author from London.[9] Forbes called his account a 'personal narrative', on account of the fact that he was there and saw things firsthand, writing feverishly. He followed the general all the way to Naples. Forbes met with the leaders, interviewed the main players, and documented the entire campaign. His book is full of maps and drawings that show the battlefields and manoeuvres. It is obvious from the striking detail of the maps that he made crucial contacts within the hierarchy of Garibaldi's army, who showed him the brilliance of Garibaldi as a soldier.

The Bourbons, according to Forbes, had access to 140 000 troops. Balanced against the accepted 'thousand volunteers' on Garibaldi's side, Forbes' account is an anomaly of gigantic proportions. There is also mention of mercenaries and spies on the side of the rulers. As the gas on the burner of the pending invasion is turned up – immediately after the bloodbath at the church of Gancia – 28 000 Bourbon troops were mustered in Palermo and its surrounds, and the shoreline was awash with naval vessels. Clearly, surprise was not part of Garibaldi's intent, or if it was the King had his measure.

Forbes explains that on 8 May, several days before Garibaldi's arrival, it was known that the insurgents – *picciotti* and anyone else ready to fight – lay in wait, in numbers far greater than the number of volunteers on the water with their general. Garibaldi then uttered his most stirring words via his letter to the people as outlined in chapter 8:

> Sicilians, I have brought you a body of brave men, who have hastened to reply to the heroic cry of Sicily . . . to arms, then! We will get muskets, but for the present any weapon will do in the hands of a brave man.[10]

Forbes has Garibaldi arriving at the port of Marsala at two o'clock in the afternoon. The inventory of both vessels is: '1002 men, 5 Hungarians, as well as 6 cannon and ammunition'.[11] Squadrons were formed from the gathered and disorganised *picciotti*, volunteers and anyone else who had their hand up to fight. The squadrons were placed under the command of a Garibaldi general, and the march commenced on 12 May. The book is peppered with stories of atrocities against locals; some were raped, others murdered, and many had their homes burned to the ground. Responsibility for such atrocities was overlooked by the author; suffice to say everyone was probably at fault. The stories are wretchedly sad.

Eventually, the forces from both sides collided: Bourbons and mercenaries, *Garibaldini* and *picciotti,* cannons and horses. Unlike musketeer Dumas, Forbes does not place himself at the battle. All we know is what he writes: that all hell broke loose and the war commenced. Our understanding of the killings is aided by the messages coming in and out of the hands of the generals in charge, under the haze of acrid gun smoke. Forbes quotes them all in his pages. Garibaldi writes a telling open letter to the Sicilians during the first days of the war: 'I counted on your fatal bayonets and I have not been deceived . . .'[12]

This must surely be a reference to what Francesco Crispi put in place, after returning from Sicily on his spy mission to gather arms and start a bomb-making militia.

Through the day, the cannons sounded, and thousands of shots whistled north, south, east and west, until, as dusk showed its face, an unexpected sight met the eyes of the *Garibaldini*: a valley full of blue-grey military uniforms running in all directions. Men bloodied, horror across their faces, weapons lost, the sun flashing a faded sparkle from their once polished buttons; the Bourbons were in an unstoppable retreat. Marshal Francesco Landi, in field command of the Bourbon forces, scribbled down on parchment a plea for help to his supreme commander, holed up in Palermo, over 100 kilometres away as the crow flies, or a three-day march as the wounded hobbled.

Forbes makes the position of the *picciotti* abundantly clear as Landi desperately seeks help. In part: '. . . there are immense numbers . . . rebels in great numbers . . . urgent request for reinforcements as the masses are numerous and they are bent on fighting . . . my column is surrounded by enemies . . .'[13] This, after only seven hours of war, or seven hours of hell. This dovetails with the frightening comment that 'men out of breath, bloodied, exhausted, pressed again like a bunch of demon-possessed, who seemed to have come out of the ground'.[14]

Landi freely mentions that the rebels were in great numbers. Why he seems to be alone in writing down these facts is curious. It is hard to imagine Landi's vivid descriptions of rebels as being anything other than *picciotti*.

As Forbes outlines in his book, the retreat of the Bourbons was both unexpected and quick; they were vastly overpowered. The battle ended with Bourbons fleeing to Palermo, and Garibaldi's troops regrouping to plan the taking of the capital. Landi and his fellow generals would garrison Palermo with 10 000 troops and cannons, with naval ships off the coast, ready for the onslaught. The maps in Forbes' book are as good as words. One map has the legend 'Garibaldini, Squadrons, and Bourbons', with a clear distinction being made between the volunteers and the *picciotti*, who are labelled as 'Squadrons'.

After days, Garibaldi took the surprise approach and entered the walled city from the southeast side, declaring that it was time for some 'guerrilla warfare' in the narrow and claustrophobic laneways of Palermo.[15] The *picciotti*, their ranks now bolstered with locals, licked their lips, cocked their rifles, and the battle raged. This time, Garibaldi's experience from his days in South America came into play. He ably deployed the thousands of *picciotti*, who knew their city and its alleyways well. The blood continued to spill as the pages of the war calendar turned one by one, cannon shot by cannon shot, until on 29 May silence came to the city, and weapons were holstered. The Bourbon troops fled, dropping their bombs as they ran.

Garibaldi would learn that had the fight continued for one more smoke-hazed day, his own side would have been the one to surrender. His troops were down to only nine rounds per man.[16] Surely, the *Garibaldini* would have been destroyed had it not been for the hasty retreat of the Bourbons.

But worry of another kind showed its head in the capital, with the petrified citizens pleading for an end to the atrocities. The rabble within the ranks of the Garibaldi army had failed to adhere to the armistice, as looting and raping ravaged a city in fear. Leaving each house, they would cut the owners' throats or send a cartridge into their bodies, then burn the abode to the stone foundations. They even stormed a nunnery and raped all within. Unabated, others joined in the criminal activities in the weeks following, while Garibaldi lost himself in armistice negotiations, press interviews and planning his escapades across Sicily.

Thankfully, Garibaldi had the good sense to end the lawlessness. He fronted his warriors and demanded all men with a weapon return to the walls of the city and hold back the defeated and the thieves.

Meanwhile, Marshal Landi was sent back to Naples to face a court-martial. There he described the warfare with Garibaldi's *Mille*, who had at their disposal armed criminals and beggars. Hence the reports of rape, murder and looting.

Fascinatingly, Forbes' book makes no mention of any of the volunteers wearing red shirts. Nor are there descriptions of the blue-grey uniforms of the Bourbons or the putrid linen shirts and sheep skins of the *picciotti*. Indeed, the thousand volunteers are scarcely mentioned, and almost nothing is written about their clashes with the enemy.

At the end of the clashes in Palermo, Forbes says there were only 600 volunteers left standing. What happened to the other 400 is, like so much about the expedition itself, a mystery. How many deserted we will never know. How many *picciotti* ran off is also a mystery, as it is for the number of Bourbons. As no journalists were allowed to cover the events, a guess is as good as we can expect. Any wonder Dumas' tale sold millions.

It is naive to think disinformation was not in play in Sicily. That Garibaldi used the earliest form of Mafia to crush the Bourbons was a good reason to roll out an author of historical fiction, Dumas. Or, perhaps, an author of propaganda and disinformation.

It's a script. It's a nonsense.

It is also naive to think that the unification of Italy, the taking of Sicily, the invasion of a sovereign state, did not have propaganda as a key weapon in the armoury. Everyone loves a hero. We all like those who volunteer for the hard tasks. Expeditions back then were exciting journeys to new discoveries. Throw in a few hard men, pepper the tale with acts of courage, moments of valour, and suddenly, the pages of the history books look like blurred images in a fun-house arcade of mirrors.

As Lucy Riall observes in her book, *Garibaldi: Invention of a Hero*, there was never any question about the support of writers for Garibaldi.[17] They were very good at creating a sense of excitement and adventure. The foreign press in particular tended to depict Garibaldi's campaign as an adventure in which the correspondent himself figured as something of a minor star. One journalist wrote: 'Garibaldi is fighting in town. I am going to chance the shots. Lots of sketches and a long letter by the next ship. One is now leaving by the harbour, Whizz! All the dust dashed up near me. In great haste.'[18]

Recording history is a responsibility for all, not just high-rankers standing at the back of the battlefield smoking cigars. It is a task for writers, authors, historians, professors, correspondents, editors and others who have a rare opportunity to document the most extraordinary events of a time. There is no justification for wild pontificating or exaggerated bravery. Likewise, there can be no hiding of dirty secrets. The books of Alexandre Dumas and Charles Stuart Forbes could not be more opposite in detail. One book, from a famed writer of fiction who wrote wild stories of musketeers and badly done-by heroes chasing freedom, sold millions of copies. The other book, by a little-known historian who put himself in Sicily, failed to sell its limited-edition first print run, and ended up on a dusty shelf at the back of a smelly archive in the backblocks of Palermo.

I know which one I believe. Viva non-fiction!

CHAPTER 10
THE JOLLY ROGER

SICILIAN SAYING:

Cani ca nun canusci patruni

A dog who doesn't recognise its owner

Meaning, somebody who works for his own advantage

As a boy growing up in Australia, the world's largest island, it was not always city life for me. There was always the bush, as we call it. The never-never. That endless horizon that entices the adventurer. Usually, at the end of such an expanse, there is an ocean, for my land has over 12 000 beaches. Hence, I was fascinated with swashbuckling pirates. My school libraries were full of wonderful tales of 'Aye, aye matey' and talking parrots on the shoulders of red-jacketed, peg-legged pirates brandishing muskets and flying the Jolly Roger flag. As the pages turned, and a Pacific island came onto the horizon, the pirates would then pillage treasure and abscond with fair maidens, before heading off on timber-hulled ships with ancient chests overflowing with coins and gold. Robert Louis Stevenson helped me learn to read with his *Treasure Island* stories of Long John Silver and Billy Bones of the 1880s. Truth be known, I would have loved to be able to read these books again and escape, even for a night or two, but somehow life became too serious, too grown up. Too Mafia.

•

Historians often say timing is everything, and I agree; there is a moment when actions are needed quickly, or the opportunity will be lost. Six months before Francesco Crispi put on his hair pieces and glasses and opened his fake travel papers to go in search of *picciotti* leaders, and well before Garibaldi conjured his *Mille* strategy, the French commenced an extraordinary feat that would stun the world. They started work on the Suez Canal. The British were livid at missing out on the spoils, or the water track to India, Asia, Australia and beyond, and likewise King Vittorio Emanuele was brimming with envy.[1]

Whoever controlled the Suez Canal theoretically controlled Europe and could tap into gold-plated wealth. As for Sicily, its strategic value escalated because its rulers could watch over trade ships, and were positioned near a new and faster maritime route for naval vessels as well.[2] At a time of much political upheaval, the Suez Canal was an advantage to power-hungry despots.

What was the real need to topple the Bourbons? And would ownership of Sicily help the fortunes of King Vittorio Emanuele, who had his eyes on not only being the first King of Italy but, maybe, with a little luck, monarch of the Suez Canal?[3] A more apt question might be, why did the Sicilian people need to be freed? Who made the decision to be their saviour?

By all accounts, life was reasonable for most people in the Two Sicilies. Palermo-based American historian Louis Mendola says: 'It would be ridiculous to conclude that life in Sicily was any better than life in Piedmont, but ludicrous to conclude that it was any worse. Or that Palermo was in some way backward to Turin.'[4] He writes that the Kingdom of the Two Sicilies was 'Italy's wealthiest state'. The first major wave of immigrants to the United States and other parts were actually from Piedmont and Genoa, not Sicily or Naples, who 'made the long journey to a strange land for a reason'.[5] Mendola makes clear that all was not well in northern Italy, circa 1860, and the regions of Tuscany, Liguria, Piedmont, Lombardy, Veneto and Rome were every bit as impoverished, and illiterate. In fact, their literacy rate was far worse than that of the Two Sicilies. In short:

It is clear Piedmont needed the Two Sicilies, or at least its gold reserves. Based on this measure alone, the wealth of the southern Kingdom eclipsed that of all the other Italian states combined, whilst its national debt was a fraction of Piedmont. This was a matter of public record, and somebody in Turin wanted the gold in Naples. And they were willing to kill for it.[6]

Despite the folk from the south often being labelled as backward or uneducated – since unification they've been called 'southerners' or *terroni*, which translates as 'dirt people' – the opposite could be said at the time of the invasion; they were better-off, proud and accomplished.

The combined value of the gold ingot holdings, in reserves for the Duchy of Palma, Venice, Lombardy, Modena, Tuscany, the Papal States, Piedmont and Sardinia, was around 229 million at the time of invading Sicily. The equivalent gold ingot wealth for the Two Sicilies was almost twice that, 443 million.[7] Additionally, Savoy was burdened with the largest debt of all pre-unitary states – 1292 million gold ingots – despite being a fraction of the size and population of the Two Sicilies.

These figures alone make it clear the Two Sicilies was better off. One northern state, Piedmont, had a higher national debt than that of the Two Sicilies.[8] Indeed, Piedmont had the highest debt in all Europe. The Two Sicilies also had just under half the overall number of university students in Italy. Not bad for a land of poor dirt people. Twenty years after unification, the same Piedmont was flourishing, in surplus, thanks to taking the Two Sicilies.

So buoyant was commerce in the Two Sicilies that the Rothschild family chose Naples in which to set up their only – prosperous – investment bank in Italy. The north had no such prosperity worth tapping into. The *Riveli* records (land records held in Palermo), for the time preceding unification, show that many more locals owned their own homes compared to the national average. Before the takeover, the Two Sicilies was the first state in Europe to introduce pensions; the kingdom also had the most printing presses, lowest taxes, largest naval yards, biggest iron-ore foundries and largest steel engineering plant; it was home to the first university on the mainland to teach economics and was the first state in Europe to bring in a constitution; and they were even decades ahead of the rest of the world when it came to glass recycling.[9]

The Kingdom of the Two Sicilies was also the first in Italy to implement gas-fuelled lighting in public areas, and built Italy's first railway line and first suspension bridge, which had other nations in awe. In the area of science, the Two Sicilies boasted the world's first seismic observatory, and its initiatives in steam shipping were legendary, as was innovation with the telegraph. Sicily also had the largest sulphur mines: ninety-six per cent of the world's total production, sulphur being a key component in industrial processes – the world needed Sicilian sulphur. Additionally, the Two Sicilies was Europe's largest market garden of fruit and vegetables, as well as wine grapes. Its textile mills and looms numbered in the thousands. At the Paris International Exhibition in 1856 – three years before the plan to unify Italy was hatched – the Two Sicilies was voted third in the world for industrial development.[10]

On a military intelligence level, the Two Sicilies was ahead of everyone in the field of marine code and submarine telegraph. Both Naples and Palermo nurtured the first botanical gardens, way ahead of those up north, and before unification the first public-housing project was constructed. In the arts, the Two Sicilies was famed for its opera houses and attracted the finest singers on the planet. The kingdom also had a significantly lower infant mortality rate compared to the north, and vast numbers of doctors.[11]

So, who was complaining? Who needed to be rescued? By comparison, Rome was far less prosperous – remember, sheep were grazing in the Colosseum!

Sadly, after unification, the area formerly known as the Two Sicilies lost most of its wealth and all of its status. The region went backwards; schools stopped growing and some were shut down under the new governance. King Vittorio Emanuele snatched most of the industry, transporting it to the northern regions as part of a massive industrial acquisition program that allowed northern Italy to play a significant role in the Industrial Revolution. Virtually all textile looms were transported to the north, along with steel production and a great deal of primary production. It's no coincidence that Fiat, Italy's premier car-maker, was founded in Turin. By the end of the nineteenth century, Italy was a shining industrial light in Europe.

In Naples and Sicily, since the first days of the invasion, tens of thousands of people were angry. Twelve months from the taking of Sicily – watching and waiting in fear as to what might eventuate – the people took to the streets, angered at the raping of their land. And the loss of their industry. Livelihoods disappeared to the north.

Rioters from Agrigento across to Palermo clashed with caretaker police, and from Catania to Trapani, students demanded a better deal. Farmers denounced the so-called liberation, and townsfolk struggled to move on, always under the watchful eye of swarms of Mafia now rooted in the landscape of southern Italy. Voices of disharmony echoed all the way to Turin and Rome, heard by King Vittorio Emanuele, and ignored. Despite newspaper headlines about disenchanted southerners, ordinary people were on a firm path to becoming peasants.

A year on from unification, the name King Vittorio Emanuele was mud, while Giuseppe Garibaldi was seen as a man who came, conquered and was chased off.

Over 5000 protestors were estimated to have been killed during the riots that followed unification; some history books say it was as many as 100 000. The Palermo Prefect report for that same period outlined widespread civil unrest: rioters were all about, people in the streets openly burning the coat of arms of their new King. There was not a main town or city that wasn't engaged in venting anger. Slogans were splashed across city walls: 'Muoia Vittorio Emanuele', Death to Vittorio Emanuele! The arrests were so numerous that the prefecture was unable to calculate them, and almost all the militants were not Mafia, not *picciotti*, but ordinary citizens rebelling against what they saw happening.

During this unrest, a propaganda article appeared in the *Gazzetta Del Popolo* saying, 'How positive is the presence of the new government as the people can live in peace without the presence of thieves, no kidnappings, no murders, no anarchy, it's a free and civilised population and young people are willing to join the ranks of the army to promote the freedoms.'[12] Really, did the King believe the plebs to be that gullible?

To silence the voices of the Bourbon soldiers captured in the taking of Sicily, King Vittorio Emanuele banished them to prisons in the north. He considered purchasing an island off Argentina to ship the soldiers, now beaten inmates, to further mute their opinions on unification. He settled for a prison named Fenestellae, an ageing, bitterly cold Alpine fortress, where the inmates were locked away.[13] After a few winters, many of them shrivelled up and died in prison, eradicating any chance of the truth seeping out. Their relatives back home were hit with an 'extraordinary' set of taxes, levied to help pay for the war effort to 'free' the poor souls who were imprisoned in the first place.[14]

After two and half years in the archive, I'd read through many hundreds of titles. Most bound in gold-inked linen covers, others in leather, they had the classic look of knowledge. The sort of books used by professors across Italy, and for those interested in Italian history, around the globe. Yet few books deviated from what could be found in the reader taught to kids who would go on to lead a united Italy – future captains of industry, politicians, farmers. A naive story of unification.

Why the truth, the real story of the invasion at Marsala has not been printed in Italian history books is an enigma. There seems no other reason for neglecting the truth than the Savoy-bred Italians of 1860 never wanted the Mafia name associated with such a significant national moment. And that Piedmont was in dire straits financially – on its knees, riddled with debt. Clearly, raiding the coffers of the Two Sicilies was the ideal solution to balance their books and industrialise quickly.

As the reason for the invasion seems more financial than a passion to promote a better way of life for southerners, the propaganda writers were busy at their inkwells. Less than ten years after unification, no money was available to improve the quality of life, no reforms were delivered.

The Neapolitans stated their independence was lost to Piedmont. They had been reduced to the status of a distant and abandoned province. The Sicilians felt the same way; even the Tuscans complained the new regime was oppressive and denied liberty. The lives of the common people became miserable. Months after Garibaldi left Naples, Piedmont security forces marched in to take control. The heavy-handed troops took over the towns of Pontelandolfo and Casalduni (near Naples). Both towns were looking for the advancements proffered by unity. What they got instead was a sheer nightmare. Homes were invaded, the army moved through the population bashing, even killing, the menfolk and raping their wives. And devouring their food and live-stock. The documented facts of the violence show behaviour that was nothing short of terrorism.

One hundred and sixty years later, such behaviour is still (understandably) remembered; both towns turn their backs on any national day of celebration. At the time it happened, crimes were ignored as the propaganda machine kept up stories of harmony, and King Vittorio Emanuele kept making enamelled street signs. Amazingly, at each step, the same propagandists served up a healthy diet of nega-tivity against badly done-by southerners, who were told how lucky they were to be living under King Vittorio Emanuele.

Five years after unification, the Rothschild bank closed its doors in Naples, vacating Italy, such was the decline in commerce.

Historian Louis Mendola mentions an African American who went through hardship as a slave in the United States in his early life, but after gaining his freedom travelled to Sicily. Witnessing the locals' poverty, the former slave reported: 'The condition of the coloured farmer in the most backwater parts of the southern states of America is incomparably better than the condition and opportunities of the agricultural population in Sicily.'[15]

Many Catholic scholars opposed the invasion and the eventual outcomes, or lack thereof. These educated Catholics were never consulted – a grave error in judgement by the King and Garibaldi. Had they sought discourse with Catholic leaders they would have possibly found views opposed to interfering with southern Italy.[16] Not one of the hopes of 1860 was realised. Italy was being run in the opposite direction to other nations that aided industry without killing private competition. The government seemed more focused on maintaining power and squandering national resources. Consuming the present and mortgaging the future.[17]

If the great scholars can be believed, the united Italy, fifteen years after Garibaldi's invasion, was going backwards, with mounting debt and no prospects without financial assistance. Soon after, the Sicilian sulphur mines, now controlled by industrialists from the north, used child labour, and would do so for decades. Kiddies shovelled orange-stained, chemically enriched dirt for a few lire a week.[18] The admired literacy rate for the south – one of the highest in all Europe – also plummeted, as education was all but ignored. So, what was the reason for invading Sicily?

•

Admiral George Rodney Mundy, the naval commander in charge of the British Mediterranean fleet, found himself aiding Garibaldi and his two ships heading for Marsala. The admiral was instructed to offer the red-shirted general safe passage and to protect British interests at the port. Once Garibaldi and his troops had disembarked, Mundy and his fleet loitered, keeping an ear turned to mainland Sicily to hear the cannons while history unfolded under the smell of gunpowder.[19] Days later, when Garibaldi's army attacked Palermo, the admiral commenced a bombing campaign to soften the general's target and encourage surrender from the Bourbons. So much for neutrality! The Palermo marina was riddled with shells as 15 000 Bourbon soldiers were escorted from Palermo under the watchful eye of Mundy, and the city became Garibaldi's.[20] There appears little doubt the victory was aided by the British and their many vessels. As one astute correspondent thought, the mystery of Garibaldi's triumph against all numerical odds – the number of Bourbon military – was 'wrapped in English banknotes'.

Days after the taking of Palermo on 29 May 1860, the Bourbon commander, General Ferdinando Lanza, brokered an armistice with Garibaldi. Lanza asked Admiral Mundy, who was now acting (oddly) as umpire, if he could gain a three-day extension to the surrender deadline after which he would have to quit Palermo. Lanza had thousands of troops tucked away in the palace grounds and there were logistics to consider.

The British admiral gave it consideration. In effect, this would postpone the surrender from 29 May until 3 June. Garibaldi agreed; however, in doing so, he oversaw the emptying of the entire contents of the strongroom of the Banco delle Due Sicilie – almost 167 billion ducati, which in today's value is more than 86 million euros.[21]

Why the Banco delle Due Sicilie was the target of the looting is a mystery, as it was a private bank, and had nothing to do with the economic management of Sicily. Nor did the funds have any link to Sicily's stock exchange. They were funds owned by citizens of Palermo, some wealthy, and many who were not. Garibaldi also forced the emptying of all bank deposit boxes, with a combined value that was never disclosed. Cash, private papers, bonds and jewellery were taken as cannon shots rang out over the bank's roof. Who counted the booty is unclear, but Palermo was well and truly in the hands of Francesco Crispi, acting as Secretary of State and Minister of Finance. The defeated General Lanza could only watch and wait in the wings as the cash was scooped up.

The next item on Garibaldi and Crispi's list of withdrawals was the Mint of Sicily, the contents of which were handed to them both by General Lanza and the Treasurer of the expelled Bourbon government, Domenico Peranni.[22] Money was needed to pay the men who fought alongside the great Garibaldi.[23] Of course, these men were the *picciotti* and their Crispi-allied leaders, who must have stood in the shadows at the back door of the Mint with their sweaty hands out. A trait that soon became embedded in their *modus operandi*.

The amount was so vast it was said to be the equivalent of half the total war fund spent by King Vittorio Emanuele on fighting the Austrians the previous year. A war that almost sent the north into bankruptcy. A war that Garibaldi partially led, for no outcome. One historian stated the amount to be above a billion in pounds sterling.[24]

Was this the side of Garibaldi that Henry Adams referred to when he met the general in Palermo? Where Adams formed the opinion that Garibaldi was acting both as 'banker and anarchist'?[25] And let's not forget Adams also thought Garibaldi was acting like a 'pirate'.

Who got tasked with carrying such a weighty sum of money – the entire bank holdings, safety deposit boxes, the cache of cash from the Mint – away from Palermo is also unclear. It just disappeared. There is no mention of the exact amount. However, it is said that Crispi supplied a 'receipt' for the sum of money he took.[26] Where that receipt went is unknown. Historian G. M. Trevelyan suggests the surrender of money to Crispi was listed in a government document of 1860, known as a *cronaca* – a chronicle of expenditure and administration. For two years, along with the tenacious Elena, I searched for a copy of that report. We eventually found it in an archive in Palermo. While the pages had faded from white to mustard, the ink was still legible, and as suspected, the report proves, undeniably, that Crispi and Garibaldi snatched the loot.[27]

Whatever the exact amount, it must have been the equivalent of hundreds of millions of euros today. And that doesn't include the gold that disappeared. I meticulously searched the archives in Palermo, along with the curator Nicolo. We spent ages trying to find anything – a piece of paper, a prefecture report, a dossier, newspaper articles – that would explain the funds taken by Garibaldi. His reason for taking workers' savings, cash and assets from the rich, as well the financial infrastructure of a nation. I even travelled to the Archivio Centrale della Stato, the national archives in Rome, to search the oldest documents, yet I found nothing.

Within days of General Lanza handing over the contents of Sicily's Mint he was banished back to Naples. Fascinated as to what he was doing in Naples, Elena, Nicolo and I kept searching. We came across perhaps 300 files addressed to General Lanza, all dating from mid-June 1860 onwards. We read each of his reports; however, they all pertained to dull administrative matters. Lanza had been reduced to a mere clerk, processing petty claims and finalising internal issues.

We kept digging, blowing the dust from files, looking for any comment on the emptying of the Mint. Seeing as the Mint was looted, we thought there might be a page or two referring to the money having been lifted. Again, nothing. One might expect that record-keeping would be minimal during a coup or revolution; however, with such a fortune, there should have been a record, a report, a notation. The more we searched, the less we found. But, then again, from my experience as a detective, robbers don't leave notes explaining their crimes after ransacking their quarries.

We did find a cache of documents regarding works undertaken on the Mint by the architect Carlo Giachery. He had been engaged in 1859 to strengthen the foundations of the Mint, which were weakening due to the weight of gold, currency and coins locked away inside.[28] The files, maybe 200 pages in all, followed the progress of Giachery's works, from early plans in late 1858 through to being finalised in early 1859.

The detective in me then had an epiphany: Giachery's works were public works, therefore public knowledge. The reason for the reconstruction of the strongroom of the Mint would have been the talk of Palermo, and perhaps further afield. Maybe Savoy? It's the type of gossip that tends to fall into the ears of those with ill intent. Could knowledge of the wealth inside Palermo's Mint have reached the ears of King Vittorio Emanuele? Or those of Garibaldi? Or Crispi? Or all three? Was this the reason for conjuring up the need to help the poor Sicilians as an invasion pretext? As we know, King Vittorio Emanuele was, financially, going belly up.

In effect, taking the fortune from the Mint would have deemed Sicily insolvent, instantly bankrupt. The pillaging of funds was inconsistent with the pre-invasion propaganda that Piedmont was desirous of helping the people, not emptying their bank accounts.

Within a couple of months, it was Naples' turn to donate to the vast coffers being gathered by Garibaldi and Crispi. They had moved on to the city, where more than 20 000 *picciotti*, bandits, thieves and rapists started to ravage Naples, a cultural icon of Europe. King Francesco and his family fled to save their lives, leaving behind their wealth: bank accounts filled with more money than can be imagined. It all disappeared,[29] making it one of the biggest withdrawals in history.

The movement of such a vast amount of cash, papers and jewellery would be a serious exercise, especially with *picciotti* running amok. From all accounts there was no law and order, just chaos, looting and bodies, from Palermo to Naples. At a guess, it would have taken many men many hours to carry the booty from Palermo and the other cities. Men, carriages and many teams of horses. To comprehend the dilemma, a million euros in bank notes and coins can be stashed in the boot of a regular family vehicle. Imagine the size of the fortune if you accept there was a hundred times that. Or more.

Someone must have seen something.

Within the ranks of the *Mille* was Ippolito Nievo, a lawyer and respected writer from Padua, who travelled with the doctors, pharmacists and students. Twenty-nine years old at the time of unification, he was swept up by the idea of the *Mille* and pressed to be part of the voyage. He was said to have distinguished himself at Calatafimi, one of the *Mille* who did well in battle. So much so that he was given the odd title of Vice First Class Intendant, a sort of hybrid role between an accountant and an auditor. He was required to document the expenses of the *Mille*, as well as each stage of the invasion. He was also commissioned to carry back to Turin the administrative documents as part of his report. All of a sudden Ippolito was a very important man.

After the surrender of the Bourbons, he handed his report to his superior, Giovanni Acerbi, and a copy of it to Garibaldi. The report seems to have been ignored by Garibaldi. What did it contain? What did Nievo see or witness that ruffled the feathers of Garibaldi? Could he have been the one brave administrator who dared challenge the emptying of the banks and the Mint?

He seemed to have been miffed that Garibaldi snubbed him, so he did something unprecedented. He gave a copy of his report to Isidoro La Lumia, director of the *Giornale Ufficiale di Sicilia* newspaper, but the report was not published. Undeterred, he wrote an article and gave it to *Perseveranza* magazine, which published the story in July 1860.[30] Did Nievo have the original receipt that Francesco Crispi wrote, after he and Garibaldi looted the bank and Mint? The scope of his work suggests he was the logical person to take possession of the receipt, and the *cronaca* document.

Nievo kept working as Palermo was conquered and the march to Naples was underway. His boss, Acerbi, then ordered him to go to Naples and officiate over matters there, which he did. Cavour, the most senior politician in King Vittorio Emanuele's cabinet, was even more worried about Garibaldi at this time. Indeed, he was at a loss to find any solution for the general and wrote to the King urging him to remove Garibaldi from the campaign, saying that it was 'necessary to save Italy from Garibaldi, and to end it as soon as possible'. Why? What were Garibaldi and Crispi up to?

What we do know is that Giuseppe La Farina, lawyer, writer, and one of the leading academics of the pre-invasion movement,[31] wrote to Cavour before the end of June to say: 'Public money is being used arbitrarily without even indicating the destination.'[32]

The vast sums of stolen monies became the subject of a hidden report made by the Neapolitan army officers who guarded the cash. There was said to have been 136 soldiers who had to step aside to allow Garibaldi unhindered access.[33]

La Farina had a vision for a new Sicily and had caught the eye of Cavour and the intelligentsia of the north. He was an obvious choice for leadership. Cavour dispatched him to the island days after the bombs were silenced in Palermo, but La Farina and Crispi were soon to clash. In short, Crispi was appointed the leading politician for the King once Palermo was conquered, and, together with Garibaldi, acting as dictator, the two men were running Sicily, until La Farina's arrival with Cavour's desire that he take over from Crispi.[34]

Soon after, La Farina complained in a letter to Cavour about Garibaldi, Crispi and money. The red-shirted general found out and put La Farina on a ship sailing towards Genoa, banishing him from Palermo. Garibaldi had no such power to do this; he was not in the Piedmont government, Cavour was. Indeed, he was top of the government tree. Besides, Garibaldi was on the march again on his way out of Palermo, so what bothered him about La Farina? What had La Farina come to know?

The history books miss some of this chronology, in favour of labelling La Farina an interfering scoundrel to Garibaldi. The *New York Times*, quoting what they were fed, broke the story on 31 July 1860 that La Farina was 'expelled', along with two senior police, as the Sicilian government (Garibaldi and Crispi) 'could not tolerate the presence of such individuals'.[35] The Turin press, in contrast, reminded readers that La Farina was supposed to have 'full power from the Sardinian Government to assume the title of Royal Commissioner'.[36] From that moment, Garibaldi was on the nose; Crispi was back to learning how to swim again in the pond of politics; and the Pope came out against the invasion. What had the Pontiff heard in his broad circle?

Garibaldi eventually entered Naples to claim victory on 7 September, arriving by train in relative comfort.[37] Prime Minister Cavour was up to his armpits trying to work through the issues the revolutionary general had presented him with. However, the sentiment to arrest Garibaldi, born back in May when Garibaldi set sail, had lost momentum. Instead, King Vittorio Emanuele sailed to Naples to meet Garibaldi.

They met in the town of Teano, where the King was said to be livid at his revolutionary. He immediately sacked Garibaldi from taking any further part in the unification process. Garibaldi was doomed.[38] Why would the King, on the day he was handed all of Italy on a silver platter, sack the general who'd made it happen? What had Garibaldi done to be dismissed so publicly? There was none of the usual pomp and ceremony. The two men, victor and benefactor, spent an evening debating the trove of issues that Garibaldi had caused. In a room that had no ears, what was said remained secret. Trevelyan describes it as a 'tense and yet melancholy' set of discussions and 'full of bad omens'.[39] Garibaldi's bloodied warriors looked on from a distance. The next day the two men walked into the spotlight of an uncertain crowd, where they said nothing. They then went their own ways, never to see each other again. Garibaldi gathered his things and went to the Bay of Naples, where Admiral Mundy and his fleet were docked. He quietly said his farewells and headed for his farm on Caprera.[40]

What happened to the money? No historian has ever been able to explain where the fortunes of this war ended up. Professor Lorenzo Nigro, an archaeologist who has worked and taught across Italy, has always been fascinated by Garibaldi's emptying of the Sicilian Mint. His book on the subject, *The Genius of Mozia: The Whitaker Saga* (2020), claims the fortune was delivered to Joseph Whitaker, a British wine merchant in Marsala, for safe keeping.[41] Makes sense, when you recall that Crispi donned yet another of his disguises just months before the invasion and headed to England. His sole purpose in doing so was to gain permission to use Marsala as the docking port for Garibaldi. As a long-standing trader who lived and worked in Marsala, Whitaker was key to Garibaldi's subterfuge and engineered the clandestine arrangement.

Once Garibaldi sailed, leaving the Bay of Naples with his reputation shattered, King Vittorio Emanuele wrote a letter to Prime Minister Cavour, stating: 'Garibaldi was neither as docile nor as honest as people say and as you yourself think.'[42]

These sixteen words might be the most telling about the red-shirted general, who, in taking refuge on Caprera, was not completely exiled. He would forever enjoy accolades from around the globe as he spoke of his victory in Sicily, and his changing of the European map. Any negative slant on his legend was either hidden away or brushed aside. As for Francesco Crispi, he bounced back like a daffodil and became Prime Minister himself two decades later. His wife, who had stood by him among the *Mille*, sadly found the scrapheap; she would learn of Crispi committing bigamy after he married an aristocratic lady. Crispi left his wife to suffer her public shame alone in her home town of Marseille.[43]

Soon after Garibaldi was sacked, Giovanni Acerbi pressed Ippolito Nievo to gather together the reports and administrative documents, those from the looting of Palermo, and to transport them back to Turin, post haste. Politicians were eager to study the facts. It was assumed – due to Nievo's honesty and tenacity– that the documents were in safe hands. Transporting such a booty must have worried him. It probably also worried others who knew how the money had disappeared.

Nievo and his papers – said to have filled three large crates – were loaded onto the waiting steamship, the *Ercole*, to set sail, heading for Genoa, then ultimately Nievo would hand over his booty of evidence to those waiting in the capital of Savoy.[44] Nievo and his cargo were believed to be the key to solving, or proving, who looted the banks and the Mint.

The saving grace was the weather that day: 'clear and sunny'. However, trouble reigned on the high seas, aboard the good ship *Ercole*, like the plot of a pirate story by Robert Louis Stevenson. What was expected to be an overnight task to transport the documents across the Tyrrhenian Sea turned into a disaster. Without warning, the ship disappeared. It turned out that the ship had sunk, taking with it the innocent lawyer Ippolito Nievo and his entire haul.[45]

News of the lost ship was kept relatively quiet, and no one –
certainly not Garibaldi, Crispi or the King – instigated a search to
retrieve the crates of documents that may well have enlightened Italians
on the behaviour of a general and his spy. Instead, everything went
mysteriously silent. At that point, Garibaldi was in the company of
his biographer, Alexandre Dumas, writing another fantastic story on
how he saved Sicily with his red shirts.

The sinking of the *Ercole* passed without further comment, as if it
had never happened.

The great-grandnephew of Ippolito, Stanislao Nievo, couldn't give
up the mystery of how his honest ancestor had gone down with the
ship. One hundred years later, in 1961, he mounted an expedition to
locate the steamer and its cargo.[46] Stanislao spent eight years trying
to unravel the mystery. (A man not dissimilar in integrity to his great
ancestor.) He threw everything at it, including scientific equipment
and research. He eventually discovered the *Ercole* 700 metres below
the surface, not far from the island of Capri. Using a mini-submarine,
he searched the vessel on the seabed. Inside were the crates, with the
documents and reports, still in place as if on their way to Turin as
Stanislao's fine ancestor had intended. The evidentiary value of the
documents was useless, however. After one hundred years in salt water
they were ruined. In his search, Stanislao discovered evidence that the
brave Ippolito was in a real hurry to get the documents away from
Palermo and to the safety of Turin.[47] He also discovered that no one
bothered to commence a search for the lost ship until well after it was
due in Genoa and authorities ultimately claimed that a fire on board,
caused by engine failure, led to the ship's sinking. Yet Stanislao saw
no evidence of fire.

When I interviewed the American historian Louis Mendola about
the vast wealth that disappeared, he made it clear that the unifiers who
took Sicily and Naples made certain that nothing was documented,
papers went missing, and reports that might have told a different story
were lost in the fog of unification. Forever ensuring that those enquiring
into what really happened would be left to exhaustive research, using
guesswork to join faded dots. In his essay 'Documentary Falsification

and Italian Biography', historian Denis Mack Smith highlights the systematic destruction, rewriting and concealment of official documents as common practice in Italian history.[48] For me, what happened to the loot represents the Herculean crime of the nineteenth century.

Not all newspapers lauded the red-shirted general when he retreated to his farm on Caprera. For example: *La Gazzetta di Roma* called Garibaldi an 'antichrist'; *Le Pays* newspaper in France saw the Garibaldi expedition as 'an act of piracy'; *L'Union* news in France called Garibaldi a 'bandit, a pirate acting for his own ends and a buccaneer'; *The Illustrated London News* called him out as being 'guilty of simple piracy'. And on it went. Likewise, some politicians spoke out, like the Neapolitan Minister Carafa, who openly accused Garibaldi of carrying out 'a fact of the most savage piracy'.[49]

•

As mentioned earlier, at the time La Farina was expelled from Sicily along with two top police officers, the Pope weighed into the fracas by going against the invasion. What had Pius IX found out? Some believe the church was privy to information that Garibaldi planned to invade the Vatican.

Another piece in this puzzle might lie with the most senior Catholic Church official in the United States, Archbishop John Hughes.[50] He had been sceptical about Garibaldi when the revolutionary lived on Staten Island ten years earlier but chose to bite his tongue. The archbishop would take an extended tour of southern Italy and the Vatican once Garibaldi had been sacked; he had talks with Pius IX,[51] becoming the beneficiary of candid facts and innuendo. It is clear from the writings of the time that the inner sanctum of the Vatican was fearful of Garibaldi; he was referred to as part of the 'vulgar'.[52]

The archbishop wrote to the Pope about La Farina's expulsion, relieved that the Pope was safe from Garibaldi. What did he mean by this? Was he fearful the riches within the Vatican were at risk? As a result of this perceived threat, a large contingent of Irish Catholics volunteered to protect the Vatican and the Pope; they stood guard from late June 1860 until the arrival of a larger contingent, well into the following year, and Garibaldi moved on.[53] Garibaldi's reaction to the most senior eyes of the Catholic Church watching his every move was to later label Catholicism as 'the religion from Hell, the Pope is Lucifer'.[54]

The Catholic Church held on to its collective worry over Giuseppe Garibaldi well into the later stages of the nineteenth century. What did these men know? Is there something inside their own highly secret archives? I was never granted permission to access Vatican records.

Another person who inherited some of this negative sentiment towards Garibaldi was Sicilian-born Dr Charles Fama, who settled in New York City. Decades after unification he was head of the city's Italian Protestant Ministers and openly called the Italian government robbers at the time of Garibaldi. He claimed in writing that there had been an exodus of Italian Catholics to the Protestant Church 'since all their beloved patriots who made Italy one – Garibaldi, Mazzini, Cavour, Victor Immanuel [sic] – are called robbers and thieves in the night'.[55] Dr Fama was aligned with the sentiments of Archbishop Hughes, though they were a generation apart and of different religions.

There must have been an extraordinary stench in Palermo, during the days of the armistice, for such views to have been held by powerful men so close to the smell. The thing that interests me about the criticism of Garibaldi and Crispi is that it all seems to do with honesty, or lack thereof. Money. Theft. Not about the obvious acts of violence during the battles, the barbarism, treachery or treason, just the taking of funds. A good amount of those funds belonged to hard-working Sicilians, the ones with the never-forget memories of injustice. They have seen so much over the centuries.

Yet the poets of the day, the writers of prose and flowery verse saw Garibaldi in a different light as they wrote romantic tales of their 'saviour'. Like poet Elizabeth Barrett Browning when she penned: 'scarcely since the world was a world has there been such a feat of arms. All modern heroes grow pale before him.' This is the man depicted in the press photographs and the paintings with his flowing red mane, ginger beard, baubles and beads on his belt, swashbuckling eyes, and red cloth from groin to cap.[56]

•

The treasure trove of documents on board the *Ercole* could have sunk many careers and answered many questions about the takeover of an island that didn't seem to be doing too badly for itself, circa 1860. It may well have explained the rioting in Palermo and surrounding cities and towns. And the birth of the Mafia.

What happened to the *Ercole* and its documents is one of the great fireside tales of the nineteenth century, and what Garibaldi and Crispi had to do with it, as well as the *picciotti*, the early Mafia, is nothing short of intriguing.

What they did with the loot from the Mint and the banks no one has ever been able to explain. Just like one of those mysteries in wonderful books penned by Alexandre Dumas, Robert Louis Stevenson, Rudyard Kipling and the like, under the flag of the Jolly Roger.

CHAPTER 11

INCEPTION

SICILIAN SAYING:

Chistu passa ù cunventu
The convent offers this

Meaning, when you have no choice

Inception is a lot like an embryo, the start of life. What causes something to exist, then grow? Perhaps it's like a newborn foal, which knows instinctively that it must get up on its feet, straighten its puny legs, lock its knees, and stand. Once standing it takes a nervous look, left and right, to gain its bearings, before its first step, then its second, each step an encouragement, until it takes on a wonky gallop into the animal kingdom.

But first, the conditions must be perfect to allow the foal to get from embryo to birth. It's the same for any species, the rule of evolution. So, what were the perfect conditions to birth the Mafia? To better understand, maybe it's worth asking where it didn't happen, where it wasn't born. There is no Mafia in Switzerland. A land of rolling, clover-covered hills, chirping nightingales, pine forests, wisps of clouds brushed onto a horizon of majestic snow-capped mountains, and the chimes of cow bells.

Nineteenth-century Sicily is like no other land, especially at the height of the Industrial Revolution, when labour is cheap and un-unionised.

It's an uncertain world behind rock massifs: the never-never of Sicily, a land of endless clay paddocks, skinny pigs and dark sulphur mines seeping vapour. In summer, crops fail in temperatures akin to a pizza oven. Miserable villages of sun-bleached white stone dot the interior, where despairing inhabitants walk bow-backed. Boyish men shuffle to work over rocks, their bodies stained yellow. They strip naked in preference to wearing sweat-soaked clothing that rubs and burns. They shovel raw sulphur and suck in the stench of anhydride. Life expectancy is only thirty years in the interior. Big-city aristocrats are deaf to their murmurs for better conditions, a few more coins – *per favore*.

The lucky few have work, share farmers who toil seven-day weeks, herding sheep across bald fields, or milking hungry cows. Any cry for a fairer deal from the barons in Palermo coffee houses is met with a whipping, sacking or eviction. The rest of Italy views Sicilians as outcasts, dirt peasants on a rock, with calloused hands and dumb minds. No one sees their decency, their aching desire for betterment. Their only encouragement comes from dour-faced padres in brown robes, with outstretched hands, a few coins – *per favore*.

Yet despite the misery, hardship gives rise to after-dark bravado by town elders. Men with survival instincts, who want to live long enough to walk alongside their grandchildren. Or to one day move away to a big city and perhaps work on a dock, or load grain in a store, or empty latrines.

As they sit, they plot and plan, while their wives make meals with what they can forage: *agrodolce* – limp vegetables and poor cuts of horse poached in vinegar, tossed with raisins – sweet and sour, like life itself. Landlords, meanwhile, enjoy the lemon-scented *cannolo* and chocolate *gelato*.

After much talk, one of the weary stands. He has a touch of grey and is considered wise. What he conjures will be the embryo of a simple plan, but a plan, nonetheless. He calls for the only rifle in the village – tucked away in a hayloft – and some buckshot. A handsome carriage of barons will roll into the piazza the following day to hurl abuse and inspect the mines and the fields. They will want to improve the output: more toil, more sweat. What the elder – now holding the rifle – suggests will, in time, become the inception.

The village will be waiting as the midday carriage arrives, and an odd angry shot will bring a halt to the day of gentry. The elder will call on his neighbours to dole out a thrashing, to beat them into retreat and to whip their horses' hinds back to Palermo. No one in that village is going to work anymore for any less.

This was how the game changed. The weak became strong. The badly done-by straightened their backs. The rules of employment changed.

From that one angry shot came an independent voice of a tired people, and from that voice came many more, over many years. The game tilted in favour of the dirt peasants, and suited city men were unwise to travel to rural Sicily. Within a generation, sulphur miners, salt workers, farm labourers took to an easier way: crime. Then, two steamers broke the horizon and a legendary general wearing a red shirt came ashore offering the missing link, the promise of a slice of hard soil, to anyone willing to stand beside him and do some dirty deeds.

It's not important as to whether the soil was given or not. What is relevant is the gathering together of so many hard men and the encouragement of their shocking potential. Then, afterwards, discarding them like sweaty loincloths at the bottom of a sulphur mine as their island erupted, challenging the fury of Mount Etna.

There lies the birth of the Mafia. Simple folk who banded together, with – at least in the beginning – an aching desire for betterment. Once their creature was born, it stood up, found its feet and walked, like an innocent foal. Then, in no time, as its path was clear ahead, the Mafia started to sprint, and no one has ever been able to stop it or pull on its reins.

Before long Italy, and the world, realised that something had gone horribly wrong.

PART TWO

Franchising cancer

CHAPTER 12

RULES OF ENGAGEMENT

SICILIAN SAYING:

Cu paga avanti mancia pisci fitusu
Who pays beforehand eats smelly fish

Meaning, if you pay upfront you can be deceived

A cut-off hand, placed on the chest of the murder victim, indicates the person was a thief. Eyes gouged out and clasped in a fist indicate the murdered person was a good shooter who had murdered a person linked to the Mafia. A prickly pear leaf instead of a wallet indicates the slain victim stole money or things entrusted to him. A handkerchief stuffed in the mouth is a signal to those staring at the miserable body that the murdered person should have been silent. While male genital organs hanging around the neck of a corpse, like an adornment, is a warning to those caught sexually harassing the women of any imprisoned *mafioso*.

Similar methods are used to terrorise blackmailed citizens who chose to cooperate with the law. A bomb attack, often more noisy than harmful, reminds a victim that they will have to pay the sum demanded, or else suffer the crippling of their pets. Oil sprinkled on a fruit and vegetable display or a shot fired through a shop window were other methods used to terrorise victims into submission. These were some of the many ways the Mafia got their message across in the late nineteenth century. Rarely was there a need for a follow-up message, such was the power of their theatre.

As the *Mille* heroes grew old, the Mafia were just hitting their stride. They had swapped their muddy, bloodstained boots for buffalo-leather street shoes, and donned frayed collars and twisted ties. Like all new entrepreneurs they would soon find better tailors, and scribble down rules and procedures to enforce them, should anyone think of stepping out of line. Within the first few decades of their shifty business, operational procedures were put in place as the Mafia got smart. They rushed out a rudimentary manifesto that made clear what their game was all about: dishonesty and advantage. To underpin their rules were any number of punishments, should anyone test the waters of disobedience. There would always be *picciotti* ready to use violence, but, as the leaders of the Mafia clans soon discovered, daily violence as an enforcement method needs real law enforcement on side to assist, ignore and protect – something fear tactics and dirty money never had any problem nurturing.

For 160 years the fortunes and successes of the Mafia have been possible thanks to a series of key unions. First, there were the connivances and common interests linking the big landowners, leaders of the Sicilian agricultural world, to the Mafia. It was in rural Sicily, after all, that the earliest incarnation of the Mafia cut its teeth.

Second, low-order or down-on-their-luck local or aspiring politicians learnt that if they wanted to achieve office, or keep their positions, they would have to do as they were told. In time, that obedience never needed an explanation as a Mafia nod was as good as a wink on a blind ballot paper. Once elected, the only time a politician would see an old bewhiskered patriarch, in his dusty grey-flannel suit and braces, would be when a land deal needed to be signed off, or a permit issued. Ask no questions and see you next year at the ballot box.

The third tier of support for the early Mafia was blanket avoidance of Mafia members by police. From the Mafia boss and his family, all the way down to the insignificant shepherd standing guard over a herd of stolen lambs.

The absolute power that could be generated through this triangle of liaisons – landowners, politicians and cops – became one of the Mafia's key business strategies. In short, the Mafia prospered and grew, not by work but through violence, deceit and intimidation, and by aligning itself to the legitimate end of town and to city hall. To this end, the connections nurtured by the Mafia in the 1870s were all-inclusive, and they tightened their grip on the spoils that came their way. Opponents entering their field met a penalty of unspeakable consequences. Few ever did.

Writing in a report in 1888, the Marquis di Rudini, a past Mayor of Palermo, believed that crime in Palermo was stronger than the law. Rudini believed 'Palermo citizens should protect themselves, yet by turning to the Mafia for said protection is giving a platform to the Mafia, the Mafia is powerful, perhaps more powerful than is believed'.[1] The absurdity is, you either pay for protection or you live in fear of the *mafiosi*, who, as it turns out, are the only ones who offer protection.

The Mafia in those early days created a monster, aided by incompetent law enforcement, slack prosecutors and corrupt politicians. They asked for a penny from everyone or threatened to let the monster off its leash. Sicily was full of police who knew who the Mafia monsters were, but no one spoke up. Prosecutions were rare. People went about their business, and lips were buttoned. Why? No one wanted to be a maverick. To be a maverick in this new system was to order a pine box.

The ease and brilliance with which the Mafia managed to override the law should not be underestimated. When arrested, they almost always managed to be acquitted for insufficient evidence. For those on the run, not wanting to roll their dice in a courtroom, there was the option to jump on an ocean liner and immigrate to the United States – achievable in the days before heavy scrutiny. The Mafia – always looking for a way to buck the system, to beat city hall – set up a smuggling racket to get *mafiosi* out of Sicily and into America, the sentimental home of their extended family. This option was reserved for members of the *cosca* – a name given to the earliest Mafia groups or clans – a Sicilian term (plural, *cosche*) for the leaf of the artichoke plant. Hard and tough, an artichoke's many outer leaves are like the skin of an armadillo, an armoured mammal that predators cannot kill. There could be many *cosche* in one region – many clans that make up the whole artichoke. Perhaps a *cosca* member had murdered someone of note, and was running from incorruptible police (a rare breed). The Mafia developed a network of ships and sympathetic captains that were happy to take the *cosca* member for a boat trip in exchange for a fee. The ships would leave Palermo or Agrigento and stop in north Africa, before journeying on to New York City. By the end of the nineteenth century, the Mafia was on its way to being truly international.

As for collusion and ties between local landowners, Sicilian shop owners and bosses of the Mafia, Mafia-like tactics were designed only to extract money and loyalty. The extraction of cash was like picking strawberries, easy work. The Mafia were in only one type of business: the tough business. Shoemakers do not make good killers. Bakers are not skilled at confrontations. Dirt farmers fall short at negotiations. Mafia-like tactics – that is, the oppressive tactics exercised by any means at any time and for any reason without the risk of having to account to justice – are the function of troublemakers in the management of standover tactics over the weak: the cobbler, baker and farmer.

To this end, a form of payola (payment) was established, one that had been in vogue with the *mafiosi* for some time but that became a standard operational procedure by the 1880s. *Pizzo* is the taking of a small fee in return for not being bashed or killed. Another word for it is extortion. In blackmail terms it is an unwarranted demand accompanied by a threat – the demand being cash, usually equivalent to a few dollars a month back then, and the threat being shocking violence.[2]

Literally, *pizzo* means the beak of a bird, a term originating in the depressed farming communities of Sicily, where standover *pizzo* became commonplace around the time of unification. The metaphor implies that the Mafia bird wants to dip its beak into another person's drink, take a sip and move on. A small sip from everyone's business – shop, farm, trade, trestle, butcher's block or bakery – makes for an extraordinary drink indeed.

After Garibaldi left the island, the art of the Mafia was to make it mandatory for all business owners in Palermo, and other cities and towns, to pass on their *pizzo*. It wasn't hard. Complain? Who to? No one's listening. Folks in Italy and America would learn that their payment of the *pizzo* was smart insurance against violence from the *picciotti* and their leaders. It is fair to say the *pizzo* was the making of the Mafia. While unification and the use of *picciotti*, along with the broken promise of a slice of land, fuelled the rage that flamed the Mafia, it was *pizzo* that funded the growth and power of the Mafia. It was their cash cow. It took the Mafia into the shops and traders of Sicily, into the commercial fabric of Italy. It also put them in the news headlines, and took them into the homes of innocent victims, who shivered over their meagre dinner table, worried about whether they could muster enough cash from their measly businesses on *pizzo* day.

Like the Church, the Mafia convinced people that fear of death could be overcome. Not by salvation and weekly prayer and a coin on the tray, but by way of a monthly visit by the neighbourhood *picciotto* and a coin to his sweaty palm. This shared mantle, church and Mafia, shaped the lives of simple folk who had nowhere else to turn.

Pizzo soon became a tax that no one could avoid. Scholars, economists and criminologists alike have tried to place a value on the collective yield of *pizzo* during that time – an impossibility, due to its black-market nature. A detective who has chased the Mafia knows the answer is simple: a fortune. The returns to the Mafia collective would have been, and still are, astronomical. Any half-decent politician, prime minister, president or chief commissioner of police knows the rivers of gold *pizzo* yields. Enough to make the Mafia the premier business in Italy. Yet no one has ever bothered to end the *pizzo*. It would be the Mafia's ace card in a deck of many dirty cards to pull in cash.

The Mafia grew its epicentre in Palermo. From there, it radiated towards eastern Sicily, and in time, all over Italy. During its passage from the countryside to the city, where landowners lived in luxury and relative safety, the Mafia maintained its original violent character, but it was also clever enough to adapt its internal organisation to its new urban environment. Palermo, Catania and Messina were no longer just the home of aristocrats. All of a sudden they were home to men with hard faces and smooth hands, thugs with toothpicks, brutes in black-and-white leather spats. The Mafia soon took up the morning ritual of *passeggiata*, a stroll along the boulevards in search of a new panama hat or pair of London brogues, or an espresso coffee and *biscotti* with the gentry. Their acclimatisation to suburban life and occupation of lavish apartments on the sunny side of the street worried their fellow citizens and commanded their silence. Salacious stories of vendettas ensured both sides of the social spectrum lived in harmony, as they still do today. It is all to do with the rules of engagement.

During this change in home and work environment, the Mafia built its organisational structure, their *cosche* – at country, city or village level – which remained fundamental to every sector of Mafia activity: pastoral stock theft, movement of contraband, standovers, blackmail, *pizzo*, and so on. Several *cosche* constitute a family, whose affiliates have supremacy only in their given region. This is a strictly enforced rule, though opposing families can form a bond, for any number of reasons, including business or planning.

It is easy to see the rural history behind the Mafia and their choice of names and words to describe the inner workings of their secret society. The embryo of the Mafia, well before unification, grew among the artichoke growers and much broader citrus trade in Sicily. Tough guys stood over growers of lemons, limes and oranges on the island, forcing a commission (*pizzo*) from fearful farmers. The citrus standovers were arguably the first form of rural extortion, ensuring the *picciotti* and their leaders an ongoing slice of the citrus pie. It was a lucrative racket, mainly because citrus exports from Sicily were popular with Britain, and traders needed a constant supply to keep up with the demand. The citrus that left the island each week was mostly from the British-controlled port of Marsala, which had allowed Garibaldi and his *Mille* safe passage upon their arrival.

•

Before 1860, one of the earliest Mafia bosses, Don Antonino Giammona, honed his standover skills on citrus farmers, violently forcing his hand into the profits of the lemon growers. (The title 'Don' was given to the head of a Mafia *cosca*, as a sign of respect. It comes from the Latin word *Dominus* and means 'lord'. Mafia movies and books invariably overuse the title Don when referring to the head of a clan or family. Most of the time, family heads are just called by their name.) At the time of Garibaldi, the forty-year-old Don Antonino made his way down to the port of Marsala with his clan and became squadron leader of hundreds of *picciotti*, fighting alongside the red-shirted general. After unification, Giammona's 'career' in Sicily could be seen as the perfect example of the fusion of politics, wealth, law enforcement, crime and Mafia. He became a captain in the National Guard, where he crushed any attempts by Sicilians to revolt against the new King of Italy. He knew the benefit of playing to the gallery and feigning loyalty to those higher up the food chain. He stayed in this role for six years. He then left the King's employ to become the head of Palermo's largest Mafia clan.

Throughout the 1870s his clan dominated a racket of extortion and violence that murdered twenty-three people. Giammona camouflaged his involvement behind a religious brotherhood named the Territory of St Francis of Assisi, managed by his dodgy brother, Rosario Giammona. In time his position was elevated by winning a seat in parliament by a narrow margin of fifty-five votes. The killer head of the Mafia was now a politician, a man of the people, and opposition was in short supply. Giammona often found his name on legal papers; each time the prosecutor referred to him as a *mafioso* and each time he walked free due to a lack of evidence. As early Mafia bosses go, he became the epitome of 'untouchable'.

A subsequent inquiry into the violence used during unification had a strange outcome. The resultant report published in 1866[3] recommended that police be encouraged to make alliances with Mafia leaders in an effort to suppress revolts against the rule over Sicily, and Giammona had made the most of this opportunity. Giammona was one of the leading *mafiosi* on the island, and his sons and extended family were *capi* in the scourge.[4] So bold was Antonino, he was known to breach the early rules of engagement, including attacking fellow *mafiosi*, which is punishable by death. Antonino scoffed at the rules he helped create and killed anyone critical of him, his *cosca* or his management. Despite his contradictions and flagrant breaches of rules, no one dared take the argument up to him.

By the end of the nineteenth century, the *pizzo* was in force everywhere, thanks mostly to the Honourable Antonino Giammona, Member for Palermo. He popularised the tickling of most cash tills in Sicily. Approaching old age, he had avoided seeing the interior of a prison cell, smashed all attempts to prosecute him, and boasted about being a powerhead in Sicily's now embedded Mafia. Aged eighty-five, he died without ever being convicted of a crime, and left, as his lasting legacy, the *pizzo*.

Underpinning the cohesion and unity of the Mafia was a code of silence (*omertà*): to not speak of any Mafia activity unless to each other, and only then to further the business plan or improve it. Any outsider contaminating this stricture faced the *picciotti di ficatu* (brave young men), who were determined to show their boldness at any cost and climb the steps in the Mafia kingdom.[5] These were killers who didn't hesitate to cut the genitals off a playboy and shove them in his mouth, to spoon the eyes out of victims, or place a prickly pear at the door of a common thief, and so on. Crime and punishment with its roots in rural Sicily, where farm hands castrated sheep, ate offal, and cleared prickly pear from the land.

The head of a Mafia clan presided over all punishments. He did not tolerate crimes or violence against another without his permission, especially against his treasured *cosca* lieutenants. Lack of respect for this rule would exact immediate punishment and lifetime expulsion from illicit activities.[6]

The Mafia boss was typically the eldest man in each clan, who had the benefit of age and wisdom after coming through the ranks from *picciotti* to become a *capo*. Like any chairman of a board, he worried about supply and demand, balancing the books, negotiating unrest, research, and developing new markets. His all-powerful role ensured his hand, or his word, was absolute. Once confirmed as a Mafia boss, he acted as the clan's capitalist, impresario and dictator. He coordinated the perpetration of crimes, set the rules, enforced the penalties, regulated the division of labour and tasks, and controlled discipline among its employees.[7] In his clan, his *cosca*, the boss was law enforcer, prosecutor, judge, juror and sentencer. His *modus operandi* had to adapt to market conditions, business relationships, human resources and the type of violence that was the best fit for the infraction.

With the consolidation of Mafia power in the countryside, and the growth of crime in the city, the nexus between common crimes and Mafia crimes changed profoundly. On the one hand, by the end of the nineteenth century, there was an increase in crimes like extortion, murder, kidnapping for blackmail, letters demanding money for protection and theft of animals. On the other hand, there was a decrease in petty theft, sexual assaults and drunkenness. However, this trend must be assessed with caution. We must not be deceived by the decrease in common crimes, which has been interpreted as implying the Mafia was asserting order, replacing the state. In other words, the man on the street was too scared to harm his neighbour for fear of being harmed himself by the Mafia. Actually, if we consider the Mafia's typical crimes (theft of livestock, murder, armed robbery, extortion, blackmail, cutting of plants and vines, arson and crippling of livestock), the statistics reveal that the localities characterised by the presence of the Mafia can still have the highest rates of these crimes.[8] They can still be dangerous wherever they operate. Their presence does not mean social harmony, as they often proffer.

Forty years after the inception of the Mafia, at a time when they had started to perfect their management skills, Sicily's crime rate was ranked fifth or sixth in Italy, lower than other regions considered socially more advanced, such as their northern neighbours. (There are twenty regions in Italy.)

A typical Mafia technique was the extortion letter, the number of which increased proportionally as the Mafia became stronger. We can even identify formulas in the language used in extortion letters. A pattern was visible that was different to other letters of demand by non-Mafia persons. The Mafia leader, aware he is feared and obeyed, therefore does not threaten but gently advises his victim, in writing, to comply with the demand.[9] The following examples are significant:

> Dear Sir, your friends pray for you, if you do not want to have the goods that you own destroyed, please send three thousand Lire. If you want to live on you must do this, send them on to the neighbouring house of Luigi, send it with your man Rosario by midnight in three days. Please don't miss it or your life will suffer. Santa Flavia, June 12th, 1886

The language becomes more pressing, more assertive if the victim ignores the warning or makes the naive decision to go to the police (naive because in many cases the police might be acting for the Mafia).

> Mr. Baron, it must be not later than April 4th that you have to send or bring fifty thousand Lire, otherwise both you and your Baroness will have a more evil death than your brother-in-law. But we want you alive, so just send the money.[10]

Invariably, the extortion demand was paid, and the victim left alone. It was uncommon for the victim to be tickled again for extortion – once bitten, twice shy. Such extortion letters were only sent to those who could afford it. Under the 'can't get blood out of a stone' rule, the Mafia picked their marks well. It was simply done: one fountain pen, one piece of paper, and a few days of patience. By the time extortion letters were rife, the Mafia's reputation for punishment ensured a near one hundred per cent success rate. While inside the archives in Palermo, I inspected copious police files on the extortion letters and observed the earliest form of handwriting sampling, a unique attempt to uncover a villain through the use of forensics. It was very impressive.

During the same period at the end of the nineteenth century, in the province of Palermo, there had been a significant increase in cattle rustling and thefts, while in the same three-year period bashings and common assaults decreased, which suggest the Mafia were the only ones doling out violence. Non-Mafia thugs were perhaps too fearful to force themselves on others, in case their victims were connected to the Mafia by crimes, *pizzo*, friendship or marriage.

Meanwhile, living standards and the potential to better oneself in southern Italy were on the skids. Times were tough, and while others from now affluent parts of Italy such as Piedmont and Lombardy were thriving, with a high standard of living – thanks to the fortunes of Sicily being taken up north – Mediterranean Italians were not doing well. The solution for those peasants and lowly thugs was to immigrate to America. In time, Mafia crime gangs formed in the United States, and the news sent back home was 'Get over here!' This small number of criminals gave birth to the American association known as the *Mano Nera* (Black Hand), whose crimes soon began to ooze into public consciousness. A new-world, copycat Mafia took hold.[11] The existing relationship between the Sicilian Mafia and the American Black Hand (or *Cosa Nostra* as it is now called) is more or less due to their participation in the same crime – extortion – and dates back to the turn of the twentieth century. The two criminal organisations have always stayed close, demonstrating that the Mafia had equal power and influence on both sides of the Atlantic.

Back home, it was business as usual as the clans got stronger and the tentacles of the Mafia spread to other parts of Italy. By the end of the nineteenth century, the Mafia associations and loyalties were entrenched in parliament, which had become a congress of louts. Expansion and acquisition were part of the Mafia business plan.

The prefecture and the Minister of the Interior at this time were accused of using the Mafia to shut down other gangs in the region, in effect wiping out the competition. It was only due to the intervention of honest police, along with the army, that gang warfare was all but halted for a time and the Mafia contained. Proof that, if confronted head-on, without the interference of corrupt politicians, the Mafia was/is a beatable cancer.

By the end of the nineteenth century, there was a rare decline in Mafia activity.

Outside of Sicily, growth of Mafia-type organisations was evident in and around Naples, an area also detrimentally affected by the unification of Italy. While the streets of Naples were awash with prostitution, produce rackets, standovers and pickpocketing (a crime perfected in Naples), the city had far fewer killings compared to Sicily. The Mafia, known as the *Camorra* in Naples, was less sophisticated in its management and structure than its Sicilian cousin. Other regions of Italy were Mafia-free, at least compared to Sicily. While small pockets of Mafia-type gangs were scattered across the country, the full Mafia cancer was yet to spread.

In Calabria, Mafia crime was confined to hill bandits and local infighting. And Sardinia was still a feudal society, squabbling over little.

As for Australia, a latter-day region for the Mafia, it was still a British colony, shaking off its penal origins as a place for Britain's unwanted convicts, and Italian immigration was minimal. That would change in the new century, when Australia started accepting immigrants from all over Europe, including southern Italy. Likewise, Canada hadn't seen the cancer yet, but its proximity to the United States ensured it would receive a franchise soon enough.

The biggest political scandal of the late nineteenth century is possibly the best example of the Mafia finding its legs, standing up and sprinting. It involved the assassination of the head of the Banco di Sicilia, Emanuele Notarbartolo. He was the former Mayor of Palermo, and a senior member of the right-wing faction of politics. He was also the son of the Prince of Sciara. Noted for his loyalty to Garibaldi during the invasion of Sicily, he was highly regarded by natives of the island. He attempted to use his political power to clean up the Bank of Sicily and sever any association with the emerging Mafia. *Mafiosi* were investing way too much in the banks for men who didn't work. His passion to wash away Mafia involvement saw him clash with his opposite number, Raffaele Palizzolo – a member of the left-wing opposition, which was keen to assume government.

There was little doubt that Palizzolo was in cahoots with the Palermo Mafia. He was bold and brazen, and his relationship with Notarbartolo was acrimonious.

On a train one night, two *picciotti* approached the stately Notarbartolo and set upon him with knives. Both were members of a Palermo-based Mafia clan that had associations with Palizzolo. They stabbed Notarbartolo twenty-seven times. His life ended in a pool of blood on the floor of the train carriage.

Notarbartolo was a wealthy man, yet robbery didn't appear to be the motive; his wallet was not touched. His murder highlighted how entrenched the scourge had become and how much clout the Mafia had started to wield; no one was immune. The public and newspaper editors across Italy wanted to know if left-wing elements in politics were involved; did they order the hit? But editors are not prosecutors, and before long Notarbartolo's murder fell from page one to page six. What followed was an absurdly slow legal process that saw the two *picciotti* assassins jailed and many questions asked about the extent of Mafia involvement. The three wise monkeys prevailed in Palermo;

no one saw, heard or said anything. The famed Sicilian blank stare was in play.

Palizzolo faced trial twice, only to walk from court both times with a grin on his face. The jury doubted his involvement, but by the end of the case no one in Sicily doubted the Mafia was a permanent fixture in their lives. It had also moved off the island of Sicily, looking to stretch out its tentacles further afield.

CHAPTER 13
THE BLACK HAND

SICILIAN SAYING:

Abbuscarisi u pani
To earn the bread

Meaning, to make a living, somehow

As dusk settled on the nineteenth century, three things became certain in Sicily: there would always be death, taxes and the Mafia. Forty years into its development, the scourge had overtaken the island and outlived any suggestion that it was a passing phase; it was a stupendously massive criminal gang that no one was capable of eradicating. By the new century, the Mafia had spread across the Atlantic to areas that would have been inconceivable years earlier, thanks to ocean liners, to anywhere there was a seaport.

Between 1896 and 1898, of the vast numbers of Italians who decided to emigrate, most were Sicilians. This became known as the great migratory flow, with ninety per cent making a beeline for America. Of the numbers that ran down the gangplanks of incoming ships, a few hundred were estimated to have Mafia ties. Thugs who wanted to make a living somehow, anywhere, as crime in their homeland was too competitive; there were few opportunities to exploit a population that was already fully exploited. Within a decade these numbers would swell to thousands.[1]

But, for all its ferocity and omnipresence, no one had been able to fully explain what the Mafia really was. Americans and the rest of the world rarely saw the word 'Mafia' in their daily newspapers. This ignorance was ideal for migrating *mafiosi* sneaking into new frontiers, like New York, Australia and Canada. Since then, as the clans took hold, many authors have tried to explain why a bunch of tough guys preyed on vulnerable people. But from my reading none have successfully defined what 'Mafia' means.

Some definitions are straightforward, while others are too esoteric, or academic. Many have relied on historical evaluation, and just as many have tried to define the scourge through its victims' voices, or those that either prosecuted Mafia players or investigated them. It is fair to say these past attempts all have merit, but the question still feels unanswered. I sat in archives reading documents that try to unravel the Mafia disease, written by people better educated than myself, books written as far back as 150 years ago.

Many contain the opinions of qualified individuals who expound wacky explanations for why the Mafia came into existence. Some of the crazier examples started out as PhD theses and ended up as books that, for my money, take up too much shelf space. By example, I recently read a thesis that linked real-life atrocities of the Mafia to the Hollywood depiction of Mafia crime, and suggested that fiction had given rise to fact. Really!

Meanwhile, a criminologist might offer a rationale for why the Mafia flourished, just as an overworked detective in the anti-Mafia unit in Rome could, and their explanations might differ considerably. A judge sitting in a busy courtroom could give their view based on an armful of trials they have heard. Even a Mafia hitman has a viewpoint, one that intrigues me more than that of the judge, the criminologist, the victim and the many journalists who have written about the subject.

Should you go to a dictionary definition of the Mafia, it will say: 'a secret association of Sicilian origin serving private interests by illicit means and resorting to violence'. Not incorrect, but, excluding the 'Sicilian origin' part, this could describe any Hells Angels chapter, or a gang of ruthless people smugglers. Personally, I like the Wikipedia definition: 'a criminal organisation whose activities are subject to a hidden collegiate leadership and which is based on a strategy of infiltration of civil society and institutions'. I would just add a clause about the use of extreme violence and the Mafia's unique ability to sustain a level of fear in the broader community that aids their illegality.

One writer who left an impression on me was Sicilian Giuseppe De Felice Giuffrida. De Felice, a socialist, was twice Mayor of Catania, up until his death in 1920. He wrote much about the Mafia, and for many Italians became the quintessential voice on the subject. For me, his book *Maffia e delinquenza in Sicilia* ('Mafia and Crime in Sicily'), published in 1900, explains the scourge, but also confuses its origins.[2]

De Felice believed the Mafia was a residual phenomenon, the result of an unresolved transition from feudalism to modernity. De Felice can also be seen as a good example of confusing who or what the Mafia is, as he states that 'due to the cohabitation of social structures and powers elsewhere – in comparison with the modernity of the state of law – behaviours capable of overturning society's regulatory role, the blocking of mechanisms of justice came about'. These conditions facilitated the creation of the Mafia – De Felice affirms that the Sicilian criminal phenomenon was the expression of an insular culture, with a particular 'psychological propensity'. He suggested that progress had 'flushed out the complex and residual criminal phenomena such as Mafia'. That's my point, he gets complicated. Whilst he writes well, and he's obviously above my intellectual paygrade, it all becomes too esoteric. I mean, we're talking about thugs!

Migration to places like America, De Felice argues, caused the loss of the strongest and most enterprising part of the population, which led to the 'degeneration of the species, since only the weakest remained, the least suited to the struggle for existence'. In other words, the Mafia who stayed behind in Sicily were of inferior intelligence. Oddly – the evidence is on record to prove otherwise – he believed Sicily had one of the lowest crime rates in Italy, and suggests the economic crisis of the late nineteenth century affected the weakest parts of society, especially in the countryside around Palermo. Explaining the Mafia as a uniquely Sicilian phenomenon, De Felice writes:

It cannot be said that Mafia is a Sicilian disease; and those who believe that Sicily is all a hideout of Mafiosi, give proof of not knowing the real conditions of the island. Mafia? It is there, as elsewhere, that the sick part of society produces and feeds it. Mafia often assumes a political form and character, serves to exert a pressure, to guarantee a clientele, to impose an interest, while other state crime gangs [meaning in Naples] aim more directly at theft.[3]

Then he says:

Once Mafia ruled in the countryside, spreading terror throughout, now it is more civilized . . . will you believe that the purpose of the Mafia is theft? Not at all! Mafia has hardly ever been involved in theft.

Further on in his book, De Felice refers to the Mafia as 'a society of bloodthirsty people': 'The Mafioso does not commit serious crimes; the field of his delinquency is most of the time restricted to fines, because of theft and rarely of crimes against a person'. So, what is the Mafia? De Felice proposes:

It is a violent explosion of popular anger, due to a collective and instinctive impulse, which unites in an almost criminal pact, many of those among the most impulsive, who, treated like dogs by society, swear that they do not trust in any other justice than the one got with their own hands. To help one another and support one another, like brothers, till death and to escape from the claws of justice. And to silence the witnesses who want to speak.

Some of what he wrote is brilliant, but just as much shows ignorance – such as his claim that the Mafia were not thieves (has he not heard of the *pizzo*?). The extent of the Mafia's crimes, their thirst for money and propensity for violence were well established. Even in America the Mafia were becoming entrenched; by 1900 there were 145 429 Italian immigrants living in the United States, so it stands to reason some were bandits on the lookout for spoils.[4]

My understanding of what the Mafia was, or what they are now, is through their disregard for law and order, justice and process, an understanding best illustrated by the story of a New York City police officer, Joseph Petrosino.

There is nothing new about police being killed in the line of duty, either maliciously, by accident, or from being in the wrong place at the wrong time, such as bumping into a bank robber on his way out of the bank. Police departments around the globe have way too many memorial plaques honouring men and women who made the ultimate sacrifice to the communities they served. I have worked with cops who were gunned down in their pursuit of criminals. One, a fellow detective sergeant I worked with, making inroads against the Mafia, was the recipient of a massive parcel bomb. He lost his life in an instant, but his lovely wife and children still grieve the loss of a good man. I have been luckier; death threats against me have not eventuated and I am here today to tap away on my laptop and tell stories of better, far braver cops than myself. The murder of a fellow cop is a sadness that hangs on to you for years.

In December 1908, 48-year-old Joseph Petrosino, the boss of the NYPD Italian crime section, obtained authorisation to travel to Sicily to investigate the phenomenon of Mafia in order to curb, if possible, the emigration of people with a criminal record, and establish a connection with the Italian police to interrupt the ties between Sicilian Mafia and American thugs of Italian origins.

Joseph Petrosino was of Italian origin and had more than twenty-five years of policing experience. Born near Naples, he saw firsthand the scourge as it took hold during the 1870s. It was a time of struggle; a great divide existed between the southern 'peasants', as they were called, and the more affluent northerners. With few opportunities for advancement, even to a simple labouring job, the folk of Naples, Reggio Calabria, Palermo, Brindisi, Bari, Catania and other once-important cities flooded the ships leaving daily for New York City, the land of liberty and prosperity. The Mafia also made good use of this same water track out of Italy, away from misery, vendettas or prosecution, to the land of milk and honey, or so they thought.

With a skinny wallet with a few useful contacts, the Mafia immigrants would soon become part of the great American crime book. Cities were growing fast, and scams were aplenty, particularly in the world of labour rackets and construction sites. Skyscrapers reached for the heavens and Mafia gangs buried their victims in the concrete slabs at their base. Against this backdrop, the spotlight shone on Petrosino. His fight against organised crime became so legendary that he attracted recognition from the Italian communities in America. The Italian Consul General in New York gave him a gold watch for the 'brave and active work aimed at discovering and arresting individuals who had escaped from Italian justice'. Petrosino arrested and repatriated to Italy over 600 criminals responsible for extortion and blackmail in Little Italy, New York City. New York's Mafia was on its well-oiled training wheels.

As a result, many Americans were prejudiced against Italian immigrants. Crimes such as murder, kidnapping, standovers and violence seemed part of their way of life. The victims were also Italian by birth or ancestry. In time, the problem – and its perpetrators – acquired a name: the Black Hand, when a prosperous Italian from Brooklyn received a letter of demand. Pay up or else your house will be bombed, signed *Mano Nera*, the Black Hand. The demand was for $10 000, later reduced to a more workable $1000.[5]

Back then, the deeds of the Black Hand were publicised by newspaper accounts, at a time when the American Mafia had not properly structured itself. The proliferation of crimes by the Black Hand – kidnappings and letters of demand – gave rise to specialist policing, with hand-picked officers like Detective Petrosino. His sidekick investigator, Michael Fiaschetti, observed the Black Hand riding the crest of emerging organised crime, fuelled by each new ship that docked in New York. Something had to be done to stop the cancer.

Petrosino and Fiaschetti had a roving brief to stamp out the Black Hand, and Petrosino proved brilliant at it, with an arrest rate that was arguably the best on the east coast. There was little doubt his ethnicity was the key. The commissioner saw merit in Petrosino schooling up on the cancer in Palermo, to understand how it all started. His trip to Sicily in 1909 was to ascertain how the suspects emigrated without proper papers and escaped Italian justice, then attached themselves to crime gangs in New York City.[6] It was also hoped that Petrosino would discover links between the Sicilian Mafia and the flourishing American Black Hand.[7]

Petrosino travelled undercover, under the name of Guglielmo De Simone, with an address at the Banca Commerciale building in Palermo. This, along with the skulduggery of Francesco Crispi in 1859, was among the earliest examples of undercover methodology involving false documents. For all the preparation and care taken to keep a low profile, there was one act of carelessness that Petrosino could not have seen coming; he had left the United States in the middle of an election period. New York candidates were using anything they could get their sweaty hands on to gain an edge over their political opponents, and a cop on a secret Mafia mission was enough to get a politician in the papers. The newspapers were fed information that Petrosino had left New York eleven days earlier to investigate immigrants of ill repute. Once the story was leaked, the press went into overdrive. The *Herald Tribune* featured an editorial on 20 February 1909, saying:

> Lieutenant Petrosino went to Sicily to obtain important infor-
> mation on many Italians who lived in the city of New York but
> should be expelled because they were criminals. Petrosino is in
> Palermo to document individual cases, and on his return, the
> Sicilian people with a criminal record will be sent back.[8]

New Italian-Americans became worried that their liberty, promised by the famed torch-bearing statue on arrival, was now under threat. Those with something to hide were put on notice, and some went on the warpath. Before the next edition, Palermo was talking about the undercover Petrosino and his mission to stamp out migrating Mafia.

Petrosino worked alone, moving across the island, taking meetings with police and building up his file against *mafiosi* who had emigrated. Five weeks into his research, he travelled to Caltanissetta, a miser-able, brutal town in the interior of Sicily that fostered the Mafia and perfected the ways of the Black Hand. Here he was confronted on the street by a thug he had dealt with in New York. He wrote in his diary that he had been recognised and was on dangerous ground.[9] (Anyone with any understanding of undercover work could only be alarmed at the potential dangers that now faced Joseph, alone in Mafia country.)

The leaders of the Black Hand gathered in New Orleans at the house of Paolo Marchese, alias Paul Di Cristina: a Mafia hood who had, thus far, turned his poor ethnic background into a lucrative American business, running Palermo-style rackets across the eastern seaboard of the United States. The meeting was attended by a who's who of early crime bosses, thugs who had a vested interest in keeping low-level standover men – once resident in Sicily – in their employ in America. They decided to send Pete DiGiovanni, a key Mafia thug, to Palermo to confer with Mafia bosses as to what should be done to stop Petrosino. Should Petrosino have been successful, the American Mafia may have been a shadow of the entity it became by the Roaring Twenties. If he had completed his task, he may have stopped the cancer from spreading altogether. The potential of his success cannot be underestimated.

Upon DiGiovanni's arrival, an urgent meeting between the emissary of the Black Hand and the Mafia bosses of Palermo took place in the grand *palazzo* of Don Vito Cascio Ferro, the head of the Sicilian Mafia, and a man now worried.

Don Vito, a native of Bisacquino in the province of Palermo, is credited with having brought the Mafia in Palermo to the level of a 'delinquency industry', an odd term outside the Italian language. In 1900, it meant evil, hard-nosed crime, with a particular specialisation in kidnapping for extortion purposes. At that time, Don Vito's enterprise and network of companies and legal entities included a fleet of fishing boats that transported stolen cattle to the Tunisian and Calabrian coasts, where his extended gang took charge of selling the booty. These same ships were also used to transport, via the coasts of Tunisia, *mafiosi* who were illegally immigrating to America. Don Vito's well-used water track across the Mediterranean Sea was not known to Italian police. They had failed for twenty years to work out the scam. It would be exposed, however, should the tenacious Petrosino succeed on his mission. The bosses of the American Black Hand, the men at the New Orleans conference, owed their own escape from Sicily to Don Vito's water track.

It was Don Vito who helped popularise the use of *pizzo*, after his mentor Don Antonino Giammona popularised the extortion game in the late nineteenth century. A similar system was adopted by the *mafiosi* who immigrated to America. Those occupying a cosy seat at the New Orleans conference forced shopkeepers, business operators, wharf dockers, stevedoring companies and the vulnerable to pay a *pizzo*. Should they refuse, they could be killed. Back then, a Mafia tariff was attached to many bakers and their loaves; every case of bananas, even a tray of meat would be *pizzo* taxed. Refusal saw the Black Hand arrange a horse-drawn carriage to pass by the disobedient business to show off the efficient workings of an automatic rifle. Spraying a belt of rounds in broad daylight usually encouraged a change of mind.

Don Vito is described as the epitome of an early twentieth-century Mafia boss. He was a tall, distinguished man, elegant in appearance, with uncalloused hands and a long beard. He enjoyed respect and prestige, being a welcomed guest at the best hotels, and honoured by important figures in politics and finance. He was often invited to join company boards, to which he brought little other than prestige and authority. It is said that when he travelled from one province to another in western Sicily, the mayors of towns on his way waited for him at the gates of their village to pay homage by kissing his hands. Don Vito could publicly boast that he had not killed a single person or harmed a hair on anyone's head.[10] His prestige was such, he could silence anyone who might have said otherwise. And no one ever did. There were no known killings by his own hand, but many by his lips.

In the meeting with the emissary of the Black Hand, who came to discuss the suppression of Petrosino, Don Vito personally took charge to demonstrate his superiority and authority. He had no other choice.

While in Palermo, Petrosino wrote to his NYPD superior to inform him that he had been received by the Sicilian Minister of the Interior, with whom he had a long conversation about Italian criminals and their crimes in the United States. The minister had declared an interest in assisting Petrosino and had instructed his chief of police to order prefects not to issue travel documents to Italians with a criminal record. A major breakthrough. On 1 March 1909, Petrosino wrote from the Hotel de France in Palermo, where he was lodging, stating that he had proof of criminal associations of certain American residents with Sicilian backgrounds, and expected to obtain more details on many others in due course. There was a great sense that the gates to the United States were about to be slammed shut on the Mafia.

On Saturday 12 March, at nine o'clock in the evening, Lieutenant Joseph Petrosino decided to take a stroll through the old part of Palermo, an area no more than 70 metres from the famed Church of Gancia, where so many Palermitans lost their lives protesting against the Bourbons in April 1860.[11]

He came upon Piazza Marina, just steps away from the harbour, and walked into the gated gardens, home to the largest Moreton Bay fig in Europe, situated alongside a large marble statue of Giuseppe Garibaldi gazing determinedly across the piazza. A few strides further on Joseph stopped to wait for a well-to-do carriage with a team of prancing horses. A tall, dapper-looking man who had just alighted from the coach strolled towards the handsome policeman. Motioning as if to reach for his hand, he instead fired three revolver shots, cracking the dusk air and fatally wounding the undercover cop, with one bullet hitting Petrosino's head. Before falling, Petrosino took his own revolver out of his pocket and fired in vain at his assassin. His gun fell to the roadway. His night and fight had ended.

An hour earlier, Don Vito had arrived for dinner at his friend's grand *palazzo*, just a short carriage ride away from Piazza Marina. Just as guests were grouping for pre-dinner cigars, he quietly took leave. Using his friend's coach, he went to Piazza Marina to kill the policeman. Afterwards, he returned to dinner with the other guests who could testify, in good faith, that they had spent the evening with Don Vito in the house of their mutual friend. No one realised that Don Vito had been missing for a short while, and in the classic Sicilian way, no one saw anything, heard anything, or was likely to say anything.

Inside Petrosino's breast pocket was his diary, a tool that all good detectives use to aid their investigations. On the last page he had written a poignant note: 'Don Vito Cascio Ferro, born in Sambuca Zubat, resident of Bisaquino, Province of Palermo, dreaded criminal'.[12] A notation that was not lost on Petrosino's colleagues in New York, and proved the nexus between the life and death of a great cop.[13]

Joseph Petrosino's investigation into the Sicilian Mafia was supremely brave, and well before its time in the methods of covert policing. (His task would be done more cautiously today, with close support.) It was also a significant challenge for Don Vito, the boss of his own 'honoured society', to meet his challenge and resolve the issue.[14] The Black Hand across the pond expected results, and their mentor showed his mettle. The water track for the Mafia remained open, and those ensconced in the Mafia in America could further their joint enterprises.

Don Vito was never charged with the slaying of Lieutenant Petrosino. The killing of Petrosino is still considered the perfect crime committed by the Mafia, one of thousands of murders they got away with. But, regardless, all cops recall their slain – it's part of our silent respect. It was reported that 250 000 New York citizens turned out for the funeral march for Lieutenant Giuseppe 'Joseph' Petrosino. Lest we forget.[15]

After being stuck inside one of the archival libraries in Palermo, I would often take a walk to get some air. I would stroll down to the harbour or visit the gated garden at Piazza Marina to sit on one of the benches and look up at the towering statue of Garibaldi, then across to two smaller busts. One of Rosolino Pilo, a *picciotti* leader, nearby to Giuseppe La Massa, maybe the first ever *mafioso*. A few feet away is a rusted metal plaque on a skinny pole in memory of Lieutenant Petrosino.[16] I thought about the association of these monuments in the one tiny area. And the hero, Garibaldi, who used the earlier Mafia in a devastating display of guerrilla warfare, overlooking a piddling metal plate for Petrosino, a man who stood against the future generations of those same Mafia, trying to keep them out of America. His marker is almost lost under the ancient fig tree.

As mentioned, I once shared a task force assignment with a detective sergeant colleague. We were working on a viper's nest of *mafiosi* in Australia, thugs who killed often and sold marijuana and white-powdered drugs by the truckload. They were considered an epidemic. Detective Sergeant Geoffrey Bowen was a lot like Joseph Petrosino: tenacious, fearless, honest. He took the fight up to a violent Don Vito type, who he caught supervising the cultivation of a massive cannabis plantation, growing in outback Australia, worth untold millions of dollars.

Geoffrey, too, was okay to go it alone. To openly pursue the scourge. He was blown up by the Mafia boss – by a phosphorus parcel bomb – for his efforts (red phosphorus is the stuff of match heads, highly flammable). He was burned beyond recognition, but his legacy survived. Like Joe's rusted tin plate under the fig tree. For cops, for me, remembrance carries real weight, about the same weight as Petrosino's diary. So, when I'm asked what is the Mafia? I brush aside the long-winded academic explanations, preferring to tell the story of Geoffrey, or Joseph, and the many other police who have been killed by the cowards who run and work the Mafia clans. The faceless mobsters who give out life-snatching orders that cause innocent children to lose a parent.

What is the Mafia? Do not try and analyse it too hard, don't waste your brain on it. Like De Felice, it will only confuse you. The Mafia is many things, but, by its members' black hands it is home to killers, first and foremost, of brave cops, from as far back as its inception.

CHAPTER 14
THE IMPERFECT PREFECT

SICILIAN SAYING:

Pi suvicchiarìa

For oppression

Meaning, when you act out of contempt

The twentieth century was always going to be vastly different to the previous one. While the nineteenth century saw the Industrial Revolution, capitalism and the rise of the Mafia, the twentieth century promised to be more risqué, more daring, and it didn't fail. In Western countries, the 1920s were the Roaring Twenties, meaning speakeasies, nightclubs, booze and dry martinis, jazz music, flappers, smoking long-stemmed cigarettes, and the start of moving pictures. The 'roar' in the twenties was very much an American invention, which was then adopted throughout Europe, the United Kingdom, Canada, Australia and most other places where cocktail shakers were sold.

But not so much in Sicily. There, debauchery was more reserved; the roar in this struggling island was mainly due to the work of the Mafia. They held a firm grip on all things that produced a financial return and couldn't be traced. Sicily was going backwards. Having never recovered from unification, its economy was under threat, with many factory workers moving north, leaving the remaining Sicilians to their misery.

The 1920s also saw the rise of Fascism in Italy. With Fascism came the strutting despot in knee-high boots, Benito Mussolini. An absolute ruler, he moved around the halls of power, mostly in Rome, wearing either a tight-fitting, pinstriped merino wool suit or his signature black military uniform with polished knee-high boots. Then there was the crop, a tiny leather jockey whip he would lash himself with as he walked. This show of power came adorned with a forest of medals, baubles and buttons, all highly polished. Benito was no laughing matter, which is probably why he rarely smiled. He was on a mission to change Italy, and the northern states were on board the train, which was moving quickly.

Mussolini ensured everyone worked in fear. It was said he had a stare that could slow a locomotive. With fear as his mantra, he reigned over his thirty million subjects for more than twenty years before he was shot dead in northern Italy in 1945.

While he was from a different time than Garibaldi, he did take one clever trait from the great general: a signature outfit. Mussolini liked his black, including shiny black silk shirts. But while Garibaldi worked with the Mafia to achieve his aims, Mussolini took the opposite approach. Shortly after declaring himself dictator in 1925, he openly declared war on the Mafia, even though the Mafia had showered his party with support to help get him into power.

It seems Mussolini became miffed when he visited Palermo in 1924 on a political junket and was met by the Mafia boss, Francesco Cuccia, of the infamous Piana dei Greci clan, who was also the mayor. Cuccia offered Mussolini protection while in Sicily, a typical gesture to get onside with the power players. The despot refused and took a cheap swipe at the top *mafioso* before heading off to give a speech to thousands. Nobody belittles thuggery! The *mafioso* took offence and passed word around the townsfolk, ensuring Il Duce ('The Leader') – as Mussolini was often called – would speak to an empty piazza. The man in black failed to find an audience, and as we know, a politician without a crowd is nothing. From that moment, Il Duce raged war on the scourge. He promised the media that he would eradicate the Mafia and return Sicily to a more productive state within the union. Mussolini set about finding the right man to kill off the Mafia, and chose Cesare Mori for the job. In many ways they were alike, excessive self-promoters.

In appointing Mori, Mussolini stated: 'Your Excellency [Mori] has carte blanche, the authority of the state must absolutely, I repeat absolutely, be re-established in Sicily. If the laws still in force hinder you, this will be no problem, as we will draw up new laws.'[1]

Suddenly, the Mafia had two thorns in their side, both dictators, with similar quirks against acceptable fashion sense. Mori was famed for wearing the shiniest black silk pants with starched and pressed razor-sharp pleats. Along with a matching shirt, and of course the boots – there were always the boots – with a matching riding crop and tin medals. A pigeon pair.

Alongside attacking the Mafia, Mussolini also wanted to hit Sicilian anti-Fascists, as of all the states Sicily had the poorest support for his government. Most Sicilians cared little for national politics.[2] They had had their fill decades earlier with the unification fiasco, and besides, as an island, they had been invaded and governed by ruthless despots for centuries. Another dictatorship meant little to a culture that had survived largely by governing themselves underground and sorting out their problems internally.

Since unification, there had been a shift in commercial interests in Sicily, mostly because the kingdom had moved up north much of what made the island tick economically. Since World War I, the Sicilians also faced a further hit: demand for their fruit, vegetable and cereal crops was in decline, sulphur was no longer as important in twentieth-century global industry, and other suppliers were cheaper anyway.[3] Civil neglect was evident in the abysmal roads and footpaths, and academia had fallen away, while malaria killed many during this time.

Naively, Mussolini thought the Sicilian slump was solely the work of the Mafia. What he did not realise was how ill the economy was, that out-of-work employees turned to crime to put bread on their tables, which caused many to turn to the Mafia. The Mafia patriarch was a viable choice of loyalty for the needy, especially in rural Sicily. A cohesive system operated whereby old-school *mafiosi* ensured the poor got something during hard times, and of course the Mafia clipped every person's ticket in the process.

Then along came Il Duce's Fascist henchman, Cesare Mori, anointed head Prefect of the island, the man to take charge of the whole shooting match. Mussolini labelled it the 'Southern Solution'. The cleaning up of Sicily.

Cesare Mori had an impressive record in law enforcement. Palermo born, he spent his early career in northern Italy, before he came home to take charge of Mafia-entrenched Trapani (before Fascism). Geographically, Trapani sits in the shadow of Calatafimi, the tiny village that played centre stage in the unification battle. Mori wore a big hat and a belt with two six-guns, and favoured horseback over a car – an old-fashioned cowboy.

Legend has it that at the time Mori took up his Trapani commission, 700 Mafia murders had occurred there the previous year. It was described as 'the worst small city in Italy, if not Europe'.[4] Violence had become a pastime. Taking on the Mafia, Mori was so hardened that on one occasion he stood his ground in a nine-gun shoot-out against a street full of mobsters and won, leaving the bodies to the local undertaker and priest.[5] Soon after, he faced off against 1500 angry salt-mine workers who were striking for better wages. The Mafia union bosses were making a mockery of Mori's cowboy routine – that's before Mori drew his firearms and demanded the rioters go home, which they did. Mori feared no one, and Mussolini needed his John Wayne methodology. By late 1925, aged in his fifties, Mori found himself in the top job, with Palermo, if not all of Sicily, his to play with.[6] He filled the wardrobe in his office with black silk shirts and went to work as head Prefect, amid a nervous population that had seen many sideshows before.

Mori's early press announcements were more for the ears of Benito Mussolini than the public. Like Garibaldi, he declared he would unite Sicily, and Fascism would clean up the Mafia. The noise of his new appointment faded away as he walked the corridors, slapping the palms of the gentry, making friends and evaluating the many factions and frictions in old Palermo. He needed to rally support and get the administrators on side. While some smiled, few listened. Most just gave him that Sicilian blank 'fuck off' stare.

He was seen on the streets, day and night, with his short-back-and-sides haircut and wire-framed spectacles, his crop callusing his thighs. On his many visits to the tiny villages that dotted the coast and interior of Sicily, Mori would take his Alfa Romeo to impress the poor. He was also known to park his car outside a town and send his lowly cops ahead to stir up the village. He'd then arrive moments later on horseback, chest out and looking every bit the cowboy coming into Dodge City.[7] Each time he showed the law enforcement flag, he also espoused to disinterested onlookers the glories of Fascism. But ultimately he was there to clean up a scourge, and Mussolini checked the newspapers each morning to see if his choice of Prefect had started his campaign.

Mori learnt much in his early days and was the first person in authority to recognise there were now two Mafias in existence in Sicily: the old and the new.[8] The old, and its ideology and methods, had roots in Garibaldi days. The old, Mori saw, had become the cosier and fuzzier of the two Mafias; its members saw currency in tradition, looking after rural people's interests, taking grievances up to city hall, demanding change, taking a reward for achieving it, then stepping back and letting the minestrone settle. However, the *nuovo* Mafia was something quite different. Mori saw this twentieth-century Mafia as hungry for the vices of the Roaring Twenties. The new *mafiosi* were envious of their Chicago and New York cousins. They wanted it all, but without the 'niceties', the politics needed to effect change.[9] The new Mafia was prepared to kill for it all, and kill often. Its atrocities were troublesome: not only were members of the public or officials being killed, but minor squabbles between locals ended badly. The new were attacking the old in an effort to gain control.[10] It was as if extreme violence was the only answer to a problem within the *nuovo* Mafia, which discarded the more traditional manner of dealing with issues, which often involved time, patience and firm suggestion.

Mori's horse and six-guns would need a bigger, tougher strategy to accommodate the changing face of organised crime in Sicily. He also made another observation, this one less intuitive than his first, which ultimately led to his downfall. He genuinely believed every male in Sicily was a member of the Mafia. That every man and boy was a *mafioso*, which he said to anyone who would listen. He took this irrational logic one step further, declaring *anyone* could be a Mafia member, including women and children.

He wrote to Il Duce and outlined his discovery, accompanied by three demands: to obtain more funding to allow him to crush the Mafia; to obtain better resources; and to pass immediate legislation making it an offence to be 'an associate of the Mafia'.[11] Mussolini agreed and proclaimed his new law, which, in effect, could be applied to any person in Sicily.

The island was aghast at the legislation. The law could be applied without someone knowing who the Mafia suspects were or what their association with the organisation was. With almost no proof needed, half of Palermo, rural Sicily and beyond, chattered their teeth. A great many Sicilians knew of someone who lived a shady life, was a declared *mafioso* or had unexplained wealth. How would the cops define 'associate of the Mafia'? How could the courts convict? Mori soon delivered the answers. His first assault against the Mafia came soon after the gossip ended.

First, he withdrew all gun licences, regardless of whether the holder was a farmer or not.[12] Then, just before Christmas 1925 – as the streets, bars, *enoteche* and restaurants of Palermo were full of festivities and religious ceremony – the trucks arrived, loaded with cops. The police rolled into town behind Mori in his polished Alfa Romeo, and, in a move that stunned the citizens of Palermo, they swarmed the bars, cafes and streets and arrested – at random – sixty-two men in one night. Sixty-two locals merely in the company of family and friends. None of the raids or arrests took place in the usual places for *mafiosi* activity, such as brothels or illegal gambling houses. No one had committed a crime.[13] Those arrested were frogmarched to police stations and charged with being an 'associate of the Mafia'. The broader community sensed the city was under threat from legislation that could have a devastating effect on everyone.

Mori then dealt the men of the city another blow – a further 142 arrests were made in similar circumstances. By Christmas, another 328 arrests, and Palermo suffered its bleakest *Natale* in history, as jails brimmed with well-to-do locals.[14]

The profile of the more than 500 arrested was more akin to lawyers and shop assistants than toothpick-chewing, hard-nosed thugs milling about in packs looking for strife. Mori indelibly stamped his name on the city when he announced to the newspapers that the men in custody were parasites, and the definition of Mafia now extended to the city's administrators as well as politicians.

The new year did not see any change in Mori's mindset, which had a damning effect on rural Sicily. A few days into January, Mori with a posse of 800 low-level cops surrounded the town of Gangi in the interior of the island. Set on a hilltop, Gangi was a miserable town fallen on hard times and had become a hub for the old Mafia, the traditional Mafia: a collection of clans that oversaw labour and farming rackets in the area about 100 kilometres from Palermo.[15] (Many of these once-sad villages have since been beautified by a different generation, with different ideals.)

The inhabitants woke one morning to find themselves a global headline. Their town was under siege. Mori had arrived on horseback to lock up each and every man for being an 'associate of the Mafia'. Men went into hiding: beneath floorboards; into the denuded hills; up into attics; down cellars; and wedged into caves that usually held contraband rather than desperate men.

Within the hour the town went quiet. Like Dodge City, the streets were deserted. Mori walked the main street to see his arrival had backfired; no one surrendered. They had all scuttled away. Mori demanded every house, humpy and shed be raided, and the houses be so upended as to make them uninhabitable.[16] He ordered his cops to eat all the food in each house; kill any chickens; shoot the livestock; drink any wine; and sleep in the beds with or without the wives or partners of the missing men. His goal was to flush the men out and make them surrender to justice as an 'associate of the Mafia'.

One of the first to be arrested was an eighty-year-old invalid, who fell to his knees where he stood, tears streaming down his face. He was carted off to prison. Then came another, then another, as Gangi and surrounding villages were trashed. Day two came and still most of the town's men were missing, lying underground. Then came a common-sense white rag of peace. The town elder, Gaetano Ferrarello, crawled out of his cave and walked into town with an offer. He would mediate the surrender of each man. A classic patriarch, Ferrarello had presided over many feuds and was the ideal person to take charge.

Mori immediately arrested Ferrarello and rushed him out of town in irons.[17] Gangi would be a litmus test for what lay ahead for the rest of Sicily, and perhaps Italy. Mori reinforced his orders: all to surrender or everything will be destroyed. In the end, the town was ruined and 400 of its menfolk, some no doubt old Mafia, some too wretchedly poor to be anything, many elderly, were arrested and sent to prison to face trial.

The only criminal charge listed in the many court records for those awaiting trial was 'associate of the Mafia'. The newspaper stories ran wild after the siege ended, declaring Cesare Mori a hero and comparing him to the mythical Hercules.[18] A moment of fame that no doubt saw Mori put more starch in his laundry and into his stride. One front-page banner called the prefect 'Santo Mori' – the saint of Sicily.[19] Mussolini declared his Southern Solution was ticking over nicely. Then came the invitations, the red carpets and champagne as Santo Mori topped the list of every socialite's dinner party invitees. Palermo was alive with praise, and 1926 roared like no other year as the aristocracy (hopefully) cheered the end of *pizzo* and standovers, and the end of being considered the poor relation of Italy. Then a member of the intelligentsia asked a simple question: Are these arrests legally sound? It was answered by more cork-popping and the appearance of more champagne glasses, then forgotten.

What goes around comes around, and that is certainly true of court cases. I recall the hundreds of cases I put myself into that ended in a prosecution. Each required a lot of evidence-gathering and documentation; it's hard work. Cesare Mori had been a busy man too. In his first year in the job, he filled the prisons beyond capacity, and it was only a matter of time before prosecutors would want to see the evidence. Someone worked out that of all the arrests thus far, eighty per cent were for the new 'associate of the Mafia' law, so, the question was, where was the evidence? Mori looked a little lost as his fingers tried to sharpen the crease in his slacks. He had to find evidence somewhere, anywhere.[20]

Then Mori had another of his epiphanies. Friends, family and associates of those who were arrested and sitting in prisons were paid a visit by Santo Mori and his posse. There were too many dirt-poor peasants for Mori to see, so he selected the most vulnerable. They were set upon and asked to make incriminating statements against their loved ones, and acknowledge they were Mafia or associates of Mafia. Many were at a loss, too low in the food chain to know anything. Others were confused about what a *mafioso* was, as the subject of the statement (a family member) would come to lunch each Sunday, and therefore the alleged association amounted to one family member being in company with another over lasagne. How could this be a criminal association? they queried. After a few hundred attempts to gather statements, even the cops started to wonder about the veracity of the massive anti-Mafia operation they had been part of, as well as the integrity of the raids and the arrests.[21] Again, Palermo went quiet, the only noise came from the overfull prisons.

A few observers thought Mori might be the victim of his own fervour, in placing the cart before the horse. Mori was not flustered, though. Never short of a bright idea, he hit the road and visited villages and towns that had had their sons, fathers, husbands and elderly arrested. He thought his best form of attack should be all-out threats. He told family members they would make statements or else they too might be considered an associate of the Mafia.

In one town, Mori received the collective 'fuck off' blank stare. He got the message and left town, only to come back with his posse, and lock up another hundred men for being associates of the Mafia. Those who remained nervously stepped forward, one at a time, to offer their statements. Eventually, under Mori's new rule – that you give up the others or give up your own liberty – Mori's lowly cops started to make some headway. However, the possibility of false or misleading statements under such pressure speaks for itself. There were statements written by peasants who were illiterate, some who had never held a pencil. The documents had been drafted by exuberant cops in fear of Santo Mori. Statements that were genuine fell into the category of hearsay, with almost no facts. Still, Mori saw it all as evidence for the prosecution, and as Prefect he controlled the entire courtroom process.

With time, another town suffered the same demise. One hundred men were arrested until the townsfolk put their hands up to make a signed statement. And so it went across Sicily. Men in their thousands arrested as associates of the Mafia, taken away to prisons and locked up. Over a few months, Sicily had been reduced to a pawn in the dirtiest game in Europe, ethnic Mafia cleansing. Homes on the island would have no food on the tables due to the loss of the male breadwinner. Likewise, frantic wives and children fell apart as communities started to fracture. Church services were packed to the rafters as mothers looked to the heavens, asking God how they should feed their children, who were subsisting on condensed milk and flour.[22] The heart of the artichoke, a metaphor for the old Mafia, was absent, and the poor were to fend for themselves, while the head Prefect attempted to answer the endless demands by the prosecutors: Where is the evidence? Find us evidence!

By the end of 1927, the statements numbered in the thousands. Four hundred were analysed, but only a few were of use to the courts. The rest spoke only of the poor, the needy, the vulnerable, who were hard-working and incapable of being Mafia members.[23]

The Southern Solution continued its *modus operandi* for another two years. Villages were raided, cafes and *enoteche* busted, menfolk arrested, pressure applied to their families to tell all, and good citizens asked for statements. The broader community, meanwhile, sat back and feared for their families; how could the poorest manage or survive? Mori had a solution for this as well. He took to touring Sicily and visiting almost every school. His purpose was to lecture students against the Mafia. What he found were miserable underprivileged kids, a stamp of extreme poverty across the island. Many were wearing three-to-four generation hand-me-down clothes. Few were eating well; a good many were malnourished. Brave teachers did their best to instruct disillusioned children and explain why their fathers had been taken away.

Mori, who didn't seem to understand the ramifications of his mass raids, lost his tact. He criticised pre-pubescent girls for failing to wear underwear, not realising their families could not afford food, let alone undergarments.[24] To instil a sense of pride in students, he offered a story-writing contest to all classes. To enter the annual prize students had to write a short story on the joys of Fascism. Mori would judge the entries and announce the winner at the end of the school year.[25] When the time came, his prize went unclaimed; almost no one had entered. Mori stepped away from the schools. When asked, he offered his own judgement to a journalist: 'Many Sicilians were morally and intellectually deficient, but they were good and simple at heart.'[26]

At the end of the two years, the only thing that had changed because of 'Moriism' was that 11 000 Sicilian men – fathers, brothers, fiancés and sons – had disappeared from the farms and dirt blocks, and from the cities and streets. They were squashed into prisons, sleeping six to a cell that was meant for two. Santo Mori took offence at the quoted number of arrests as he felt certain it was 13 000 rather than 11 000. Nonetheless, most of Sicily had been turned into a community of single mothers and grubby kids. Il Duce, meanwhile, stood on a dais in Rome on Ascension Day, raised his arm and declared to a gallery of journalists that the Mafia had been broken, and the victory was due to Fascism and Santo Mori.[27]

While 1928 brought the rest of the world Disney's Mickey Mouse and Charlie Chaplin's Little Tramp, Italy was entertained by Il Duce and Santo Mori, a double act to rival a cheeky mouse and a slapstick genius as they wrote themselves into the history books and newsprint of the day. So confident was Mori, he let it be known that anyone who challenged him would be considered an enemy of the new Sicily, an associate of the Mafia.

Any philosophical position or ideology the old Mafia thought they held was gone, shot. The word 'Mafia' became the ultimate put-down. The moral indignation that came with the word – now whispered sideways – destroyed those who chose to hang on to it. Sicily was deeply divided. And scared. One side supported Moriism, mostly the gentry, while the other side were so poor that they wore the badge of the Mafia through their thin faces and tattered clothing. They were seen as desperate ambassadors for the traditional values of the Mafia. Yet so many of these desperate folks were nothing more than collateral damage to Moriism. Police who processed the thousands of arrests ensured their fate. They wrote alongside their arrest sheets the word '*mafioso*' for all to see regardless of whether evidence might come to light. The psychological slump felt by innocent men, wrongly labelled, lasted until death.

Mori should have been worried about his lack of evidence and the thousands of courtroom trials before him; instead, he went on the attack. It was time for him to bring in a new law, one that would, once and for all, shut the door on the Mafia. The legislation declared that any Sicilian could shoot a *mafioso* on sight without prosecution. When announcing the law, Santo Mori offered another one of his ingenious prizes to anyone who dared kill a suspected *mafioso*. Many 'winners' claimed the prize. One peasant killed a man he believed was a *mafioso* and wounded another – enough for Mori to pin a silver medal to his chest.[28] Vigilantism joined Moriism. Lunacy arrived in Sicily, until someone had the good sense to repeal the law.

Mori officiated over a system of justice to rival any communist country. He barred Sicilian judges from sitting on trials and appointed instead hand-selected judges from the northern regions, which had the highest popular support for Fascist policies. The only people called for jury service were employees of the state: administrative workers, bankers, businessmen, doctors, accountants, friends of Fascism and well-to-do citizens. The final coup in his court process was to reduce the time allocated to each accused person by having mass trials – 150 defendants at a time. The courtroom became a cattle yard.

The domestic reaction to his draconian process was mixed. The international reaction was virtually non-existent. There was uproar among the local legal fraternity, who demanded individuals be put on trial singly. Apart from their protests, no one else seemed to notice, or no one wanted to be labelled an associate of the Mafia by doing so. The community went silent.

Steel cages were built to house the accused. These were attached to the outside of the courthouses while evidence was heard inside the packed courtroom.[29] Few inmates were able to speak their piece, and some complained of a lack of representation. Most mass trials lasted a day or two, three at most – a few minutes for each '*mafioso*' defendant.

So confused was the process, the system so overloaded, that many defendants were at a loss as to what the evidence was, or how it related to them. One case, if the newspapers can be believed, involved a boy who was only three years old at the time of his arrest. Another accused a priest of being a Mafia member. Others claimed women were members. Another prosecution used a single photograph of a man sitting on a borrowed horse and holding a borrowed rifle as evidence; he must have been a *mafioso*![30] The newspapers of the day were awash with such stories. Then came the case where a woman pointed her finger at a nest of so-called Mafia men. She was an inmate of a 'lunatic asylum' – she'd been locked away for killing her baby – and her reliability as a witness was questionable. One mass trial of 161 accused men centred around a small box of letters written by one of the accused. The prosecutors stated that the letters proved an association between the men, therefore proving they were Mafia members. The man who penned the letters denied being a *mafioso* and died in prison waiting for justice. Some thought the contents of the letters innocuous, with many of the men merely seeking introductions to other men about horse breeding. Regardless, the law of the land swiftly found guilty all but thirteen of the men – most had never met – and gave them sentences of between seven and twenty-three years.

And so the sideshow went on, case after case racing through the courts. The only constant was the sound of the judges' gavels, slamming down after each 'guilty' verdict, as Mussolini sent the chief justice and Mori an urgent telegram to hasten the trials.

After three years, men were dying in prison awaiting their day, or minutes, in court. Some suicided, losing hope and their standing in the broader community, such as Gaetano Ferrarello, the elder from Gangi who had tried to mediate a surrender.[31] Despair clouded Palermo for months as the trials continued. The saddest part of the Mori system of justice lay in the sentences; many received life in prison. Others were lucky to get away with thirty years, some blessed with twenty, and so it went.[32]

By trials' end the island was full of poor, misjudged and shockingly mistreated Italians, yet no aristocrats came to the aid of any of the accused. The newspaper headlines on the final day of the kangaroo courts said it all. *The Times* in London ran the banner: 'Mussolini has throttled it [the Mafia] with success.' The *New York Times* offered: 'The

Mafia is Dead, a new Sicily is born, the Mafia may have begun as a philosophical group . . . but it degenerated into a criminal organisation.'

Once the dust had settled and the gavels went quiet, life returned to Sicily, though it was not the same. People stepped gingerly through each day, eyes looking sideways, and fingers crossed in pockets. For all the damage Cesare Mori had inflicted on the Sicilian community, there was one bright note. When he had taken office some four years earlier there had been 224 murders and 312 robberies in the capital in that year. Now that he had locked away half the male population, the rate had dropped to thirty-five murders and fourteen robberies. Was this statistic a measure of a successful campaign against the Mafia? Or was it a product of the fear that shrouded the island?

Torture had been the secret weapon of Mori and his lowly cops in extracting the confessions of many of the accused.[33] Stories of barbarism surfaced as whispers passed from one inmate to another. Some reported that during their interrogation they were placed inside a *cassetta*: a small, purpose-built wood-slatted box. Naked, they were whipped into confession, their bodies were cut and bloodied and smothered in brine – salt and olive oil – before they were basted for up to three days in the scorching Sicilian sun. Of a night they were heard gasping for water as they lay near lifeless, their bodies blistered.

With this medieval torture method, the salt bites into the open wounds while the oil cooks the flesh.

Mori, hearing the same story getting louder and louder, ran from his martini-sipping dinner party to his office to formulate an answer.

Sir Ronald Graham, the British Ambassador, heard the same story one too many times and put down his martini glass to enquire. He broke the silence of the patricians and wrote a shocking report openly questioning the Southern Solution. He also believed any victories to be had against the Mafia were due to Santo Mori making deals with the heads of the Mafia, deals that spared them from arrest, while Mori instead focused on helpless, lowly peasants. Innocents who had no voice, whose only connection with the Mafia was that they had been forced to obey their orders. Mori got results by using the most doubtful means, including fabricated police evidence and mass trials.[34]

Graham went on to say that hundreds (more like thousands) of men were victims of a miscarriage of justice. Even Santo Mori's closest confidant, Signor Laschiavo,[35] declared that Mori had 'lumped hundreds of men and criminals together indiscriminately'. The British socialite Tina Whitaker, a member of the Whitaker wine and marsala export family in Sicily, and friend to Mussolini, also scrutinised Mori, saying, 'grave injustices have been inevitable in the wholesale imprisonment of citizens', and that 'Mori's methods were drastic and merciless, and important *Mafiosi* have been left at large'. She ended by saying, '[u]nder the ashes, burns and smoulders the fire of resentment'.[36]

As Mori's world started to crumble, a new and powerful man entered the fiasco: military hero and commander Antonio Di Giorgio. Mussolini had lined him up earlier for the top job in the military and was anxious for his report on Mori's apparent catastrophe. Happy to assist, Di Giorgio got out his big guns and aimed them at the Prefect. He informed Il Duce about a false legacy, questionable methodology, torture and scandal. He made it clear that innocent men had been condemned, and, in his opinion, Mori had acted out a private vendetta against poor rural folk who had no interest in Fascism. Gobsmacked, Il Duce dismissed Di Giorgio and sent him back to Palermo without any suggestion of a resolution.

Di Giorgio went home, wondering what the dictator from Rome would do about the dictator from Palermo. On his arrival, the military man and the Prefect faced off, one a whistle-blower, the other a blower of wind up Mussolini's proverbial. Only one would walk away from this battle with his reputation intact. Mori had one last trick up his sleeve. He labelled the army hero an associate of the Mafia, and all ears in Palermo turned towards Rome. The next day Mussolini sacked Di Giorgio and sprayed the news across the media, ending any negative press about the revered Southern Solution and sending a message to the petrified island that anyone could be dethroned at the hands of Mori or at the whim of Mussolini.

Soon after, an election took place in the interior of Sicily. Resurrected, Santo Mori felt it was the ideal time to wave the flag for Mussolini's Fascism, so he went into the country areas that had been stripped of men and stood over whoever remained, demanding they vote for the Fascist candidate.[37] Trucks were loaded up with 'lambs' (disciplined voters) and transported to the polling booths to guarantee an outcome Il Duce would relish. What Mori did not plan on was the connection of the old Mafia in the flash city offices of the barons and aristocrats of Palermo. Let's not forget, the old Mafia had spent generations establishing relationships with barons and saw squabbles and demands resolved. There was a currency to these old relationships, years in the making. The old Mafia used this tradition to point the finger of concern towards Mori, to highlight the wrong they saw in the imperfect Prefect. The gentry went wild, screaming about vote rigging. Mori had nowhere to hide, no rock to crawl under. He was left standing alone.

All the starch-suited man could do was run from one socialite to another, from politician to businessman to the end of his dark, lonely laneway. Everyone turned their backs on the man who was in fear of no one, except, finally, himself. The end was anti-climactic. One miserably hot day in 1929, Mussolini sent a telegram to his protégé announcing that his services were no longer needed; please vacate your office.[38] And so he did. Mori packed up his medals and baubles, sold his horse, and boarded a ship to the most northerly region of Italy to write his memoirs. Mussolini, meanwhile, turned his eyes to another man who could entertain his ego: Adolf Hitler.

The ruthless actions of Prefect Mori caused a wave of emigration, both legal and illegal. No one wanted to be in Sicily during his four-year reign; no good could come of it. Low-level Sicilian mobsters took the clandestine water track that had been in play since Don Vito's time and sought refuge in the United States. Once there, however, it was not easy to integrate without an introduction into the already existing gangs.

Estimates have been made of the mass exodus of Sicilians in the 1920s. Certainly, tens of thousands found a home outside Sicily, mostly in New York City, Chicago or Philadelphia, bringing with them tales of the madman known as *Prefetto di ferro*, the Iron Prefect, as well as stories of lost brothers or uncles and the ruination of scores of families. Ultimately, Mussolini and Mori's efforts only galvanised the Mafia, and entrenched it as a way of life.

For all the jail time the pair exacted on thousands of badly done-by Sicilians, none of it was a deterrent, as most were mere plebs. And the Mafia just got stronger.

CHAPTER 15
SLIMY OCTOPUS

SICILIAN SAYING:

Chiù scuru i menzannotti un pò fari

It can't be darker than midnight

Meaning, never give up

In my second year of research, I spent time at Palermo's magnificent Gancia Archivio, situated in The Kalsa district. This area was once home to the city's poorest people, as well as many north Africans who settled there in the nineteenth century, bringing with them their culinary habits and colourful clothing, which still forms part of the rich tapestry of Sicily. Much Sicilian street food has Moroccan and Tunisian influences.

The Gancia Archivio took over a former convent. Built in 1601, it sits at the back of the Church of Gancia. The archive is home to more than a million documents, reports, early publications, parchments and the like in a network of rooms and corridors so vast it defies description. Whenever I was allowed to open a vault and step inside, I fell into a rapture; I will never forget my time in this wondrous place.

Each day I walked into the archive, I was aware of stepping on the same paving stones where twenty locals were murdered by the Bourbons in 1860 and could envisage the spilt blood and hear the death cries. It was an experience that, for me, epitomised being both a detective and an investigative author. The head curator of the archives is a very fine Palermitan called Nicolo. Over three years, this forty-something-year-old and I became good friends. He holds a master's degree in archival studies and had embraced the mammoth task of managing the cache of documents that make up the history of the city. He was the only staff member who spoke fluent English and was allocated the task of meet-and-greets with international English-speaking scholars, historians and writers. Initially, like all Sicilians, he gave me the blank stare routine; you know the one. Then, after a time, he became innovative in his searching. Like Enza, he knew I was like a bad penny; I was always going to come back.

Daily, I would sit in his tiny reading room in silence, along with a few serious-faced historians, turning brittle pages as staff sat to one side of the room watching my every move. This was how they did things at Gancia – no trays of *biscotti*, no small talk, just reading. After a couple of months poring over prefecture reports – careful to make sure the pages didn't break or crumble – Nicolo tapped me on the shoulder. He wanted to see me outside the quiet zone of the reading room. He handed me a dusty old folder and suggested I might like to read it, emphasising the contents had barely been read since it was written in 1938.[1] While he was doing some housekeeping, a few years earlier, rearranging a section of documents, the folder fell to the floor. Nicolo peeped inside. It was, he joked, a Holy Grail of Mafia activity, a rare document on the darkest moments in Mafia history: the 1930s.

The report was bound in bright red leather with gold lettering and had been prepared by the Sicilian Carabinieri for Benito Mussolini. It would have contrasted so well with Il Duce's black silk shirts.

I wrote many reports when I was a detective and task force team leader, after investigating serious crimes. I had neither the budget, nor the audacity, to cover my reports in red leather. This red report was signed by forty-seven Carabinieri chiefs; clearly it was special. It certainly hooked me in. The first page was a declaration of sorts, under the name of its principal author, the head of the Carabinieri in Sicily.

An extraordinary document; in effect, it was a briefing paper on the position of the Mafia up until 1938. Seeing the forty-seven names on the 180-page report made me think of the lone Giuseppe Di Giorgio, the army hero who blew the whistle on the treacherous Mori, only to be dismissed from office. Some years later, the most senior officers in Sicily stood together to tell all about the current state of affairs. A clever ploy, as surely Il Duce would not risk sacking so many top cops.

The red report made my fingers twitch as I put on my clean white cotton gloves, turned to Agata, my translator, and readied myself for what would be a four-week exercise, reading the report. In translating this document, I chose to keep the wording as close as possible to the sentiment of the original, but bear in mind that nuances suffer in translation.

They opened by stating that despite the wave of actions by police and lawyers over time, the Mafia has never stopped. It gives the occasional illusion of peace, however this illusion is a trick, so the police would assume that calm had been restored. In reality, the actions of the Mafia have never waned or ceased. While the Fascist government tried to convince people the organisation had been defeated, this was not the case. The ignorance of police, in also believing the Mafia was gone, was not smart as the police, in turn, went into the community in an attempt to convince them that the Mafia had been dealt with. Fascist propaganda helped this. The government controlled the newspapers, what information the public read and heard on the radio, and before long there was an incorrect and widespread belief that the Mafia had been ruined. The Mafia was instead driven underground.

The report then highlights some of the more active regions where the Mafia was complicit in crimes. Trapani, the seaside town at the centre of Sicily's salt industry, is mentioned as a Mafia stronghold. The report defines the Mafia as 'terror': a name used by the common people when talking of the scourge. It then outlines the action the Carabinieri put in place in an attempt to stop the Mafia from the 1920s and the period of Cesare Mori, and into the 1930s. Mori claimed he removed the Mafia like a 'trunk of a tree'. But, said the red report, the tree was only pruned; the roots were untouched.

The reason the tree stayed intact is because the Mafia had influence over the social elite of Sicilian society. The Mafia had become more difficult, more dangerous, and their activities were spreading because they had become aligned with powerful people. Apparently, the Fascist regime failed to understand the weaponry or methodology or workings of the clans. Yet Mori said that the Mafia had been defeated, the effort against them had been 'victorious'. Nonsense, says the report.

It highlights the arrests of the many so-called Mafia by Cesare Mori before 1928 – the thousands in mostly rural regions. After the mass arrests the police backed off, believing they had done enough. From then, policing of the problem slowed down. They felt Mori's arrests were of people below the Mafia structure, who lived on the fringes, low-level *mafiosi*, some from the Piana dei Colli clan (on the beachside, north of Palermo), a violent area where mobsters, to quote the report, 'made waves of blood and filled the main streets of Palermo with dead bodies to show they were in charge'. The Mafia clans that operated in the rural areas surrounding Palermo were particularly murderous. They were responsible for an incalculable number of deaths. It was common to see the butchered bodies of *capi* and even bosses of the Piana dei Colli clan obstruct the footpaths each morning as the infighting raged.

The Carabinieri were suggesting that links between the ruthless heads of Mafia and the elite *bourgeoisie* of Palermo should have been investigated and smashed, instead of picking on low-level individuals.

One Mafia boss who was more cunning than most, Ernesto Marasà, and his henchmen and brothers, Francesco and Antonino, were ignored, yet they were the most dangerous, being connected to the rich end of town.

The report is adamant that the *bourgeoisie* were, in effect, protecting Marasà, and their commercial partners. The rest of the red report is about the investigation of Ernesto Marasà and his large clan. The report makes it blatantly clear that Ernesto was a secret mobster, hidden due to the ways of Mori. Despite the obvious presence of Marasà, the Prefect was selective about who he would prosecute, name or declare as a *mafioso*. He never once pointed towards Marasà, but in actuality, Marasà was the *generalissimo* of all Mafia on the island.[2] The *capo di tutti capi*.[3] (This translates as the boss of all bosses; it's a term seldom used, and denotes the title of the supreme leader.) In fact, the report names Ernesto Marasà as the 'slimy octopus' of all Mafia. Into everything, slithering everywhere, wherever there was a chance to make money, Ernesto was there, with the help of his murderous brothers.

The Marasà regime was the important missing link in the global story of the Mafia.

During Mori's attack on low-level Mafia and plebs, the Marasà clan went underground, and restructured, as the *bourgeoisie* watched from their leather chairs, cigars in hand. One of the first things Marasà did was construct a power base inside the prisons to manage those who had been incarcerated. This created a new and flourishing organisation whose numbers replaced those previously arrested, awaiting trial. All this under the blind eyes of police (Mori), who were distracted by the need for 'evidence' for the mass trials.

Marasà rebuilt the organisation by using the prison population as a resource, initially causing conflict within the various clans, resulting in infighting and many deaths. Heads of clans were not spared during the killings, and the smarter ones fled to Naples to escape vendettas against them. Some went to America. Clan murders increased, until an amicable solution for control and management could be found. In reality the Piana dei Colli clan reformed, only more dangerous, and with a defined structure.

Tranquillity returned to the greater Mafia, but only for a moment. Typical of mob bosses, clan heads became unhappy with their territory and the returns on offer. Gangland killings and street violence increased and there were more ferocious crimes and vendettas and reprisals than normal within the Mafia. The Mafia had also come to better arm itself, with superior guns and equipment. The escalation of violent crimes showed no signs of abating, and police simply labelled the murders as symptoms of a systemic problem of the time. From 1933 Mafia crimes and violence were extreme.

The report highlights how under-resourced the Carabinieri were to turn the tide, suggesting it was time for Rome to step in, as the island's security was in serious disarray. While the report acknowledges that Rome sent in a special force to assist police, they came and went quickly, leaving the local Carabinieri with the same old problem with the same old lack of resources.

At this stage, the report states that from 1933 Sicily had a 'sad phenomenon' and was losing the war against an emerging, more dangerous Mafia. This echoes Mori's comment that there were two

Mafias: the old traditional Mafia going back to Garibaldi and the new twentieth-century Mafia that was utterly ruthless. At this juncture, Ernesto Marasà was a 52-year-old and at the height of his power.

After the police were denied resources by Rome, the report tells of the innovative ways the Carabinieri banded together to take on the scourge. (It is not surprising that Mussolini and his honchos in Rome ignored the Carabinieri's requests. To acquiesce would be to acknowledge that the Mafia was not defeated. Il Duce would have been a laughing-stock.) From September 1933, the Carabinieri pulled together an elite squad trained in military-style fighting. The manpower was divided into twelve sections, one for each region, united against the scourge, and sharing what resources and intelligence they had. The hand-selected men from the Carabinieri were transferred to an Inspectorate, and set about establishing relations with local police. (In modern terms, it was a task force.)

The task force responded to Mafia-linked crimes and took over investigations with a carefully thought-out plan. They analysed the clans to better understand the 'sad phenomenon' and their *modus operandi*. In effect, the twelve regional Inspectorate offices were given autonomy to end the criminality in a way that should have been done decades earlier.

The Inspectorate soon had the confidence of the public, and cooperation between regions started to uncover a network of criminals happily going about their illegal business. The Inspectorate chose Messina as their first target city and methodically built up a cache of evidence that, after a night of raids, netted 130 *mafiosi* at their game. This both stunned and stunted the Messina Mafia, whose members believed policing on the island was one corruptible officer on the beat; they never figured on such a concerted attack on their operations. (Indeed, the red report makes it clear that the Mafia thought they had absolute control over the island.)

But for every action comes a reaction; the Mafia fought back, and across the land there was a massive escalation in crime in order to build up the coffers to fund the defence of their 130 brothers. In retaliation, the Inspectorate regrouped and hit Sicily hard. There were dozens of raids in key towns, such as Palermo, Agrigento and Trapani, as well as villages throughout of the interior. Three hundred *mafiosi* were taken into custody, joining the others. Cattle rustling was attacked head-on. Stolen goods, guns and exhibits were seized. Then came the stalemate; crime had stopped. The message had been accepted, or so the Inspectorate thought. The Mafia bosses and their managers – the *capi* – were forced to re-think; they realised they faced a force to be reckoned with.

The Inspectorate did not slacken, escalating efforts to a dangerous level. One side was bound to break. To get into the deepest roots of the Mafia, the Inspectorate had to be smart, and that meant gathering evidence, unlike the Mori tenure when evidence didn't exist. The Inspectorate ensured the goods seized, the evidence, matched the crimes they would allege in court. Their hard work was ready to go to trial, and the exhibits were loaded into the police truck to be transported to Messina for a series of hearings. Late the same night, as the truck cruised along a dark country laneway between the village of San Biagio Platani and Casteltermini, it was forced to stop by gun-wielding Mafia lying in wait.

Within minutes the entire load went missing, snatched by a team of *mafiosi*, ensuring the criminal charges against the hundreds of accused would be tossed out. The Inspectorate received no assistance from Mussolini, just the ridicule of headlines across the country stating that the Mafia were back and more organised than ever.

Of the Mafia clans that took part in the truck raid, it was found that none of them knew each other. They only came together for this one audacious act. The Inspectorate also discovered that the planning for the raid had been in progress for many weeks, proving that the Mafia was just as resourceful as their new enemy. The *capo* who arranged it all and rallied the others was Ignazio Alessi. Alessi had been called to a special meeting by the Mafia bosses and given his orders – in a letter – that the truck was to be intercepted and the exhibits stolen. The Inspectorate found the letter in a follow-up raid intended to bring those involved to justice.

Later they would find another open letter, addressed to all the *capi*, to unite, to put an end to their grievances and save their energy to fight the Inspectorate. The same document instructed all Mafia members to commit as many crimes as they could in an effort to fund the defence of those arrested. This open letter was seen as a galvanisation of the Mafia. The slimy octopus was becoming more brazen, in direct contradiction to Mussolini's declaration that the Mafia was dead.

(This series of actions – the raid of the exhibit truck; the clandestine meeting of *capi*; and the order to commit crimes for the greater good of the incarcerated – marked the existence of the new twentieth-century Mafia. Indeed, Marasà's fearlessness became a feature of future Mafia incarnations worldwide.)

One outcome of the truck raid and the uniting of the Mafia was a reorganisation into defined Mafia sub-regions. Drawn up and ratified by the many bosses, the regions agreed to end their squabbling to concentrate on the business of crime. This was followed by the creation of rules and protocols, which became a mandate for all *capi* in a region. Many *capi* could exist inside one family, which controlled a region. It was the role of *capi* to grow the family, and to this end they were required to contact runaway *capi* in America and other countries, to ensure everyone was across the big picture.

The red report openly, and boldly, criticised the government for its inaction, and its idiotic position that organised crime in Sicily was a thing of the past. The police chiefs called it 'a plague'. There were 250 known Mafia members in the region of Agrigento alone, and on it went. (Simple maths tells the reader the extent of the problem.) The Inspectorate considered Palermo to be the capital of the Sicilian Mafia, which was still the nation's dominant Mafia at that point. Crime escalated to the point where it was ingrained in every Sicilian's way of life.

The red report analysed the minutiae of how the Mafia worked. When arrested, for example, Mafia thugs would state their occupation as 'farmer', despite having no land or farming business. Even city thugs would say they were farmers. This was thought to be a reference to the old Mafia and rural Sicily. It also suggested prejudice by police against workers of the land, a clever defence ploy.

The Carabinieri kept up the pressure as more *mafiosi* faced jail, and for a time crime figures actually dropped. But this didn't last long enough to have an anniversary.

Guiseppe Garibaldi, the great revolutionary who led his 1089 volunteers to Sicily to take on the massive resources of the Bourbons, aided by a secret team of pre-Mafia criminals.
(Alamy)

Francesco Crispi, arguably the first ever spy, who was magnificent in gathering criminals to aid Garibaldi.
(Wikimedia Commons)

Joseph Petrosino, the brave New York police officer who went undercover in Sicily in 1909 to understand the workings of the Mafia, with a view to halt their immigration to New York City. He was executed for his efforts.
(Alamy)

Typical of the thousands of aged files the author studied to expose the story of the birth of the Mafia. (Author's collection)

One of eleven archives where the author sat for 44 months to unravel the Mafia mystery. (Author's collection)

Possibly the first ever image of the Mafia: criminals banded together in 1860 at the gates of Palermo who, within two years, were calling themselves Mafia. Their leader, on the far right, is considered the first Mafia boss – Giovanni Corrao. (Museo di San Martino, Napoli)

Benito Mussolini, the despot who fooled the world that he had killed off the Mafia in his 'Southern Solution'. (Getty)

Cesare Mori, the highest-ranked law enforcer for Sicily from 1926–1930, and torturer to thousands of peasants who then became Mafia. (Getty)

The murderous Marasà brothers, with Ernesto standing. He went on to write the manifesto for the modern Mafia and his criminal network ruled Sicily for more than twenty years. (Courtesy Marasà family descendants)

An aged Ernesto Marasà standing in the courtyard of his *palazzo* after it was hit by US B-17 bombers in 1943. Undeterred, he went on to rule for another decade. (Courtesy Marasà family descendants)

Al 'Scarface' Capone, the first US *mafioso* to open the door for non-Italians to become part of a Mafia network. (Alamy)

The brilliant Charles 'Lucky' Luciano, the architect of the modern global Mafia and contemporary of Ernesto Marasà. (Wikimedia Commons)

Frank Costello, a standout US Mafia negotiator and patriarch from 1930–1957. Politically savvy and socially connected, he himself survived a Mafia assassination attempt in 1957. (Wikimedia Commons)

The aftermath from a 600-kg TNT explosion that massacred Judge Giovanni Falcone, his wife (also a judge) and three police security personnel. (Getty)

The magnificently brave Investigative Judge Nicola Gratteri, prosecuting 355 Calabrian Mafia in a mass trial between 2020–2022. (Alamy)

The bravery of Alfonso Sabella, Investigative Judge in the Anti-Mafia Pool, is almost without peer anywhere in the world. (Getty)

A mural on the side of an apartment building in Palermo of much-revered Judges Giovanni Falcone and Paolo Borsellino. This same image appears constantly throughout Sicily. (Author's collection)

Then came a breakthrough that would forever change how the Mafia was investigated: the introduction of the *pentito*, the supergrass, the informer, the give-up, the snitch – the answer to solving organised crime. Arrested gang members started to talk, giving evidence against their brothers. The Mafia bounced back by appointing a *capo* in each region to dole out punishment for any snitch or informer. Death was usually the only option. Despite the counter-punch, cracks began to appear in the galvanised hide of the new Mafia. For the first time, police gained crucial (collective) evidence by *pentiti*. Disharmony crept into the Mafia. All they could do was call a conference and work out a way to end the increasing number of snitches within their ranks. The most important meeting ever called by the Sicilian Mafia was convened at the Hotel Vittoria Palermo.[4] (I would often take my espresso there on my morning walks to the archives.)

It was this meeting that ratified Ernesto Marasà as the *capo di tutti capi* – the boss of all bosses. He would draft and enforce a network of internal laws. A resolution that made sense, as Marasà was the chief architect of the Piana dei Colli rebirth. And, of course, he had his two hitmen brothers by his side to ensure his laws were obeyed. (Marasà, as an aside, was so under the radar of police that – I was told – there was no picture of him anywhere in police files.)

An important ruling came out of the meeting that night: the ways of the old Mafia were declared dead and buried. Tradition had no more place among the *mafiosi*. There was a bigger picture out there, and being aligned with rural peasants was a thing of the past. Marasà's new Mafia was the future, and anyone who planned to disrupt his dictatorship would face certain death. The regional Mafia bosses welcomed the dawn of the contemporary Mafia. In a move that would have ramifications globally, Marasà openly threatened to kill insiders who played with cops. His laws were passed down the line, across Sicily and into Naples, and on the first ocean liner heading to New York City.

This was a true contradiction of character as the report revealed Marasà had a history of informing police about thugs he wanted eliminated, so he could grow his power base. (This made Ernesto Marasà the first supremo, indeed, the most dominant *mafioso* of all time – yet, paradoxically, the most secret and highly positioned *pentito* in Mafia global history, to that point. An extraordinary contradiction.)

The red report disavows the Mori period, and tells of the brutality of the new *mafiosi*, now under the guidance of the 'slimy octopus', Ernesto Marasà.[5]

In time, Marasà would enforce his will on Sicily, and the rest of Italy, and influence his cousins across the Atlantic. The report also testifies to the way the aristocrats of Palermo had, for generations, protected the Mafia bosses, allowing them to buy themselves respectability, while their gangs killed in the name of power and profits.

By the middle of the report, it is all about Marasà, his new Mafia, and his efforts to ensure his Mafia would rule for all time. Little has changed from the Marasà model. His laws were, in hindsight, perfect in holding together the rank-and-file *mafiosi*, as well as entrenching, for the first time, *omertà*, the code of absolute silence. *Omertà*, while in existence for decades, had never quite become Holy Writ for the Mafia, until Marasà declared it gospel.[6]

The Inspectorate called the Marasà rules the 'full reconstruction of the Mafia'.[7] There would be no more misguided loyalty from the old *mafiosi*.

By 1937, the Mafia clans were branching into new crimes such as loan sharking – offering loans to desperate people at interest rates so high debtors end up paying a thousand per cent on the original loan, or else are killed off part way through the arrangement. *Pizzo* was still king and would always be, and kidnapping had become as common as prawns. Almost every Sicilian was paying their penny, directly or indirectly, to the Mafia clans.[8]

In time, the Mafia bosses started buying real estate as they embarked on a program of growth by acquisition, while attempting to hide their wealth. One scam was ingenious in its simplicity. They bought land for a fair but low price, then within three months resold the land at more than a hundred per cent profit to a buyer – a cousin or distant relative, who would act as guardian of the land – while the original Mafia owner pocketed the profit. Simple but effective money laundering. Some of the land scams involved hundreds of citrus crops, and sulphur mines were also a target of Marasà. Another dirty scheme was intimidating innocent people to hand over their meagre savings or property. The police were too under-resourced to put an end to the practice. Ernesto had his tentacles everywhere.

The crimes of the *mafiosi* were highly rewarding and impossible to get a handle on. Mussolini, at that time, was consumed with the politics of a pending war and newspapers had no column space for repetitive Mafia stories. It became a bit like the boy who cried wolf: no one wanted to hear about crime.

Because of the apathy, Marasà ramped up his crimes to include bank heists, armed robbery and anything involving lots of cash, all with the aid of a growing cancer in the community: police and judicial corruption. As the Inspectorate states, the Marasà boys became a 'three-headed monster'.[9] Antonino took charge of persuading politicians it would be best to do what the clans asked. There was little resistance as the brothers benefited from weak-hearted politicians who were only too keen to help with the *pezzi grossi* – the 'top brass' – leaving the smaller stuff to government officials. Brother Francesco was more the down-and-dirty type. He took control of the scams, as well as the violence. That left Ernesto to watch over his flock from arm's length, 'his bulging eyes watched everyone, everything, every minute of the day'.[10]

In all, there were 175 *mafiosi* earmarked for prosecution, the entire Marasà gang. The Inspectorate got on with the business of gathering evidence and taking valued testimonies from the *pentiti*, who – due to the selfishness of the Marasà brothers – had vowed to kill off *Generalissimo* Ernesto. But the wheels of justice turn slowly.

The final words of the Carabinieri were exactly what one would expect from a competent law enforcement authority: 'There must be no holding back against the evil that is the Mafia – that is dishonouring Sicily. The state must wield the scalpel.'

As someone who has faced off the Mafia and spent years investigating the organisation, I was impressed by the sophistication of the report. The Carabinieri were the first in the world to understand the value of gaining informers – *pentiti* – to speak out about the inner workings of the secret society. They were also the first to infiltrate the methodology of the Mafia, and to work out their *modus operandi*. Whereas their

American counterparts in that same period were lost to speakeasies, corruption and sore necks from looking the other way.

While the red report makes a mockery of Mussolini's Southern Solution and his misguided efforts to curtail the scourge, it becomes obvious that had he embraced the Carabinieri effort, the Mafia may well have been crushed and the red report never written.

The red report rewrites the Mafia story, thereby questioning much of what had already been written, especially for the period 1920 to 1945.

Fascinatingly, there is no mention of the word 'Godfather'. Proving that the term is an invention of authors and screenwriters. In my view, too much emphasis has been placed on titles, and all the underling roles and positions. There is the boss (Godfather), his second in command (under boss), a *capo* or two or more, and the many soldiers scrambling over each other to curry favour from above through their dirty deeds. And a *consigliere* (or two) who acts as an adviser on finance and/or strategies. As I say, do not try and analyse it too hard, don't waste your brain on it.

Likewise, there is no mention of the name '*Cosa Nostra*', demonstrating that the Mafia was not called this before World War II. As I have always suspected, *Cosa Nostra* (literally, 'Our Thing') is an Americanism, born out of New York City after the war. However, since the 1970s *Cosa Nostra* has – oddly – become the adopted name globally, including in Italy.

As a postscript, I was anxious to know what happened to the Marasà mobsters. I was also perplexed that there were no known pictures taken of Ernesto. I consulted everyone on this oddity: the history faculty of Palermo University – global experts on the Mafia – every archive across Sicily and Rome, ancient libraries, online photo studios that sell images from the Fascist era, newspaper libraries, and on it went for a year. I even sat in the Biblioteca Centrale in Palermo for two full days, reading every page of the two main newspapers of that period, on microfiche, dated from 1937 to mid-1943, determined to find the brothers Marasà. *Niente*, zero. They had become enigmas. But surely there must have been one photograph of Ernesto? The missing link in the global Mafia story. Arguably the greatest Mafia boss of all.

Nicolo from the Gancia Archivio also wouldn't let go of this missing link, using his spare time to search, everywhere.

Then came a truly serendipitous moment. Just as I pressed 'save' on my manuscript for the last time, just as I was about to send it off to my publisher, a text message dropped onto my phone, with the simple comment, 'I found him!!!'

Although it had been half a year since I spoke to Nicolo, I didn't need to ask, 'Who?' Then a picture pinged alongside the message, of an innocuous-looking, but very fat, brown folder, obviously old; it bore the index number 4135. And the words, 'Procedimenti Penali Anno 1942'. Meaning criminal proceedings for 1942. Then came another image, with the index number 4136, and on it went, five in total. Five fat folders. The last image was of Nicolo – a selfie – standing in one of his four massive vaults. The picture showed a room as big as an aircraft hangar, with shelving stacked to the roof, with an estimate of 40 000 folders all identical-looking in colour and size; the only thing differentiating each was a number. Although there was work in progress to log each file into a searchable system, it was currently impossible to know what was in each folder.

Seems Nicolo had spent months opening each one, looking for any mention of Ernesto Marasà. He refused to give up. And, on a sunny spring day in 2021, he sent me the sweetest run of pictures.

Living in Luxembourg at the time, I caught the next flight to Palermo, one way!

CHAPTER 16

JUDICIAL CORRUPTION

SICILIAN SAYING:

C'è i chianciri

The only thing to do is cry

Used when a situation is desperate

In trying to understand the Mafia and its trajectory, it's important to recall the reaction of the rural plebs of Sicily when their 'Garibaldi promise' of land was extinguished. It is equally important to attach that rejection by society to what Moriism did to the ancestors of the same plebs. What happened as a result of Mori's actions must land at the feet of Benito Mussolini; his course of conduct – linked to the torture of thousands of plebs – set the future path of the Mafia.

The Mafia hierarchy were ignored, as they swam in the dark waters of corruption, enjoying their spoils and toasting Moriism.

Mori boasted of arresting 13 000 Mafia members, though official figures differ.[1] The editor of a mainstream newspaper of the time put the number at 30 000: many of them honest fathers and their families who were treated as collateral damage and 'condemned for centuries of prison time, tortured, their innocent screams could be heard from behind prison walls'.[2]

By the end of the Mori period, entire families would be incarcerated and tortured, while landowners, aristocrats and the real Mafia remained untouched. One journalist wrote, '. . . if the police don't stop arresting criminals (in hindsight most were not), all that would remain is the prickly pears of the cactus plant . . .' [3]

What happened to Ernesto Marasà and his killer clan? To find those answers I had to sit in the reading room with my dedicated translator Elena and read upwards of 4000 pages, the sum total of the five folders found by Nicolo.

As I mentioned in the previous chapter, Ernesto got smart and reworked the standard operational procedures of the Mafia – known as the manifesto – on how the Mafia clans would operate. Some of the rules had been around since the previous century, but Ernesto tightened them up. Then slammed them down on the table, for all to adhere to.

Each Mafia brother shall:

- Offer total silence on all activities, breaches punishable by death, *omertà*;
- Have shared pride and defence of other brothers through an act of revenge or committing a crime to support the brother;
- Know that no obstacle can ever stop a vendetta, even if it takes years and involves travelling to a faraway location;
- A vendetta can be transferred to another member in another country;
- Obedience to each *capo* is indisputable;
- All brothers are men of honour;
- Each brother has to display a mark or symbol that others can recognise;
- A simple soldier can only commit a crime under the orders of a *capo*;
- Committing crimes without *capo* sanction will result in harm to the soldier;
- Anyone seen to get close to police is to be killed;
- Each clan of brothers can use or request resources from another clan, but only at the request of a *capo*;
- A simple soldier must obey any instruction and undertake any crime asked of him by a *capo*; there is no way out.[4]

The manifesto made the position of soldier and brother clear, dropping altogether the old Mafia word *picciotti*. It also explains that each *capo* commanded ten brothers – a chain of command. The manifesto also stressed that a Mafia boss had autonomy over his clan, which in turn had several *capi*, and many 'brothers'. Indeed, the report offers the new title *Presidente Generale*, the supremo – Ernesto Marasà.[5]

A ceremony was developed to encourage brothers and soldiers to understand the seriousness of being accepted into the Mafia. This 'blood ritual' had a touch of the macabre and a hint of a poorly scripted Shakespearean drama. After completing a series of preliminary tasks – such as murder – the *nuovo* soldier would attend a gathering for his initiation. This involved cutting his palm to create an open wound that could draw blood.[6] He would drip the blood onto a card or piece of paper that pictured a saint of the inductee's choice. Once the card was saturated in blood, it was placed on the inductee's open palm and set alight to burn to ashes. At the same time, the new brother would recite: 'I swear to be loyal to the brothers and to burn my body for them, to die for them like this piece of paper is being burned right now.' As the card burned down to fine powder, the inductee would hold his own, refusing to flinch.

The Carabinieri opined that the *nuovo* Mafia had, by 1938 – and under the rule of Marasà – become a thing of 'criminal beauty'. In his tailored suits, with the mask of a gentleman, Marasà was untouchable.

In reading the source documents of how the manifesto, *omertà* rule and initiation ceremony gained prominence, I spared a thought for all the movies, books, works of fiction and TV dramas that had written these structural points into their stories. Obviously relying on word-of-mouth tales to build their stories. Yet, here it was on corn-coloured paper, written and sworn by a key *mafioso* of the time, the Marasà rules. Circa 1931. To me, an aficionado of the Mafia, it was everything Nicolo said it was: the Holy Grail of the management structure of the modern Mafia.

The filing of the red report (late 1938), was followed soon after by the outbreak of World War II, and Italy was immersed in another form of violence. The five folders Elena and I were now looking at were written a few years later. In essence, these five folders are, firstly, the front folder that outlines the prosecution case, maybe 1000 pages. This is followed by the back-end four folders which contain all the testimonies, evidence, facts and search warrants. In other words, the case against those charged, many thousands of pages.

The back-end folders were where the real gold was found against Ernesto, Francesco, Antonino and their cousins, Lorenzo and Girolamo, the executive of the Marasà clan, and their 175-gang *cosca*. It was a repetitious listing of murders by the clan, so many (I estimate) it would take a team of criminal analysts months to link them all, and trace them back to each killer under the Marasà banner. Of the more than fifty murders mentioned, most were revenge killings, and many involved the death of fellow *mafiosi*.

Then came the lists of countless blackmail rackets, testimony by hundreds, who spoke of standovers, *pizzo*, violence and criminal damage. And continuous livestock theft, the mainstay of the rural gangs. Also, stories of the use of guns and the movement of weaponry within the gangs. The *pentiti* statements were a triumph, vivid, with no holding back. The five folders are an extraordinary body of investigative work by the forty-seven Carabinieri police chiefs and its Inspectorate.

It appears the Inspectorate did take the scalpel to the Marasà brothers. The island's Carabinieri raided the homes of each *mafioso*. But, oddly, of the 175 men who were raided, Ernesto Marasà was one of the last to face a visit from the police. In fact, most of his gang had been rounded up months ahead of Ernesto and his brothers, as the police picked off their targets, leaving the *Generalissimo* to the end. I find this strange. From my background in task force investigations, it's always best to cut off the head of the gang first, leaving no one in authority to hold the lower levels together. More chance of destabilising the group.

The first Marasà to fall was Francesco, who was arrested on the street and remanded. The next was Antonino, who was 'confined', which means 'domestic exile' – held in the confinement of an island prison.[7] With the two main tentacles removed it was now the turn of the head of the *slimy octopus*. Trouble was, Ernesto had fled. And would stay on the run as a fugitive while war raged across Europe for the next three years as the prosecution floundered, bouncing from one desk to another. This one act of administrative blunder – deciding to arrest Ernesto last – would be detrimental to the outcome of the judicial process on the 175 *mafiosi*.

We kept reading. With little happening on the file, two years later, a report was filed, Francesco and Antonino applied for parole, pending their trial.[8] Soon after, a junior prosecutor wrote a sixty-page summary of evidence, outlining the case against the Marasà clan. (Odd to have a junior having carriage of such a powerful document.) However, the same prosecutor omitted to mention any murder, any killing. One single incident involved the killing of eighteen men and attempted murder of another twenty. Instead, all that was mentioned were the softer offences of dishonesty and damage. What was happening here? I thought. The junior prosecutor would go one giant step further by stating in his summary that there was insufficient evidence to support any prosecution against any of the 175 Marasà clan suspects.

Elena and I couldn't believe what we were reading, so we reread the back-end folders, and yes, copious evidence about copious murders had been omitted. The evidence was all there! I smelt a rat. Just days after the junior prosecutor's decision, on 22 August 1940, Francesco and Antonino were set free from their holding cells, allowed to go about their business. The judicial process got weirder. A few months later, the same junior prosecutor signed an order that all persons held must be freed, and any fugitives should no longer be pursued. Yet no judge had seen the file, or read the evidence.

On 31 May 1941, Judge Giuseppe Grisafi was presented with the summary. He singled out the name Ernesto Marasà and made a hand-written order to no longer seek his arrest, as he was no longer considered a fugitive from justice.[9] There were no other individually named orders on the file. It appears Ernesto got the royal treatment. Within weeks, the same judge would declare that all accused had no case to answer. The prosecution was dead in the water.

In modern detective speak, the forty-seven Carabinieri had been given a snow job, their work had suffered a whitewash; ten years at the grindstone had been all for nothing. Passed over by judicial corruption. Let's not forget, this happened at the height of World War II, when all eyes and minds were on survival. The Marasà court decision was lost in the fog of war. It is remarkable the power that Marasà and his large *cosca* had.

Ernesto Marasà crept out of hiding to domicile in his luxury Palermo *palazzo*. And business went back to normal.

The criminal genius that was Ernesto Marasà would continue to walk the streets of Palermo, on the sunny side, with gold rings on his fingers and in a fine woollen suit; he had become highly protected by all. Historically, by the stooge Cesare Mori and, indirectly, his superior Benito Mussolini.

However, each wild story usually has an even wilder postscript. As war marched on, Marasà and his clan got down to stamping their authority over Sicily, with little resistance as many of the island's police were fighting in Mussolini's losing army. Then, one late spring morning in Palermo, the Allies arrived, in their tens of thousands. But not before they softened the soil with a massive display of aerial bombardment. On 3 May 1943, bombs rained down on the once cultured city, tons of metal falling from the sky; death was everywhere. One bomb landed on the gorgeous *palazzo* of Ernesto Marasà and blew it off the map. But the *slimy octopus* would survive once more, crawling out from his cellar, to find his brothers and to fight another day.

One of the main newspapers of the time wrote, '. . . it is a necessary instrument of dominance [the Mafia] over big land owners . . . accept or die out of hunger . . .'.[10] The same article advocated the benefit of the Mafia to play a role between the big landowners and the small farmers. With this sort of sentiment influencing the thinking of post-war Sicilians, is it any wonder that Marasà continued his run?

As an aside, 1943 was a good year for causing angst, near-death or misery to heads of the Mafia. Don Vito Ferro, the Palermo boss of all Mafia activities at the turn of the century – the man who gunned down the brave Lieutenant Joseph Petrosino of the New York police department, back in 1909 – also found himself at the mercy of Allied bombers. He had been arrested earlier on a string of charges, including murders unrelated to that of Petrosino. His arrest was at the height of the Marasà era. Rumour has it that old Ernesto had had a hand in Don Ferro's demise. It seems logical; they were arch-enemies.

The old Don was languishing inside a remote prison when the bombers came flying above, dropping their deadly metal, destroying the prison. Some time afterwards, the dapper Don would be discovered dead in his cell. Not from the bombardment, but from extreme dehydration. Trapped by his confinement, with everyone else either dead or having fled, he was unable to access water.

As an example of Ernesto Marasà's survival instincts, in 1947, with the *Generalissimo* long past his sixty-sixth birthday, an atrocity unfolded in the countryside just out of Palermo. It was Labour Day and a well-known bandit, Salvatore Giuliano – often mistaken as Mafia, when in fact he was a murderous thief who hated communists – gathered a team of equally capable bandits and surrounded a family-day picnic, where men, women and children were gathered to celebrate a political victory. With machine guns, rifles and grenades the criminals mowed down the defenceless crowd, killing eleven and wounding scores.[11] The same Carabinieri as those who had seen their prosecution of Marasà dismantled rushed to the massive crime scene and set about finding suspects. One Ernesto Marasà was seen, overlooking the atrocity like a sheep dog watching over his flock. The police listed him as 'belonging to the mafia and a supporter of Salvatore Giuliano'.[12] But no further action was taken, against Marasà, Giuliano or anyone. The way of Palermo cops, back then.

As a side note, during my research for this book, over three years I wrote countless times to the Palermo University history faculty, seeking interviews with the main professors, known globally for their work in unravelling the back story of the Mafia. I outlined my police background and desire to write about the earliest Mafia. Not once did I receive a reply. In an act of desperation, I harassed the head researcher of the faculty and begged a meeting; she kindly acquiesced. This academic, on the verge of her own professorship, explained that she was barely aware of Ernesto Marasà but had no knowledge of the five folders, indeed she felt there was no material in the Gancia Archivio that could assist me, nor was she aware of material elsewhere.

I went back to the Gancia Archivio and checked the files again, and something jumped out at me: pencil marks, or the lack thereof. Scholars are known to place pencil marks under key paragraphs and passages as they read important files to be used in their theses. It's a quirk that is tolerated in archives; I've done it myself. There were no pencil markings on any page. I then checked the Reader Lists, which offer the name of each scholar who has gained permission to study the files.

No researcher had ever read these same five folders. Except Elena and myself.

•

Nine months later: October 2021. Having left Palermo, I knew I would be leaving behind unfinished business; I had failed to locate a photograph of the slimy octopus, Ernesto Marasà. I had to accept that there simply wasn't one in existence. The *Generalissimo* of the Mafia would become a Sicilian thistle embedded in my side as I lost myself to studying the American Mafia and all its machinations.

But the thistle sting soon got the better of me. I had to return to Sicily for one last try. Dottoressa Francesca D'Pasquale of the Gancia Archive would oblige my obsession and Elena and I waded through countless more folders over many days. Nothing but dusty sneezing. Surely, it was time to walk away. Out of frustration a Palermo film director friend of mine, Salvo Cuccia, and I took a long drive to the ruins of the Marasà *palazzo* that had been bombed in 1943. We had a slim hope of being pointed somewhere, anywhere that might yield an old family picture. But first we needed to take the advice of the police; after all, we were putting ourselves back on the hunt of the *capo di tutti capi*. We were told to stay away, to go home. Instead, we drove to the old *palazzo*. It was now a mix of automotive and electrical retail shops, a horse-riding school, a reception centre and a maze of flats. By nightfall – after knocking on way too many doors and getting that 'fuck off' blank stare – we went home, empty-handed.

The next day Salvo took up the challenge again and opened his laptop. He went into a frenzied online search of the locations we had door-knocked. Then, bingo: a Facebook link to a distant relative who had posted – years earlier – a picture of the bombed *palazzo*. We were on the scent, talking to a suspicious great-nephew of Ernesto Marasà. Once the waters were smoothed over, this thoroughly decent man would assist this story and supply pictures. He also offered to introduce me to his 96-year-old mother, who was Ernesto's niece and had known him for the first twenty-three years of her long life.

A few days later the *nonna*, the great-nephew, the filmmaker, my translator, a cinematographer and I sat in the sunny courtyard of the Marasà *palazzo* remains and openly discussed a patriarch who, until now, had been missing from the global puzzle of the Mafia. The ultimate *mafioso*, who lent his hand to the emerging Italian crime scourge in America with his manifesto and rule of *omertà*.

On a personal level it was a great moment for this once anti-Mafia detective to be munching *biscotti* and taking notes inside a crime boss's castle, albeit now ruined. It was as if the walls of the old *palazzo* started talking once the *nonna* found her voice, at times lost in her struggle to recall, other times locking her eyes onto me, perhaps wondering what would finish up in the pages of this book.

Her recollections confirmed and vindicated the story already laid out, and supported the red report. She recalled her uncle as a fugitive for three years at the time of his prosecution. He hid out in a luxury suite in the Grand Hotel et des Palmes, the best hotel in Sicily, located on the main street of Palermo. Enjoying the comforts of the hotel he, apparently, was looked after by local police, who were with him daily. She explained that should Ernesto want a visit from his family or friends, he would ask his police friends to disappear as he took in his guests. Then, afterwards, they would return. This dodgy arrangement remained in place until Marasà managed to wriggle himself, his brothers and his gang out of the prosecution that Elena and I studied in depth. Hearing of such complicity made me think again of the red report and how the heads of the Carabinieri knew Ernesto Marasà was the supreme *pentito*, the secret weapon of local cops, getting rid of thugs he needed out of the game, so he could control his empire.

The most surprising fact that we learnt was about Ernesto's age. It is stated in many archival documents that he was the eldest of the three brothers, but in fact he was the youngest of four. One brother was unknown to prosecutors. The *nonna* explained that, by 1910, Ernesto had assumed the role of patriarch of the family, when he was only thirty years old. It would be another fifteen years before the full fury of Ernesto would bloom, as he took on the other Mafia leaders and killed his way to his 1938 prosecution. On the day of the Allied bombing in 1943, the eldest brother, Francesco, would take a massive shard of shrapnel to his neck and die by nightfall. Four months later, Antonio would also die, aged sixty-three years. Ernesto would dominate crime in Sicily until his own death in 1948. It appears Ernesto and Antonio were childless and villainy was bred out of the Marasà family.

During our talk the *nonna* kept hold of an aged leather-bound book which she eventually decided to share with me. It was a business journal of the many export shipments the Marasà brothers had made of their citrus fruits to New York, Boston, Philadelphia, Chicago and New Orleans. Details down to the weight and cost of consignments and the names of each ocean liner, dating way back to 1887. It all started to make sense, as I recalled that Don Vito Ferro had created a water track for *mafiosi* thugs to stow away on ships going to America. Don Vito controlled the Sicilian Mafia during the earlier part of the twentieth century, and instigated the extortion rackets of the Black Hand in New York, crimes that led to the execution of Lieutenant Joe Petrosino. Obviously the Marasà clan were part of that water track, disguised by their limes, lemons and tangerines. It was then that I viewed black and white pictures of the funeral of Ernesto; an impressive send-off, hundreds of mourners following behind a casket atop an ornate carriage pulled by horses, led by ten padres and other ceremonially dressed priests, some carrying thuribles, as well as a crucifer. One picture showed four horse-drawn carriages laden with flowers and wreaths. The mostly dour-faced adult male mourners had the appearance of extras from central casting, pulled together for a Francis Ford Coppola movie.

Lastly, the *nonna* twice fell to giggles before regaling us with the story of the expulsion of Mussolini from a public meeting in the early days of his dictatorship when he visited Palermo. Apparently, the Marasà family were involved and she talked of the Mafia-affiliated Mayor Francesco Cuccia, who snubbed Mussolini, ensuring the despot would have no listeners at his rally.

Before long, dusk had started to fall over the *palazzo* and the now-tired matriarch and we would bid farewell to history and to a truly delightful family who gifted me their honestly and an unforgettable memory.

CHAPTER 17
FRANCHISING CANCER

While most of the world was embroiled in war in the first half of the twentieth century, the Mafia enterprise continued to grow. As the eminent author David Critchley once said, much of the information on the Mafia during the war period, 'is founded on speculation, exaggeration, hearsay evidence and ideological preconception'.[1]

No heroes from either World War I or II came from the ranks of the Mafia. Its members avoided military service by getting exemption certificates from amenable doctors. This cowardly strategy was essential to the spread of Mafia interests during this period. As well as in Italy, the scourge was able to implement their criminal activities across the pond in New York City and beyond. The incubation years for the franchising were 1920 to 1945. The well-worn water track ensured thousands of *mafiosi* were entrenched in cities like Chicago, New York, Miami, New Orleans, Boston and Philadelphia. The exact same cities that took shipments of Marasà citrus fruits. While the majority of thugs originated from Sicily, many came from Naples and other areas in the lower leg of Italy. Two additional factors encouraged migration.

The first was the policies of Cesare Mori and the black-boot strutting Il Duce, and the second was Prohibition in the United States, which banned the manufacture and sale of alcohol from 1920 until 1933.

Prohibition was a poorly conceived law that only fostered crime. Instead of improving society, it created opportunities for gangsters. In short, it was a gift to the Mafia.

The Sicilian Carabinieri's claim that 'the tree was only pruned, the roots were untouched',[2] after Mori's Mafia purge, made me wonder what became of the tree and its saplings. It seems the Sicilian tree had dropped seeds in the United States and, once planted, they grew as strongly as the original tree, resisting the axe of honest police, as the seeds became rooted across the country.

By the beginning of World War II, America had felt the rod of the Mafia in many forms, from countless murders on the streets and the corruption of public officials, to the darkening of the squad rooms in police departments as the Mafia expanded their network of dodgy contacts to aid their operations. The Mafia system of crime and business in America more or less followed Don Ernesto Marasà's manifesto as set out in the red report of 1938. The skills needed to implant a Mafia organisation in a new frontier required a certain type of individual, and throughout this period a number of ruthless mobsters rose to the occasion.

The annals of the American franchise of the Mafia are full of hundreds of tough guys who reigned during the Prohibition era – men who killed and masterminded rackets, as well as bosses who ran clans of mobsters. This period – the spring of *mafiosi* in America – however, is best told through the criminal careers of three men who each had a firm grip on the scourge during its maturation. Individually, they were masterful at their trade; collectively, they had law enforcement fooled.

The first is the infamous Alfonso Capone: a short-ass thug with a long scar across his cheek, the result of a switchblade fight as a young punk in a bar on Coney Island. Scarface, as he was called (though not to his face), was not the classic *mafioso* mobster; he was instead the perfect example of the contemporary Mafia man. He could attach himself to anything, and more importantly, anyone – Black, White,

Jewish, Asian, Eastern European, public official, greedy cop. He even had a judge or ten tucked away in his back pocket.

Traditionally, Italian *mafiosi* dealt almost exclusively within an Italian circle; this was the Sicilian way. I knew this well as an undercover cop who penetrated an all-Italian Mafia clan in Australia. It was ridiculously hard to break through, to get my targets to engage with me, and ultimately conspire with me to commit crimes or allow me to be part of their crime circle. The difficulty was, they saw me as a 'skippy' – a kangaroo – as the Italians call Australians. They were sceptical of Australians (even more so now). It is a smart way to do business: stick within your own ethnic group where everyone is part of the same family tree. One can vouch for another, tap a cousin on the shoulder, whisper about someone, and confirm the trustworthiness of a fellow thug. A shared language and culture helped make the American (and Australian) Mafia.

The son of Italian immigrants from Naples, Al Capone was born in Brooklyn, New York City. He was one of the first gold-plated *mafiosi* who was not born in Italy. As a kid, he ran at crime on the tough streets of New York, mixing it with Jewish gangs and the sons of wharf workers. It was in Manhattan that he befriended another name on my list, Charles Luciano, before setting the crime world alight with his tough-guy routine and thirst for ill-gotten gains, and putting his stamp on Italian organised crime in Chicago. His interests in crime across America became legendary. The keys to his success were *pizzo* standovers, prostitution, gambling rackets, sly grog and bootlegging – the making of cheap booze from black-market grain and shipping it across state borders for sale, a federal crime thanks to the Prohibition laws.

His book of associates confirms his versatility as a mobster and modern criminal. His closest associates included – until they were murdered, shot by police or jailed – the Jewish pimp and financial wizard Jake Guzik and the dapper Russian Jew Meyer Lansky, who ran a massive illegal gambling racket stretching from Las Vegas to Cuba and on to London. All gangsters, and few of them making it to old age in the shoot-'em-up days of Prohibition. Treacherous Al rose to the top of a killer crowd to run one of the meanest crime gangs in America.

Capone's reputation was built on the way he eliminated his opposition. The Irish gang on the north side of Chicago was run by the
madman George 'Bugs' Moran. He and Capone had snarled at each
other for many years until Scarface had his closest ally, Jack McGurn,
arrange the mass slaughter of Moran's gang inside a warehouse filled
with dodgy whiskey. Known as the St Valentine's Day massacre, seven
of Chicago's worst were executed in broad daylight on 14 February
1929, as Capone sat on a banana lounge in sunny Florida sucking on
Havana cigars. By the time Capone returned to Chicago, the police
were chasing their tails on how he got away with it, as the Great
Depression fell over America. Not to be deterred, Scarface tapped
into the misery that followed, offering gambling and prostitution as a
relief for the downtrodden. He even had his dodgy unionist colleague
Murray Humphreys exploit children's milk supplies. Anything that
Capone could make a dollar from, he turned into a fortune.

Capone's shocking criminal deeds inspired President Herbert Hoover
to anoint a mini task force, under Treasury agent Eliot Ness, to bring
down America's pin-up mobster. This contest, Ness versus Capone,
lasted two harrowing years and became a model for task-force policing
across law enforcement in the United States. Daily newspapers sold
out as journalists followed their ever-changing exploits. Even a young
Ernest Hemingway, a cub reporter at the *Toronto Daily Star*, followed
the Capone capers. Throwing everything they had at Capone, however,
still failed for the task force. Ness himself looked second best in the
two-man war and his boss, United States Attorney George Johnson,
encouraged Ness to push on, to close down Capone.

Having avoided serious prison time throughout his colourful
career, Scarface ultimately came to a fitting end after an honest judge
imposed an eleven-year sentence for taxation avoidance in 1931. This
saw Capone do hard labour at the toughest of all penitentiaries, San
Francisco's Alcatraz prison. The little gangster didn't fare too well in
jail. Men tougher and bigger than the legend relegated him to the back
benches of the exercise yard, and he wielded limited authority. He
died, after snaring parole and living out a lonely life on Palm Island,
Florida, in 1947 aged forty-eight.

As a purist in regard to the Mafia and its workings, I would suggest that Capone was not Mafia. By the codes set down by old-school *mafiosi* and reinforced by Marasà's laws, Capone, strictly speaking, was merely a crime boss. Some might argue the subtlety, but let me explain. The man with the scar on his face changed the face of crime in the United States.

Nowadays, the American Mafia can mean many things. The gangs of *mafiosi* are, when business suits them, integrated with many other nationalities, such as those in Latin America, Asia, Russia and so on. Just as the US Attorney can pick many different investigators from many skill sets to form a gang, so could Al Capone. Ethnicity was unimportant to him.

Alfonso was the first to understand this, by using who he wanted for whatever he was trying to achieve. When you look at today's Mafia membership, not all the names appear to have come from the Palermo telephone book or the Naples electoral roll. It is all about business, the making of money and keeping one or two steps ahead of landing in prison. This skill involves liaising with who can best assist you, who can keep you flush with cash, and who can free you from a police interrogation room – whatever their family background might be. That's the definition of a crime gang, not the Mafia in a traditional sense.

Italian Mafia tradition up until the late 1920s dictated that only Italians could be Mafia members, but entrepreneur Capone smashed that mould. By the next decade tradition would fall by the wayside. You did not have to be born in Trapani or Palermo, or a miserable little village in the Sicilian interior, to join the Mafia. Nor did you need to have come from a hard background, from, say, a family in an upstairs cold-water tenement in the slums of Naples, who survived on five-day-old *bruschetta* and low-grade olive oil. Hard-luck stories became a thing of the past. Anyone could find a chair at the American Mafia table, even a tough guy born into a nice family in Brooklyn. As a 'fatty', Capone was tired of being picked on, so he joined a gang of street kids, and through kiddie extortion rackets he punched his way to the top of a Mafia that he would change irrevocably.

The American Mafia from the 1930s onwards could mean anyone in crime who was tough enough to take control of his own patch. For example, the ruthless gangster James 'Whitey' Bulger was the head of the famous Irish gang in Boston for forty years. He fought against and worked with Italian Mafia mobsters throughout his career. Or Henry Hill, a square-as-a-butter-box New Jersey kid who grew up inside a Mafia clan washing their cars. He would go on to make millions with his Italian-mobster mentors, most of whom were second or third generation Italians. Today, the contemporary Mafia in the United States is made up of many ethnicities, thanks to Alfonso Capone.

While Al Capone is arguably the most infamous American gangster, care of TV and movies, Charles Luciano was definitely the smartest. Luciano was born in Lercara, a stone village in the harsh interior of Sicily, which donated hundreds of *picciotti* to fight alongside Garibaldi. Luciano spent his early years in Lercara, where his father was a labourer in the sulphur mines and life was 'struggles-ville' for most of his childhood. When Luciano was nine, he and his family moved to Manhattan, and his landscape changed from hot, treeless, red-dust villages to a big city full of apartment towers and wallets. As a teenager, he befriended Al Capone and they both set off on a trajectory of crime that would last the next three decades and revolutionise American organised crime. By the time he was twenty, the Sicilian had become his own crime boss with low-level rackets all over Manhattan's Lower East Side. Soon he would be called 'Lucky', a nickname that came about from his luck at surviving a vicious thrashing that almost killed him, as well as his luck with the horses.

In his sixty-four years, Lucky did more, I believe, for the contemporary Mafia than anyone else, other than Marasà before him. For whatever *Time* magazine knows about the Mafia, they ranked Luciano as the second-most powerful Mafia boss of all time. (Who was listed as their number one, I never bothered to find out.) While he was impressive as a criminal, he was even more so as a strategist; he was the chairman of the US Mafia board and his entire life was crime.

While still a teenager, he became a competent smuggler, moving hard-to-get goods and booze around and off the wharves of Manhattan and Brooklyn. His gangster, union and stevedoring contacts came in handy in later life. Names like Bugsy Siegel and Frank Costello would stick to him like Velcro. By the time Charles hit his mid-twenties he had truly become lucky. His gang is reported to have earned twelve million dollars a year from his black-market rackets.

A man capable of developing a corrupt enterprise of that magnitude is a man who should be listened to by Mafia seniors. He became counsel to many. This position is called a *consigliere*, the person who gives strategic or financial advice, a most valued asset. So far, so good, until Luciano got arrested for dealing narcotics, a new form of contraband for an uncertain Mafia, and bosses started looking sideways at the little tough guy. He countered any negativity by buying scores of bosses and thugs front-row seats at a world title boxing match, but not before dressing his guests in new suits from a nearby tailor. Before the knock-out punch was delivered at the fight, Lucky Luciano had pulled off his finest strategy. A reported 200 mobsters considered Luciano too smart to mess with. His future was assured.

At the time of Fascism in Sicily, the American Mafia had become full of wannabe *mafiosi*. After settling in America, they became embroiled in a Mafia power war, the struggle of the old versus the new Mafia. Lucky was a modernist like his chum Capone and knew the value of aligning himself with those who could aid his criminality. He would do business with a rat if it had a gold tooth.

The result was the same as in Sicily. The traditionalists were gradually being pushed aside or killed, and Lucky's position ascended as bosses turned to him for his criminal moves and shakes. The days leading up to the Great Depression saw many moves on the Mafia chessboard. The game changed almost daily as bosses, *capi* and anyone with an eye to a senior position in the Mafia – particularly in the New York boroughs – got themselves killed off if they were not aligned with the ways of the new breed. Lucky was also ready with his Thompson submachine guns to counter any attack that came his way. In doing so, he opened himself to internal criticism as he delved into crimes that old-school *mafiosi* would never touch, such as keeping a string of low-class brothels, selling drugs and racketeering – crime frontiers that challenged even Frank Costello's loyalty, who as a teenager with Luciano had bashed Jews for standover money. Frank had grown to become a powerbroker in the new Mafia and is the third Mafia figure worth highlighting, alongside Lucky Luciano and Scarface Capone.

Costello (real name Castiglia) deserves his inclusion on my list for many reasons. He was a brilliant hierarchical figure, calm-thinking and hugely respected. It was said he never needed to kill; he could negotiate anything. Frank was also not Sicilian by birth or ancestry; he was born in Calabria, across the Messina Strait. Up until Frank's era, it was unheard of to see a Calabrese in any prominent role in the Sicilian-structured Mafia. Considered quintessential Italian peasants, the Calabrese were slow to get their gangster licences. Apart from centuries of feudal fighting, tough-guy 'hillbilly' stuff, they never became organised in crime until well after the Great Depression. It was mobster icons like Frank Costello who changed that, and the Calabrese Mafia today is consider the world's most dangerous, dominant and ruthless. (Make no mistake, the Calabrese Mafia is more deadly than a pit full of copperhead snakes. I know, it was two clans of the Calabrese Mafia that I infiltrated and gained evidence against for three years, when I went undercover.) For a Calabrese-born thug like Costello to get into a senior position in the American Mafia – back in the 1940s – he would have to possess something unique.

That fact was not wasted on Costello. He had been a thief since arriving in Harlem as a kid. He married a Jewish girl, and after a short jail sentence made the decision to do away with hard-nosed violence and to think his way through and out of situations. He would, as a twenty-something punk, learn to dress a cut above the rest, dine well, and align himself with the future kings of organised crime: Capone, Luciano, Vito Genovese, Gaetano Lucchese and other big-hitters. Costello, for me, was the George Clooney of crime – smooth. The epitome of a modern Mafia board member.

In his formative years, as other thugs searched the streets for rackets to uncover, Frank created his own money-making schemes that would impress his close friend Luciano, such as running 20 000 slot machines, in bars, bus stops and petrol stations across New York State. However, his real talent was in bringing into his organisation corrupt cops and city hall officials, and that meant ongoing delicate negotiations. Together, Luciano, Capone and Costello were the perfect team. Costello also took advantage of Luciano's strong links with homeland Sicily, and once Lucky set up his own 'family' of mobsters, he and Costello set up a fund to assist Sicilian comrades facing imprisonment. They both knew that being closely aligned with Sicily was better than the alternative. It was Costello who breathed life into Lucky when others may well have ended his life due to Lucky's grab-all approach to crime spoils.

Luciano and Costello's vision of a new Mafia helped reshape the old Mafia families, who went from sloppily run ethnic clubs (of bad men) to, in a period of ten years, tightly run franchises that saw the pair's status escalate.

Luciano was the architect of many executions of Mafia *capi*, and his killing of kingpin Giuseppe Masseria during an after-lunch card game in the early days, in 1931, elevated his status even higher, with the deadly help of his friend, hitman Albert Anastasia. It was impossible to estimate how many killings Anastasia performed in a time of hundreds of Mafia murders. He killed time and again, in a breath, for his close friend Lucky over two decades. Anastasia, another Calabrese immigrant, was so deadly he started the infamous Murder Incorporated, a kill-for-hire business. Mafia thugs booked him in to kill anyone they fell out with. This absurd venture operated for eleven years until it ran out of clients, all dead. (It raises the question: where were the police and FBI in all this?)

These two decades in the history of the American Mafia saw a rebranding in name, as well as ideology. The term 'Black Hand' got tossed aside; it was too aligned with the old Mafia, and for years the name Mafia held its own ground, until ultimately – in the 1950s – a modern name seeped into the Mafia vocabulary at a franchise meeting: *Cosa Nostra*, 'Our Thing'. A name that would eventually stick, at least in the United States. Much later, in the 1970s, it became the global name for all Mafia with Sicilian roots or liaisons. Indeed, names like *Cosa Nostra* and Godfather are now seen more as Americanisms, dotted throughout news stories or cinema depictions. (In my three years inside the Mafia, not once did any *mafioso* use the word 'Godfather'. Whereas in all my travels to Sicily over three decades it is common to use and hear the name *Cosa Nostra*.)

As strategists, Costello and Luciano were keynote speakers at Mafia conferences, giving advice on keeping one step ahead of law enforcement. Now in their thirties, the pair helped ace mobster Salvatore

Maranzano mastermind the renovation of the rag-tag family structure of the American Mafia into five families, each with a strict territory and autonomy. Maranzano had been running his scams in Brooklyn and answered a challenge from Don Vito Ferro, the boss of the traditional Sicilian Mafia, to undertake the task. They both went back to the bad old days in the Sicilian town of Castellammare del Golfo, where tradition was everything. So had the now-deceased Giuseppe Masseria. But tradition seemed to come second to Masseria's greedier ways, and he constantly clashed with Maranzano. Clearly, he had to go, and the Mafia would face their first spring without him.

It's a fascination that at this exact moment in time Ernesto Marasà and his murderous brothers were hard at it, blooming their contemporary Sicilian Mafia. The brilliance and dogged determination of both Marasà and Luciano cannot be dismissed as sheer coincidence. Clearly, they shared a vision. The five New York families were finally named Maranzano, Profaci, Gagliano, Mangano and Luciano, which became the Genovese crime clan much later. While some of the families went back to the old days of the Sicilian Mafia, they all agreed to bounce the new ball as part of the contemporary American Mafia. Trouble was, old or new, Mafia tend to fall out with each other. As soon as the five families were named other crime bosses were angered that they were not part of a ratified family. Envy, ego and power started to take over and the inside killings increased.

This left the fringe-dwelling Mafia clans – the gangs outside the postcodes of New York City – such as the Buffalo family – to fester or form allegiances with one of the five core families. Any modern-day CEO of a multinational company could see the flaws in this structure, it was too New York City–centric. In hindsight, the five families should have been ten families and spread nationwide.

Luciano and Costello did away with the *capo di tutti capi* role in controlling all the families, a role Salvatore Maranzano ached for. Luciano killed him instead. And Maranzano's lowly security thug Joe Valachi sided with the survivor, Lucky Luciano.

Costello and Luciano favoured the Ernesto Marasà structure, whereby each family had one overall boss, followed by an underboss, a number of advisers, and a football field of soldiers and up-and-coming wannabes.

To finish off this structure, Luciano set up a Mafia commission, which guaranteed each family boss a seat at the table. The commission oversaw the direction of all Mafia crimes and rackets, and, by the 1940s, outsmarted all law enforcement attempts to stop the growth of the Mafia in the United States. Lucky Luciano's and Frank Costello's finest achievement – the franchising of the American Mafia – is still, with a few tweaks, in existence today, only there has been a name change to the five. They are now: the Bonanno, Colombo, Gambino, Genovese and Lucchese families, and, like the original blunder of being New York–centric, no family from outside New York is part of the inner sanctum, although they still wield extraordinary power when they want, and can turn to the commission for help.

During World War II, Luciano's world changed drastically, as did Costello's, though in different ways. Luciano had been incarcerated for running his prostitution racket, which saw him relegated to the Mafia back seat, while Costello moved into the main chair to run the Luciano family. (Luciano had a weakness for prostitutes, something the old *mafiosi* frowned upon.)

During the war the US Navy believed German agents may have infiltrated the port of New York. Luciano, along with Mafia hitman Anastasia, who was now a crime boss himself, still held an iron-fisted control over the union labour that worked the wharves. US naval agents asked Luciano for help to liaise with Mafia hierarchy to ensure the port's protection. Both Anastasia and Luciano had a long history of smuggling illicit drugs through the ports for a decade or more, so their know-how was crucial to the war effort. Luciano is said to have agreed, in exchange for getting a transfer from the high-security Sing Sing Prison to a softer prison in Great Meadows, where fraudsters, cops and paedophiles usually served out their time. It was more a holiday camp than a prison; police call these jails 'sooky' prisons, because really hard inmates are conspicuous by their absence.

Later, in 1943, it was widely reported that Luciano aided the Allied effort to enter Sicily when Mussolini was on the run, and the war had turned a corner. The story goes that the US forces who had landed on

Sicily were seeking Mafia assistance to allow them to get across the island and the Strait of Messina and onto the leg of Italy. Luciano, from his Great Meadows minimum security cell, put word out to his Mafia contacts to assist the US forces. A yellow silk handkerchief embroidered with a black silk 'L' was air-dropped over the tiny village of Villalba, where a US Army contingent was waiting, to signal that the Mafia would help the forces.

This fantastic story has found its way into many history books over the decades and adds to the legend of Lucky Luciano. The Mafia boss was promoted as a patriot, doing right by his nation and the Allied forces. In my research, I must have read of Luciano's 'heroics' countless times. Yet US Colonel Poletti, who was in the village at the time, said the story is rubbish, an invention. Likewise, Luciano himself went on record to say the story was 'all lies'.[3] He would have benefited greatly had the fable been true, using it to lift his image, which was in tatters due to his incarceration. Besides, it is difficult to see how useful the mobster could have been to the army while sitting in prison peeling potatoes. A Sicilian journalist – who I won't name as he did some great work otherwise – resided in the village of Villalba, and seemed to have made great mileage from the Lucky handkerchief story. He claimed to have seen it fall from a passing aircraft, before witnessing the US Army springing into action.[4] Historians have dismissed his tale as a fantasy, as do I; it is too Hollywood for my taste.

As an interesting sidenote to the patriotic fable of Luciano, the famed author of hard-boiled detective novels Raymond Chandler had a sit-down with Lucky in the late 1950s; they took over a bar in a swanky Italian hotel and drank. Chandler needed a new book deal and Luciano, by this time living in Italy, needed some PR because the Italian authorities were on his case. It was during this interview that Luciano dismissed any role he was believed to have had in assisting the invasion of Sicily. Chandler wrote a note of his interview and remarked, 'all that Luciano could have told them [the Allies] about Sicily was that it was an island'.[5]

Luciano was paroled the year after the war ended, on the condition he be deported. He was put on an aircraft soon after. It was a requirement of his parole that he live in Sicily for the remainder of his years.

Soon after arriving in Italy his criminal curiosity got the better of him and he jumped on another airliner. His aircraft landed in Cuba; Luciano had listened hard to his fellow inmates in prison. He knew Cuba was untapped, ripe for exploitation.[6] His confidant Meyer Lansky convinced him of the cash-cow potential of casinos in Havana. Luciano then organised for the upper echelons of the Mafia crime families to attend a getting-out party in his honour. With his guests sequestered in the luxurious Hotel Nacional in Havana, he turned the party into a week-long conference where the business of ill-gotten proceeds and gambling in Havana were discussed and divided up among the crime families. The world's most famous crooner, Frank Sinatra, provided the tunes, and it was business as usual for Charles Luciano, and his old friend Lansky.[7] Within months, Luciano had almost single-handedly turned Havana into a massive gambling den, with a constant stream of *mafiosi*, other mobsters, B-grade Hollywood stars and every ten-cent hood who could rustle up an airfare on one of the eight flights a day into the city. Havana would go on to lubricate the wheels of the American Mafia – until Castro showed up – and Sinatra would be called to give evidence at the US Senate Committee on Mafia in America.

After months of newspaper stories across the globe focusing on Luciano's new-found business interests in Cuba, the US government stepped in and threatened sanctions on Cuba. Lansky would move on to develop Las Vegas, ensuring his legend within the American Mafia scrapbook, and Lucky moved on to Italy, where he remained. A month after arriving he was arrested in Palermo and confined to prison, pending a court hearing. However, he was released, given the soft option of being of good behaviour, and was set free to grow his global *mafiosi*. I cannot help but wonder if Ernesto Marasà had used his police and judiciary contacts to improve Lucky's good fortune to escape a longer confinement.

Flipping his time between Naples and Palermo, Luciano played a key role in facilitating relations between the old-school thugs, who didn't speak English, and the smooth-talking 'wise guys' of the US Mafia families. Free to do what he wanted, without the FBI or a US Senate Committee breathing down his neck, he explored the heroin trade and set up key liaisons with shipping agents for Marseille-French and southern Italian mobsters – who bought and moved boatloads of heroin. His smarts would see the start of widespread heroin use, and those who benefited were his allies, Frank Costello and the American Mafia families, particularly those in New York City. Charles Luciano became untouchable as police corruption (and incompetence) in Italy ensured no one would end his run. Surrounding himself with bodyguards, he had a lifestyle only billionaires could imagine. Although he had a few skirmishes with the law in Italy, he brushed them off and kept building his version of a global Mafia. (The front cover of this book shows Luciano being escorted around Palermo by a team of thugs, as well as a *capo* from the ruling *mafiosi*.)

Lucky's next achievement was truly international. He pulled in other Mafia clans in the lower leg of Italy – namely, the Calabrese Mafia and Neapolitan Mafia. Until Luciano brokered a liaison with them, they had been mostly a rag-tag bunch of thieves who lacked the vision of the Sicilians. Famed for inventing pickpocketing and selling smuggled cigarettes, they needed a lecture from the boss of all bosses, and encouragement to become more entrepreneurial. Known throughout Italy as the *Camorra* – a name from the nineteenth century that translates as 'fight' or 'bandit's jacket' – the Neapolitan crime scourge is said to have started around the time of Italian unification. The *Camorra* assisted Garibaldi's invasion of Campania, en route to Naples to seek a surrender from the Bourbons. However, once the rush of blood to the head in the victory over the Two Sicilies subsided, and the looting ended, the *Camorra* lacked sufficient structure and managerial skills to become anything more than a loose bunch of criminals.

It would take another sixty or more years before they saw the trees from the woods – the potential in widespread, organised crime. Even then, Mussolini's assault on crime gangs in the Fascist era kept most of the early *Camorra* from becoming too bold. Many of them fled to the greener pastures of America, some went to Canada and smaller numbers to Australia. Then, one day in the late 1940s, a man named Lucky Luciano walked into their office and sat down.

The Mafia of Calabria, the *'Ndrangheta*, dates back to the days of the horse and cart. The name stems from a Greek word meaning 'society of honourable men' and is sometimes said to mean 'heroism and virtue'; the Calabrese, like their 'Ndrangheta name, have always been a bit different to other Mafia-affiliated regions. They band together in gangs, and most gangs are not affiliated. Their structure is very flat, compared to the hierarchical structure of their near neighbour, the Cosa Nostra. The 'Ndrangheta's version of the criminal scourge is also based on their obsession for vendetta – the ritual to kill anyone who wrongs them, a classic feudal mentality. Their members are short, stocky-looking, and brutal by nature, and nothing more than wild – aggressive mountain men who have learnt to ply their criminal ways in towns and cities, to the point of taking over, due to fear and a willingness to destroy those in their path. Calabria is made up of dozens of 'Ndrangheta family dynasties which go about their business. Rarely do they go to war against themselves, preferring instead to run their rackets, minding their own business. The standout attribute of Calabrian mafiosi is their solidarity, a trait that allows them to grow in an over-crowded underworld of global crime.

The 'Ndrangheta's early days of unlawfulness focused to a large extent on what I call 'survival crime' – petty crime committed in order to live, day by day – stealing sheep; attacking a neighbour to steal his chickens; starting up a cattle theft racket; and so forth. Certainly, Mussolini's attack on Mafia gangs had an influence on Calabrese criminals – they mostly committed only minor crimes – until politics and time opened the door to bigger and better crimes. In the late 1940s, Lucky Luciano was standing on the other side of that door.

Luciano saw a need to bring the Camorra and 'Ndrangheta into the Cosa Nostra fold, or at least to have them as close affiliates, when needed. This may well have been his finest criminal achievement, linking each Mafia organisation across Italy and sharing these links to his crime cousins in America, which only strengthened the overall reach and workings of a global Mafia. By the 1950s, the broad franchising of the Mafia was complete, albeit the 'Ndrangheta and Camorra ran independently of their Sicilian cousins. As a law-breaking scourge, the Mafia was everywhere, either represented by the Cosa Nostra, 'Ndrangheta or Camorra or other less dominant clans such as the Sacra Corona Unita cosche in Puglia or other opportunistic clans scattered through Italy.

I make the point, though, that far too much is made of the different strains of the various Mafia, whether it be a network of gangs from Calabria, Campagna or Sicily. Or indeed, from Puglia, Sardinia or in New Jersey, Florida, Buffalo, Stuttgart, Amsterdam, São Paulo or wherever.[8] I don't understand this need to differentiate so finitely. Italian organised crime, wherever it might exist, is the worry, not the geographics.

While each Mafia sect in the 1950s was autonomous – ran its own rackets and went on to build its own global empire – each was known to link arms when it suited them, such as when they were hatching a joint conspiracy.

The *Cosa Nostra* exported its cancer to America, Canada and South America. Germany and other EU regions would also buy into the franchise. The *Camorra* would also send their disease to the Americas and – in time – all over Europe. The *'Ndrangheta* introduced their strain of cancer to the shores of Australia and Europe's Riviera, Amsterdam and Germany, where they now flourish. They have also impacted across Spanish cities and beachside resorts, investing in high cash-flow businesses that can succumb to laundering money.

The versatility in each Mafia was an asset too. And law enforcement would often be lost to the many dialects spoken by the countless families and clans. This characteristic cannot be underestimated as a key reason for the global growth of any or all forms of Mafia. For example, Australia is a classic island country, with one official language, English. Italian dialects fall into the too-hard basket for many detectives.

Additionally, each Mafia had penchants for certain crimes. Not all favoured drug dealing, some preferred the trafficking of contraband, others chose extortion, transport heists, or kidnapping, such as the *'Ndrangheta*, who, in the early days, hid their victims in caves in the honeycombed hills of the Aspromonte in Calabria. I have been all over that mountain range; it is a network of thousands of caves, some the size of houses, some interconnected, ideal for hiding tonnes of drugs, weaponry and banks of cash. And GPS tracking devices, the type employed by law enforcement, have limited to no effect in tracking contraband in this rugged mountain range. As *pizzo* has been the he *Cosa Nostra*, the caves of the vast national parkland of the Aspromonte have been key to the growth of the *'Ndrangheta*.

One *'Ndrangheta* kidnapping that could be considered the most controversial relates to the 1973 snatching of the sixteen-year-old grandson of the American billionaire John Paul Getty. Living in his family home in Rome at that time, the grandson was grabbed from fashionable Piazza Farnese and whisked away. A ransom demand (often wrongly defined) of $20 million was made and the world media descended on the Eternal City as the Mafia clock ticked away. But the grandfather refused to deal with the Mafia – in fact, he refused to speak publicly, despite the amount of money being a mere drop in the ocean to his fortune. As months passed, the victim languished, winter set in and the media savaged JP Getty, calling him mean, miserly; it never let up.

Strategically, the billionaire's dogged refusal to pay was, in my view, completely correct. But few could see the importance of refusing. Rome, indeed Italy, has always been a playground for the rich and famous, not to mention home to wealthy movie stars, fashion designers and globe-trotting business people. The same can be said for its nearest neighbour, France, and Europe and Great Britain as a whole. Had John Paul Getty paid the high price of ransom, there would have been no guarantee his grandson would be returned alive, but what would have been guaranteed was the opening of the floodgates for kidnapping those who could afford the inconvenience. It must be remembered that the Mafia are bloodthirsty opportunists: if they can exploit a racket, especially one so lucrative, they would rush at it. Every scheming *mafioso* would have undertaken surveillance of someone important, the spillover would have been horrendous.

After five months the teenager was released, only after the Getty mogul parted with a tiny fraction of the original demand, and kidnapping fell into the Mafia's too-hard basket. Trouble was, the grandson came home missing an ear, severed by his captors, and psychologically scarred. He lived a troubled life.

I liken the differences in the three key Mafia organisations of Italy to that of canine breeds. In my view, the *'Ndrangheta* can be seen as a local breed, one that hides his bone in the mountains, a vicious pit bull terrier, whose bite could take off a leg. Whereas the *Cosa Nostra* is more cultured, used to the best, a touch of *bella figura* about them, with an international flair, like a Doberman. The *Camorra*, which would rather walk past an opera house en route to a junk yard, could be a Neapolitan mastiff, fearless, able to survive in the toughest conditions. Regardless, they are all hard breeds, capable of going feral. And, like dogs, they are never solo players on the prairie; they need each other, their packs are essential to their survival.

•

The 1950s further enhanced the fortunes of Frank Costello and Charles Luciano, as the Mafia bolted itself to the floor of organised crime to the point that no law enforcement agency or prosecutor's office was able to loosen it.

The killing mongrel, Albert Anastasia, had been running the defunct Mangano Mafia family for some time only because he murdered Vincent Mangano and his brother, thereby claiming the family for himself. Sometime later he found himself in familiar territory – another Mafia boss was pissed at him. Costello and Anastasia were close allies, having both emigrated from Calabria and made good in New York. Both were now at the top of the American Mafia and glued to the hips of Lucky Luciano, their trusted business partner. The three of them had cut their crime teeth on scams when they were twelve-year-old boys. The man who wanted Anastasia's throat was Vito Genovese, who would go on to take over Luciano's family and rename it in his own honour.

Vito was ambitious, but he was thought to be too old-school. He had tried knocking Costello, only to fail, an indication that things were getting tense in Mafia HQ. So a series of meetings was called in an effort to end the hostilities. If things went truly feral between Genovese, Costello and Anastasia, the American Mafia could implode to the point of going out of business. Luciano directed them all to pack a suitcase and get to Palermo. Such was his influence. (This fracas highlights the big difference between the *Cosa Nostra* – always squabbling, at war with itself – and the *'Ndrangheta* – more laidback in approach, preferring to accept its flat management structure and get on with making fortunes. Ego versus business discipline.)

Luciano booked twenty rooms at the best hotel in Palermo, the Grand Hotel et des Palmes. No prizes for guessing who recommended the hotel to Luciano; Ernesto Marasà had holed up there almost twenty years earlier whilst a fugitive and it had served him well. The hotel made its name in the previous century as the sentimental home of the composer Giuseppe Verdi, who wrote two of his operas while in residence. The Luciano-run Mafia conference was held in the Verdi Lounge. The agenda was mixed, ranging from heroin distribution to territorial rights, to ending the issues circling Albert Anastasia.

The most important American matter of the day was the appointment of a new *capo di tutti capi* of the US Mafia. Names were tossed around and hard men with big bellies cast their ideas and votes. Michele Pantaleone, a Sicilian journalist, collected the list of names in attendance, and was gobsmacked. In the end, not one person was given the homeland nod, although the smart money was on Vito Genovese. They would have to wait until after a similar conference in New York later that month.[9] The real winner was Luciano, who, after engineering the meeting, had solidified his position as the most powerful gangster to walk the planet.

I've stayed about six times at the Grand Hotel et des Palmes, one of the great hotels of Italy, and know it well. Some years back, after I had just finished breakfast in the Verdi Lounge while imagining Lucky Luciano's conferences, I returned to my room only to have a heart attack and almost die. I was rushed back to Australia for a quadruple bypass. While I have been to Palermo many times since, and lived there to research this book, I can never return to the hotel, or even walk past the front door. For me, there will always be something not right about that hotel.

For all the expense and fuss of the most prominent Mafia men in the world travelling to Palermo to soften the angst levelled at Albert Anastasia, their efforts would be in vain. On return to New York City, Anastasia was sitting in his favoured barber shop when three Gallo brothers – wise guys aligned to the Colombo family – walked in and shot the Calabrian dead.

The 1950s was the most head-in-the-sand decade of American history with regards to the American Mafia. It was the heady days of McCarthyism, when thousands of good Americans were publicly questioned about their politics under the fear of communism infiltrating American society. For years, people from all walks of life faced ridicule, ruin and shame, including those in the spotlight, politicians and actors, as Senator Joseph McCarthy doggedly pursued them with his witch-hunt tactics. Nothing much came of the public hearings other than destroying countless reputations. In parallel, the Mafia was building its franchises, step by step, murder by murder. The 1950s was also the time of the US Senate Special Committee to Investigate Organized Crime in Interstate Commerce to see if America had an organised crime problem. Millions of dollars were allocated to this mammoth inquiry, and thirty million people watched in their lounge rooms as hundreds of wannabes, mobsters and law enforcement professionals were interrogated on live television. In the end, the committee concluded:

> There is a crime syndicate branched out across the country. There is a mysterious criminal organisation under the name of 'Mafia' so fantastic that most Americans find it hard to believe, the public office corruption has reached a level never seen before and, finally, the infiltration of criminals into legitimate business has reached alarming proportions.[10]

A lot of money wasted for such an obvious outcome. Fascinatingly, during the hearing the committee was told of the term *capo di tutti capi*, no doubt a reference to Sicily, to Ernesto Marasà, or the copying of his title for American use.

As the findings started to resonate with the public, a Mafia commission meeting was held in the town of Apalachin, about 300 kilometres from New York City, at the 20-hectare property of Mafia boss Joe Barbara, another Calabrian. The get-together had a number of purposes, including the fortunes being made in Cuba, the fast-growing heroin markets, and to finally ratify Vito Genovese as the overall Grand Poohbah of the American Mafia, the *capo di tutti capi*. Thugs as far away as Cuba and Italy were in attendance. Seventy-one voting mobsters were seated, their fat fingers wrapped around glasses of cheap wine, waiting to raise their hands, while Vito straightened the knot in his tie in preparation for his acceptance speech. Then the police arrived, acting on the well-founded suspicion of patrolman Edgar Croswell of the New York State Police. Noticing sixty-three luxury cars scattered about the property, he thought something was not quite right.[11]

While the worst US Mafia heads in the world fled on foot across muddy fields – some falling over, most too slow to get away – others claimed to be visiting their sick friend Joe. The FBI heard of it second hand, later. Finally, after years of denial J. Edgar Hoover – the director of the FBI – was forced to admit that America indeed had a Mafia problem.

One that would not go away easily.

Vito Genovese would, however, go away. In 1959, he was convicted of breaking federal narcotics laws and sentenced to fifteen years' imprisonment. As luck would have it, Joe Valachi was also doing time in the same cell block. Up until that time Valachi was a nobody; he never really elevated himself above the gun-for-hire level. And he was paranoid. So much so that he killed an inmate, believing he was about to be killed himself, and received a fatter sentence, one that would ensure his death within the confines of concrete walls. It was then that he brokered a tell-all deal with federal police and became a rare *pentito*, snitch, causing the media to go wild with Mafia stories. What followed should have been described as the end of the halcyon days of the US Mafia, as mobsters scrambled to cover their tracks and alibi themselves, waiting for a sledgehammer to hit their front door and a search warrant team of cops and agents to run through the sanctity of their cosy oversized houses. But, in reality, nothing of real consequence happened. Law enforcement was still in the Dark Ages as far as keeping up with Italian organised crime. And Valachi? He lived in a government-funded safe house, smoking cigars and watching poorly made Hollywood movies about himself until he died.

CHAPTER 18
MINESTRONE SOUP

SICILIAN SAYING:

Soccu veni ni pigghiamu
You take what will come

Meaning, you accept your fate

It's always interesting to look over the family album and chart the progress of loved ones; then, once you get to the back page, there is a moment or two of reflection before you close the album.

It's the same for the five main Mafia families of New York. Like all families, they have a tree worth following over ninety seasons in the soil of America. As a young detective during the 1980s, I spent time in the United States on a work exchange program with the New York Police Department, as well as the Drug Enforcement Administration, studying the Mafia and the workings of their gangs. At the time, stories about the Mafia were daily front-page news. It seemed as though there was a bombing or *mafiosi* execution each week, such was the ferocity of the American Mafia wars.

To talk of the 'wars' is to make mention of the social decay that was swallowing up New York. For a ten-year period the Big Apple was rotten. It hovered over bankruptcy as City Hall struggled to pay the extraordinary wage bill for hospital, transport and emergency service personnel. Successive mayors were (mostly) ineffective, as social infrastructure fell away. Even police recruitment had stopped and fire and police veterans were laid off. It seemed cutting costs was the only way out of the mess, and criminals took advantage, which means the Mafia had a field day pushing their drugs and committing brazen crimes like long-haul truck hijacking, and union standovers. Police corruption was rife. So dire were circumstances that the city suffered a massive electrical black-out at the same time that sewage banked up to the doorways of businesses scratching for a living. And hills of garbage were stacked up at each intersection. Enter looting and rampant street prostitution. Drug-addicted twenty-dollar hookers plied their trade down unlit laneways, as pimps stood by to rip off the johns. Parts of the city were lost to crime; you could only guess at the escalating murder rate and the accompanying low clearance rate. This once gorgeous cosmopolitan city had become the ideal incubator for Mafia crime.

One story of a big shot who rose to fame only to come crashing down involved Henry Hill, a Brooklyn-born Irishman, who, as a kid, used to watch a clan of the Lucchese family from his bedroom window in his parents' upstairs apartment overlooking Euclid Avenue. Many years later, in April 1980, the adult Henry found himself in a detective's interview room in front of a tape recorder. He was under arrest, about to accept his fate. A special police unit were interested in a gang run by *capo* Paul Vario. His scam was fronted by a taxi and limo yard that gave legitimacy to prying eyes. Most Mafia clans have a string of businesses that come in handy to wash excess cash, or to cook the books in case tax investigators come snooping. Vario was a fine cook.

Vario was respected, and his returns into the Lucchese family were better than most; he could be considered their most lucrative *capo*. His main man, Jimmy Burke, stood over the day-to-day twists and turns and dealt out bashings or killings when required. As a family snapshot, the Vario clan is a good example of how Alfonso Capone saw the American Mafia: a collection of gangsters from any nationality who can work together for their greater good. Ethnicity was not the key to success, criminality was. Hill, being of Irish descent, proved that; he grew up to be a great crook. Jimmy Burke also reinforced Capone's theory; he was born to Irish parents in New York, nowhere near Palermo. He was suspected of killing upwards of forty fellow gangsters within the various Mafia circles. His reign was at the height of the Mafia wars in New York. Any *mafioso* with a mouth tended to keep it shut or suffer the wrath of Burke. Vario was third-generation Italian and eventually rose to the dizzy heights of the Lucchese family.

On that April day, two of New York's finest played a tape recording for Hill. The police had secretly recorded his partner in crime, Jimmy Burke, plotting to execute Hill. The 37-year-old Hill – who had washed Jimmy's taxis and polished Vario's limos as an eleven-year-old – had a decision to make, and there was really only one option: to become a snitch – *pentito* – and tell all on the Lucchese family in exchange for witness protection. Hill had a lot to offer, as the two smirking detectives opposite him knew. Hill nodded as they took the cellophane wrapper off a fresh box of cassette tapes, and the three of them got busy as Hill's jaw started working.

The life and times of Henry Hill are a bit like minestrone soup: lots of ingredients with various flavours. Many are spicy, others more subtle, and occasionally there is a juicy morsel floating around that makes you salivate. That could be a metaphor for all *mafiosi* clans globally, too. As the twentieth century matured, Mafia minestrone included violence, extortion, murder, mass drug dealing (importation and distribution), warehouse robbery, kidnapping for ransom, payroll robbery, illegal gambling rackets and, of course, the *pizzo*, always the favourite spice. Crime was everywhere and every crime had a Mafia ingredient in it.

And what of law enforcement? New York City's district attorneys and police faced dire circumstances in the 1980s. But to their credit – and due to the determination of a small parcel of honest, civic-minded attorneys and detectives – the tide was slowly turning.

Henry Hill – depicted by actor Ray Liotta in the Martin Scorsese film *Goodfellas* – gritted his teeth and started telling bad stories about bad men. From widespread cocaine trafficking across the east coast of America to the first intimate breakdown of the entire Lucchese family structure, to the role of each clan and the crimes they controlled. What the grinning cops wanted was the truth behind two of the biggest cold cases on their books. The first involved the theft of a small fortune in cash from an Air France cargo plane at JFK Airport in 1967. The second case, from 1978, was the theft of a box of jewellery and millions of dollars in cash from the strong room at the Lufthansa cargo hold, also at JFK Airport. The Irishman's tell-all confessions would decimate the Vario arm of the Lucchese family and send most of its members to prison (including Burke), if they weren't internally executed first, that is. Hill lived out the rest of his life in witness protection until his death in 2012. Clearly, Henry Hill hadn't heard of Ernesto Marasà and his *omertà* rule of silence.

The so-called Godfather of the Gambino crime family, John Gotti, knew to respect the code of *omertà*. He was old-school Mafia in the new world of crime in America, and though he never ratted on people, he made the mistake of talking about himself a lot. In his office, in his car, in the street, he wouldn't shut up. He bragged about his exploits to his *capi* and henchmen, while being secretly recorded by the FBI. With an ego the size of the Empire State Building, Gotti only had two subjects he liked to discuss: the massive fortune he'd made through crime and how clever he was. His own mouth was his downfall.

I saw that a lot when I was undercover with the Mafia. Italians born into poverty, who, when they finally got some greenbacks in their wallet, were all big-time talk from then on. It was as if they needed to gloat, to tell anyone and everyone how much money they had and how clever they were.

Growing up in Queens, New York City, the short man with the chip on his shoulder chased crime as a teenager. As the 1960s moved to the beat of the Beatles, John Gotti – known as 'Dapper John', for his stylish dress sense – rocked to his songbook of scams, mostly standovers and narcotics. His pet racket was theft from trucks, as white goods became the consumer items of choice in American households. Everyone wanted a new refrigerator, washing machine or hi-fidelity stereo to listen to the Rolling Stones. His dominance over small-time crime rackets when in his teens caught the eye of Mafia bosses like the mongrel killer and head of the Gambino family, Albert Anastasia, and Joseph Massino of the Bonanno family. Gotti learnt quickly that admiration from New York crime bosses and offering them respect was a fast way to the top. He perfected his sleaze moves accordingly and was soon nominated to be a *capo*. He also educated himself on the other attribute needed to get ahead in the American version of the Mafia: murder within the organisation, learning to kill those who got in his way. As he climbed the ladder, he ordered the demise of many, until he ran out of opposition in 1985. He then became the boss of the Gambino family, ushering in a new dawn of Italian organised crime.

Gotti, more than anyone else, lifted the stakes of the Mafia during that time. What the public saw was grainy black-and-white photos of car bombs, gangsters' bodies, police mug shots, and burly cops marching overweight thugs out of plush houses in good neighbourhoods. Gotti, on the other hand, with his coloured ties and tailored suits, would branch out into commercial construction, adding it to his portfolio of extortion; in time, no one could build a skyscraper in Manhattan unless they first paid off Gotti, whose wealth was becoming as big as the high-rises he approved.[1] Overnight, Dapper John became an instant celebrity, and the paparazzi followed his every move. With fame came an even better tailor, an attentive hairdresser and an Italian cobbler. Enter Teflon Don, the man on whom no police department could make a criminal charge stick. His influence on the jury system was legendary, as trial after trial failed to convict a man more popular than Ronald Reagan.

Then came the FBI tapes and Gotti talking about his exploits. His mouth was big enough to fit both his feet, and among other things he spoke badly of his loyal henchman, Sammy Gravano. A thug who had killed a dozen times for him. Nothing but a 'mad dog killer', Gotti said. He also said Sammy had to go, get whacked. Sammy heard the tapes, and, at first, didn't believe what Gotti had said. The federal agents persisted. Sammy sat silent, listening to the unmistakable voice of Dapper John, and, like Henry Hill, he too forgot all about *omertà*. Sammy's only concern was to broker a good deal for himself with the cops. Again, in went a fresh cassette tape, and out came Sammy's sordid stories. Arguably the hardest tough guy in the modern-era American Mafia, he told all, including his involvement in nineteen murders. His evidence ended the careers of thirty-six thugs and murderers, including the big one: Dapper John Gotti.

The Teflon Don's run as the boss of the most profitable Mafia family in all America lasted seven years until his arrest. The hundreds of secret tapes that captured him boasting about how many men he had had killed – including blowing up the car of a fellow *mafioso* – was his undoing. Ironically, he died of throat cancer in prison in 2002. The director of the FBI at the time of Gotti's conviction, standing in a New York bar full of cops, was heard to say: 'The Teflon is gone. The Don is covered in Velcro, all the charges have stuck!' Bravo to law enforcement and perseverance, I say.

Gotti died wearing prison calico clothing to replace his cashmere suits and $2000 patent leather shoes. The Gambino family and its tribe all ended up in jail or dead, and the paparazzi went off to chase something or someone else.

While Mafia bosses from America struggled to obey *omertà*, there was one boss, Vincent Gigante – who became head of the Genovese family – who held out. Vincent had the usual Mafia pedigree: he was born poor and grew up poorer on the Lower East Side of Manhattan to immigrants from Naples. He was a big guy with a talent for boxing that kept him off the streets until the lure of money put him back there. With a few rated fights he was capable of doling out a thrashing. His then-boss, Vito Genovese, grabbed him as his driver. In time, he got the nickname 'The Chin' due to his oversized chin, and how it could take a punch. By the time he was twenty-five, he had the ideal CV for a mobster, having been charged with stealing, gambling offences and arson, as well as carrying a handgun. Punching his way into trouble and police squad rooms was also an attribute.

At the time of the Mafia wars, Vito was in strife with the high-flying Frank Costello, who was boss of the Luciano family. The tension was mounting as they both wanted the top job. As a remedy, Genovese called in the fearless Gigante to end Costello's run. The Chin lay in wait at The Majestic apartment building, where Costello lived. As Costello ambled inside late one night, Gigante fired a shot, but did not kill him. It was a monumental stuff-up, one that would see many deaths, two sides go to war, and end the career of some of New York's hardest men. As for The Chin, he would get over it, as Vito did, and tough it out. By taking a shot at the boss of a family – 'making his bones' – Gigante became the number one son to the mobster who finally changed the name of the Luciano family to Genovese. Naming rights are everything in Italian organised crime. However, the cops moved in and charged The Chin with attempted murder, despite Costello never incriminating him; he was a very rare aficionado of *omertà*, believing what comes around goes around. Costello would wait for his revenge.

The Chin was acquitted of attempted murder, and the pieces on the chessboard started to move sideways. Then, oddly, Costello opted for retirement and took his fortune, along with his misfortune of the attempted murder, and trotted off into the sunset. A strange end to a brilliant career. This left the Genovese family to run drugs across America, and the family changed their *modus operandi* overnight. Long enough for the Feds to get on to it, and to have both The Chin and his boss jailed for drug offences.

The Chin got early release in 1966 and was given the role of *capo* to the family while Vito Genovese's jail time ticked over (he died in jail in 1969). Gigante moved Genovese's Mafia operation to a swanky office in Greenwich Village. I have walked the streets he operated in and was surprised at the elegance of the neighbourhood; it was high-end fashions alongside low-grade thuggery. Gigante vowed never to go back to jail or let the FBI get the better of him again. He had become the boss of the family, and needed to come up with a more cunning way to survive, as by the early 1980s the joint FBI and NYPD task force on Mafia was becoming embedded with smart cops. The Chin let loose the most clever deception in Mafia history: in front of the FBI surveillance cameras watching his every move, he played the insane ticket. For years he pretended to be crazy, incoherent, unpredictable and unstable – and fooled everyone. At first light, he would walk to his office along the sidewalk, wearing his pyjamas and slippers, talking madly to himself and waving his arms, until he arrived at the end of the street. The very picture of an unbalanced man. Then, behind closed doors, he dressed in his $3000 woollen suit and tie and went about running his crime empire, in a strict, hard-nosed environment. With locals wondering what had happened to their high-rent village.

His motive? He figured the courts would never convict an insane man for a crime, and he was right. He had the authorities fooled, and the public scared of the big thug shuffling the streets. For two decades, his 'insane defence' worked in court; newspapers laughed at the cops and made a suburban curiosity out of the boss of the Genovese crime family.

The curtain finally fell on The Chin's 'crazy' scam – a performance worthy of an Academy Award – after 30 years. In 1992 after three decades of shuffling around, dribbling and looking blurry-eyed, the pressure became too much. Too many of his family and friends were under a dogged investigation by the FBI, which wanted to expose Vinnie's nutso routine. Too many faced the possibility of serious jail time for offering false evidence on the sanity or insanity of their relative or boss. So, The Chin walked back into court, abandoned his defence of insanity and copped his sentence on the chin.

For all the millions The Chin made – including, at one point, from being a king of extortion in the construction industry – he suffered at the hands of yet another Mafia honcho – another *capo* who ignored *omertà*. With nowhere to run but a jail cell, Vinnie 'The Chin' Gigante was locked away to serve a twelve-year sentence. He died of heart disease in 2005, but he is remembered in the Mafia family album like a goofy uncle, one who always fooled around. A brilliant and successful mobster, with a touch of real cunning.

There would be no such theatrics for Carmine 'The Snake' Persico, who found himself sitting in a jail cell in 1987, staring at his calendar and working out his parole date. He had 136 years to serve. The Snake was the sort of mobster that TV shows nominate as one of the worst killers in Mafia history. How many did he kill? The exact number went with him to his grave, though Persico is thought to have disposed of twelve of his 'brothers', despite looking like a bookkeeper. In fact, his father was a legal stenographer from Brooklyn, and Persico should have been the son who went to Harvard; he had the genes, but from the age of seventeen he was rotten. His rackets, as he moved through the Mafia ranks, included union scams, loansharking, and anything else he could make a greenback from.

He would see the changing of the guard in the Profaci family, due to Mafia wars in the 1970s, the killing of many of his associates, and the reshuffling of the decks. The Profaci clan came to be known as the Colombo family, the baby of the five families of the New York Mafia, and some say the weakest family with rackets in the Big Apple.

The reason for the Colombo family slump was simple: Persico was a supremo *pentito*, he ratted them out. Another example of how a gold-plated tough guy failed the *omertà* exam. He sold out seventy of his colleagues to save himself and his son, all along climbing the ladder until he got to be the boss. Once he had full control, he didn't realise that he had lost the respect of his *capi* and soldiers. They too took the easy way out; ten of them ratted on their brothers as well. The entire Colombo family was a nest of rodents. They were either killing each other or talking to the Feds about – as the Mafia say – who was up who, and who was paying rent. They were so vicious they even plotted with John Gotti (the boss of the Gambino family) to execute the lead prosecutor for the office of the District Attorney, Rudy Giuliani, who was heading a team of investigators and lawyers smashing their way through the America Mafia.

Even though Carmine sat in prison until his death in 2019, he didn't let go of the reins; he ran his crime family from inside, to the detriment of his crew, who all fell to successful FBI prosecutions. The Snake was not only a mad killer and a power-hungry *mafioso*, he was also a fool unto himself, holding on until he went to Hell.

If the *Guinness Book of Records* had an entry for the longest prison sentence, it would probably be for Anthony 'Gaspipe' Casso, who made killing an art form through the 1980s. He ended up facing down 455 years and was still ticking them off when he died in December 2020. Born into the Mafia in 1942, though not from Italy, he was another son of Brooklyn. His career saw him quietly kill as many as thirty-six people, mostly colleagues. As detectives might say in the sanctity of their muster room, crooks killing other crooks is not necessarily a bad thing. Cynical prosecutors might be heard to say: 'What's the offence?' Either way, Gaspipe learnt well. His father was a tough guy too and sorted out his rivals with a length of cast-iron gas pipe – like father, like son. After once trying to kill John Gotti, Casso rose to be underboss of the Lucchese family, but not before putting his stamp on the American Mafia. He teamed up with Victor Amuso, and the two of them were known for their dependability at killing off mob rivals. For years, they plagued air freight companies and unions, as well as construction sites, making a fortune. The mobster with the matinee looks, Gaspipe was rolling in money by the time promotion arrived at the age of forty-five. Due to his propensity for violence, Casso was the one who others stayed shy of. The one who tough guys watched out of the corner of their eye, should he walk into the barroom. As they should have, not so much for his killing skill but for his failure to abide by *omertà*. He ended up being one of the most feared snitches in US crime history; his evidence sent a cattle yard of criminals to prison.

The last in the photo album is the Bonanno family, a warring, infighting team of thugs who got their invitation to be one of the five families when they ran with the legendary Lucky Luciano and Frank Costello and Luciano killed off Salvatore Maranzano, the boss of his own family. This allowed Joseph Bonanno to fill the empty chair and put his name to the family. Indeed, the Bonanno family, as a mix of thugs, goes as far back as the end of the nineteenth century when the Mafia were more about traditions than wholesale killing. Later in life, they became so unruly, mostly due to their internal squabbling, that they were expelled from the American Mafia commission. The catalyst for their demise was how they allowed an undercover cop into their ranks: the bravest of them all, FBI agent Joe Pistone, aka Donnie Brasco, the cop who was played by Johnny Depp (appearing alongside Al Pacino) in the movie that told of his infiltration of the family. Interestingly, they slowly clawed their way back and in the 1990s became the most lucrative of the five families. Until a lack of understanding on the rule of *omertà* saw them giving evidence against each other again.

While *mafiosi* have proven themselves as killing experts, few are good at administration. Their human resources skills need a shake-up; there are few Mafia figures who have done well at motivating or inspiring their team or efficiently managing the day-to-day chores of thuggery. The Bonanno family, however, might just be the biggest failure in this area too. Often running around more in fear of each other than the police, they would get into shootouts over internal feuds, and the death count climbed in the late 1970s. It was during this run of misman- agement that Donnie Brasco saw an opening. And that's exactly what infiltration work is, finding a way into the maze. During my undercover career I set great store by the past success of Donnie. I learnt much about how he achieved something that no other cop on earth had done, up until that point. I would learn that, if supported, infiltration into crime gangs can bear the best results. However, today, law enforcement commissioners fail to have the patience for such stealth. It is worth drawing the parallels between Donnie's infiltration and my own.

•

Donnie was a natural to covert work, it came somewhat easier for him due to his upbringing as a guy who could handle himself on the mean streets of New Jersey. I, coming from a dirt-poor family from Struggle Town in Melbourne, saw crime first-hand from the circle my father and uncle – both drunken thieves – moved in. Donnie married his life partner and they had three children, while I perfected the art form of failed marriages but maintained a very close relationship with my only child, a daughter. Donnie and I both wanted to make a difference, and in that, we both wanted to take that giant step further and try infiltrating. We acutely understood the differences between infiltration and undercover. The former being a dedicated study into the mindset of our targets, using a methodology that involves taking years to embed oneself, through hundreds of baby steps. It's the trick of the light, the sleight of hand of undercover work, whereby the target is oblivious of being infiltrated until sometime later, perhaps even a year, he realises that he has a new close friend. One he can't recall cultivating. Donnie spent fifty-seven months ingratiating himself, as he plied his extraordinary skills and gathered his evidence, against one thug, then another. I spent thirty-seven months, and again, like my mentor, I moved from one Mafia family – chasing evidence of conspiracies and drugs – to another, where bombs, police murder and manufacturing drugs were my motivations.

Before we both put our respective toes in the Mafia water, Donnie spent months perfecting his cover story, that of a dodgy jewel thief – the ideal lure, as bad men are attracted to bling. I chose art, only because I knew my subject well and art lent itself to my cover story of laundering dirty money through my art gallery. Like me, Donnie jumped on the back of his highest-ranked *mafioso*, riding him up the ladder until he got where he wanted to go. But that requires total dedication, which means disappearing from family life and sacrificing the niceties of marriage. And it means a lot of drinking and socialising and more. We both broke rules and found dark moods inside empty booze bottles, and questioned much about the organisation we worked for. Donnie spent seventeen years with the FBI; I spent eighteen years inside my police department.

The height of our success was around our fortieth birthdays, proving that age is an advantage if you want to infiltrate the Mob. You don't see many twenty-somethings in the upper echelons of the Mafia!

Both of us were told to end our investigations prematurely, when both of us were adamant that we should keep going, as we knew such methodology may never be accepted again, by the cops or the bad guys. (It hasn't been; long-term infiltrations are now a thing of the past.) We both clashed with our hierarchies, believing them to be lacking in empathy, and neither of us received any accolade worthy of our effort. Our bosses were all promoted on the basis of our achievements; we were not. Donnie would spend years giving evidence, long after quitting the FBI. Likewise, I was still giving key evidence in 2021, in a Mafia murder trial, after it took twenty years for the case to find a courtroom. Neither of us received remuneration for any of this.

Donnie's principal targets received fifteen years' imprisonment, while mine received thirteen years on a plea bargain. We also shared the discomfort of years of overt and veiled death threats. I slept for ten years with a sawn-off shotgun under my pillow, until satisfied the threat was gone. I cannot speak for Donnie. The highest-ranked *mafioso* that Donnie befriended was shot dead for introducing a cop into the fold. Likewise, my Mafia boss, who was shot dead for the very same reason. Both murders remain unsolved. Donnie and I have integrated back into our worlds very quietly, shunning public life until we were ready. We have both found catharsis by writing of our experiences, when government psychological support was not offered.

After Donnie had spent twelve months within the Bonanno family, he latched on to a *capo* in the crew and spent years working schemes with his chosen targets, who had their eyes on each other and Donnie's diamonds instead of being alert to the infiltration. Oddly, I was welcomed into the upper levels after eleven months, then came the offer of pure cocaine, and shifty business deals, the wire taps and so on. Once Donnie's targets were all locked away, one Mafia boss went on record to say that he bore no ill will towards him, that Donnie was only doing his job. Likewise, the head of my clan called me to his jail cell and said almost identical words.

Whoever was left, after Donnie ruined the Bonanno family, the Bonanno crew finished off themselves; many of them became *pentiti* and spoke to the FBI, sending their Mob family and friends to jail. I was less fortunate – none of my Mafia contacts opened their mouths, preferring to do their time. I guess it's the difference between *Cosa Nostra mafiosi* and *'Ndrangheta mafiosi*. While Donnie and I were a generation apart, it's clear we were on the same wavelength, and shared something unique that no bumbling police hierarchy can ever remove.

•

And so ended the Bonanno family and our brief look at the album of five families. While there are many other, lesser-known Mafia families in America, still active across the nation and just as dangerous, the progress, treachery and outcomes of the five New York families is representative of the contemporary Mafia in the United States.

Today, the collective American Mafia is a shadow of its former self, thanks to three factors: a now highly talented team of honest cops and clever prosecutors who do their best to stay united in the face of the complexities of law enforcement, with the help of the extraordinary law enacted in 1970, known as the RICO law, which allows police to group the many criminal activities of the Mafia together in order to defeat them. RICO allows prosecutors to put criminals before the court should they be involved in a cluster of criminality, an enterprise of crime. This allows for a higher sentence being given to the guilty party, the key to breaking the back of the Mafia. And, thirdly, the wonderful results that can be gained in funding the long-term infiltration of mobsters, using cops of the ilk and tenacity of Joe Pistone, the greatest covert of them all.

But, to me, what happened in the heady days of the American Mafia in the 1980s, which resulted in a partial decimation of Italian organised crime, indicates a diminished gene pool in Mafia ranks. Surely Ernesto Marasà's bones would be rattling around inside his weathered coffin, decades since he laid down his manifesto. A rule book that was given the royal assent by Lucky Luciano as the only way the American Mafia would do business.

It's fascinating to look at all those in the American Mafia who were murdered by their own brothers or were squealed on and sent to prison. Or who found safe haven as witnesses for the NYPD or FBI. Almost none were born in Naples, Calabria or Sicily. Most were born on the northeast coast of America, except for a sprinkling of other ethnicities: Jewish, Polish, Irish and others. It's an unsure organisation that tampers with its gene pool. No longer home to direct immigrants from the Mafia homelands, the five Mafia families of New York are at least two or three generations away from their Italian origins. A bunch of hybrids that would sell out their brothers for a get-out-of-jail-free card. Or shoot them dead in the street. None had the proven fibre their forebears developed over decades of tradition, going back to the days of a general in a red shirt.

Not forgetting, American-Italian Mafia men like cooking. A truism can be drawn from that. Italian cooking requires a deft touch, just the right amount of ingredients, not overdoing anything. Minestrone is the same; it needs good Trapani salt and a sprinkling of Messina pepper to lift the taste of the Palermo-grown celery, and spices from Naples, and a pinch of Calabrese chilli. As Italian diners know well, you cannot leave out a key ingredient from any recipe. Without it, the soup is mere stock, coloured water lacking substance, that certain *je ne sais quoi*. Ernesto Marasà's *omertà* is that key ingredient for a functioning Mafia crime family. The *capi* and bosses in the crime kitchens, from Miami to New York, Philadelphia to Los Vegas, Boston to New Orleans, didn't follow Marasà's recipe book, brought over from the homeland decades earlier. When the shit hit the fan most of them requested to get free of the heat from the kitchen, and told all, to save themselves. And the American public are better for it!

What happened to the five American Mafia families was not unexpected. It is hard to imagine the five families will ever see the halcyon days of Mafia crime again, à la Al Capone, Lucky Luciano and Frank Costello. Thank God for that!

CHAPTER 19
TRACTOR AND SHORTY

SICILIAN SAYING:

Panza e presenza
Belly and presence

Refers to the greedy ones who only want to take

As mentioned earlier, Corleone, in the interior of Sicily, houses the Anti-Mafia Museum. Run by students, the museum documents *mafiosi* stories told by a collection of grainy black-and-white photographs from (mostly) the 1970s. A great many of these pictures were taken by one very brave and talented woman, Letizia Battaglia, who has been using her camera lenses to chronicle the horrors of Mafia warfare. I have to admit to getting emotional at the raw, harrowing quality of her work: bodies lying in pools of blood, or bombed cars, the aftermath of murder. But it's the looks of dismay on the faces of passers-by that bring a tear.

The people of Corleone are tired of their town's reputation as the home of the Mafia, as depicted in the *Godfather* films, and of *Godfather* tragics expecting to see young Michael Corleone walking down the street. However, life eventually would imitate art; the town of Corleone did play a key role in the Mafia story after all. As an aside, locals will say the name of their town means 'heart of a lion', yet I have been told over and over during my research that it means 'seed of the fruit', which makes sound sense, once you read on.

In the 1980s, the Sicilian Mafia was at war with itself; blood was spilt on the streets and laneways across the island as the great realignment of the scourge went on for years. A new breed of ambitious *mafiosi* wanted to change the old ways, the manner in which the Mafia had been run since the reign of Ernesto Marasà. Here we go again, a touch of *déjà vu*. In typical Mafia fashion, bloodletting was as normal as a sunny day in Sicily.

The Mafia wars of that period were utter mayhem; the official death toll is said to be over a thousand people, mostly bad men. That's whitewash nonsense! I believe the real figure to be easily twice that amount, and so do others who study the Mafia. But, should we accept one thousand, then let's appreciate the magnitude of that number: it's thirty-five Palermo commuter buses, all full.

This was the time of Tractor and Shorty: the two maniacs who'd had a powerful grip over the Sicilian Mafia since the early 1970s. This period was known as the *Corleonesi* reign, because most of the killers originated from that town. Tractor and Shorty were two greedy thugs who wanted to take everything. Together they can claim a good number of the thousand-plus murders of their era, either directly or indirectly, by suggestion or design. While there is nothing good to say about either individual, their stories are fascinating. And for Francis Ford Coppola fans, they were both born and raised in Corleone.

As adolescents they were only casual friends. But in their senior years, they became close and jointly controlled the entire island. Shorty, being the outright boss until his arrest, was the smaller but nastier of the two. He dominated crime until his arrest in the 1990s, then handed over the reins to his partner, Tractor.

Who was worse? Who cares? That's my opinion. Both men devastated families, instilled fear in children and women, and forever changed the landscape of crime globally. Nothing that went on in the five New York Mafia crime families compared to the thuggery and bastardry of the Tractor and Shorty *Corleonesi* period. What it must have been like as a child, playing in the streets of Palermo to the sounds of gunshots, bombs and screams, is anyone's guess.

The mayhem of the Sicilian Mafia wars was – in the number of deaths and sheer bloodthirstiness – not dissimilar to the atrocities on the streets of Northern Ireland at the same time. The difference being, there seemed little official or police control in Sicily, as the body count climbed and pine forests were cut down to make coffins.

The first of the villains, Tractor, was born Bernardo Provenzano in 1933, around the time Ernesto Marasà was spreading his manifesto. As a young punk in dirt-poor Corleone, Provenzano idolised the Marasà boss and in the 1950s fell into cattle and livestock theft to fill his wallet. A leading Italian newspaper, *La Repubblica,* dubbed Tractor the ultimate *picciotto*. His colleagues recalled him as the man who could shoot like a god, yet he really shot like the devil. He was fierce, feral and sadistic.

An accomplice told the story of first meeting Provenzano as a young man. They worked side by side in the stinking putrefaction of a tannery's boning room, removing rotted flesh from cattle carcasses, before hoisting the skins into putrid bubbling vats to dissolve the remaining flesh before the skins went off to be made into gorgeous designer handbags. The vocation of hard men, or future Mafia murderers, perhaps. Their nine-to-five wouldn't last long, as the two wannabe gangsters soon dropped their knives and entered the world of crime, electing to kill humans instead of clean rancid livestock hides.

A fellow *mafioso* associate, let's call him Michael, told how Provenzano earned his nickname, which was given to him by Michael's brother. Provenzano really enjoyed ploughing down his victims. Wherever he went, he was like Attila: after he had arrived, killed and left, 'the grass would not grow back again'.[1] Corleone has a graveyard near the centre of town. I have been there and read through the names – many from the same families – of men who did not reach middle age, sad stories of lives cut short. Tractor put a good number in that graveyard over the years. It is impossible to know how many, despite the best efforts of many journalists and investigators. Why? The code of silence: *omertà*. While the American Mafia made a mockery of *omertà*, in Sicily it was still the key survival code. It was not a thing of honour, however, as it is depicted in the media or in movies. It was a thing of utter fear. A mandate that you either lived or died by. To break *omertà* was to call up your own death. A slow, macabre and agonising one, often at the hands of Tractor and his boning knife skills, or Shorty. And if the snitch who broke *omertà* ran, and the Mafia didn't find him, they – the Sicilian *Cosa Nostra*, the Calabrian *'Ndrangheta*, the Napolitano *Camorra* – would even the score by wiping out the entire family. The ways of Italy's Mafia were (and are) vastly different to those of their American cousins in the late 1980s, when tough guys clambered over each other to talk to prosecutors. There were no cashmere-wearing, coiffured and media-hungry John Gotti types in Italy.

According to another accomplice, Provenzano enjoyed standing over his victims with the barrel of his shotgun pressed onto their faces. Then, staring into their eyes, as their mouths went dry and their eyes widened, he would slowly pull the trigger and end the horror.[2] He would then quietly walk away. There have been few like him, thank God.

As his crimes escalated and his violence defined him, Provenzano decided to take up with Shorty – Salvatore 'Totò' Riina. A man whose legs were disproportionate to the rest of his body. Standing less than five feet, five inches tall, he was also nicknamed The Pony.

It is hard to see how this pony-sized thug got such a reputation; however, it is all about the handgun and a willingness to use it. (History is full of hard men who were small but had big guns.)

Shorty was thought to have killed, or ordered dead, hundreds. But his impact on crime globally and the actual number of people who ended up dead was far greater. While many he killed were either *mafiosi*, involved in crime, or Mafia fringe-dwellers who wronged someone along the way, there were exceptions: innocent citizens who suffered at the hand of this wretch. Whereas with Tractor, his sins were the killing of colleagues on his march for power.

Had Shorty and Tractor focused their mayhem only on the public, then perhaps they would have attracted the same reaction as the paramilitaries in Northern Ireland, with soldiers, helicopters and armoured vehicles breathing down their necks.

For Shorty, meeting his boyhood associate Tractor again during their formative crime years was the making of both men; they were so similar. Both were cold-blooded murderers, with a burning need for power; the difference was in how they wanted to run the Mafia.

At the mid-point of his crime career, Tractor took to the Mafia city of Bagheria, which was lawless and lacked effective administration.

He effortlessly became a part of this criminal world. All he wanted was to commit crime – the classic career criminal. Yet, as ruthless as he was, he was the first to take a step back, as opposed to stepping into a deadly situation. However, due to the world he lived in, deadly situations arose on a daily basis. Killing was his solution, not his mantra. It solved his problems but didn't become his problem.

Shorty, however, wanted to control it all, wanted to take on anyone. A classic small man with big ideas. He saw little benefit in the old-fashioned ways that oversaw Mafia activities. A system of control had been in vogue since Ernesto Marasà's days, and Shorty thought it was worth altering, so that he, along with Tractor, could run the entire shooting match. In an era of streamlined management practices, Shorty had hit on a good idea; however, I suspect it was more about greed, as opposed to wanting to micromanage the Mafia.

•

I saw the ilk of Shorty and Tractor, albeit not as violent – there are few in history as murderous – in my time when I was undercover in the Mafia. Plebeians from peasant stock (like myself) who shared an ethnicity and insatiable desire for betterment. Yet, the same men declined the hard work and dedication of honest toil, preferring to snatch what they wanted, when they wanted, so they could be princes in their own community. Men to whom killing came easily.

Desire can be a festering emotion that's hard to push aside, to suppress when you are on the wrong side of advantage, when your contemporaries wear Rolexes and live the high life in luxury apartments with a sunny balcony. I recall my number-two Mafia boss, whose dinner table I sat at dozens of times: he was the patriarch of a ruthless clan that killed and bribed police and built an empire from drugs and intimidation. The same thug thought himself a prince, strutting about, rushing from one conspiracy to another in his shiny red Porsche Carrera, wearing mismatched fashions and weighed down by gold bling. I wanted to whisper in his ear that he stood out like oversized dogs' balls, but he would have silenced me, forever. My point being, Mafia thugs ache to be seen, or at the very least – in the case of Shorty and Tractor – they ache to be respected. That's what drives them, haunts their self-esteem, sets them on a broken road to purgatory. Trouble is, they have no comprehension that the man or woman in the street can, at a passing glance, see right through them. They are that transparent.

As most detectives say in the sanctity of their muster room, *you can't turn shit into chocolate*. I am certain Shorty and his ruthless partner fell into that same category: dead-end vultures who took from everyone. And worked out very quickly that to obtain the power, baubles and notoriety they desired in life, was to walk a path carrying a gun, and to ruin as many lives as necessary along the way.

•

Tractor and Shorty eventually agreed on a management structure of five men, so as to have less internal fighting. (Until this point, each region had had many Mafia bosses, often bumping up against one another.) Naturally, two of them were Tractor and Shorty, who acted like shepherds watching over their flock. This structure annoyed the other bosses, as it upended what they knew. No thug wants to give up what he has killed and worked for, hence the Mafia wars, and so began the rise of Tractor and Shorty. It's one thing to have a grand plan; it's another to implement it. Riina and Provenzano decided to persevere and push their plans onto all and sundry, so they worked together.

They used their five-man team to get rid of their problems. For example, disguised in police uniforms, the five stormed an office building to kill the owner, who was also a heavyweight criminal who opposed their plan. The owner returned fire and there was a shootout. Undeterred, Provenzano felled four innocents with his Beretta 38, then went to walk out, job done. The gunfight, though, wasn't over; the main victim hadn't died, so – should Provenzano's accomplice be believed – Tractor emptied dozens of shots into the victim and hit him about the face with the butt of his weapon.[3]

With the victim now well and truly deceased, the invaders left, but not before carrying the dead weight of one of their own. One of their *nuovo* five management team had been killed in the melee. Provenzano and Riina burned their friend's body, instead of burying it, to hide the evidence from any police investigation. The ways of a new Mafia.

The two, Provenzano in particular, were like ghosts – rarely did they come out of hiding. To understand their level of rotten, it's a case of knitting together written accounts from the few associates they didn't kill. From the 1970s, Provenzano's story is unremarkable, except for the killings, mostly because he was rarely seen. He remained incognito for over four decades. When someone has such a powerful influence but is not around, it builds paranoia. Victims, police, prosecutors came to worry about a vendetta he might have towards them. Some were so in fear that the tales about him kept getting taller. Frightened folk labelled him an enigma, halfway between Attila the Hun and Hannibal the Cannibal; he was the most feared bogeyman in Italy. Whereas Riina remained slightly more visible, but still on the move in case of police. Only stopping long enough to kill or bark orders.

Even though Provenzano was a fugitive, he still met with crime associates, attended gang meetings, planned and committed offences, and even had a social life. Once his tasks were done, he disappeared again, sometimes for months, not seen, anywhere. I suspect the reasons for his not being caught were twofold. First, he had many contacts within the police department and mayoral office. He was known to be a close friend of the Corleone-born Mayor of Palermo, Vito Ciancimino, who walked the corridors of power for many years, and kept Riina and Provenzano in the know. Second, many from Palermo and its surrounds were petrified at what Provenzano might do to them, should he be flushed out of hiding. Best to let sleeping dogs lie.

His extraordinary cunning was surprising for other reasons. He left school at the age of ten. He could only scribble basic words and could barely read. Instead, he got his education from the school of hard knocks and in the back paddocks, and late at night while he learnt cattle rustling. Those back paddocks were his road map, as he went about his daily job of avoiding arrest. Known to have a network of shepherd's huts dotted across the island, Tractor may well have been just that: an innocuous tractor in the field, unnoticed by those passing by. Yet he married in that time and fathered two boys, who both grew up with an extraordinary sense of confidentiality. They never missed a beat, never told a school friend, the kids on the street, or nosy neighbours about their father, or where they visited him a few times a year. His wife, Saveria, was the epitome of devotion; she never strayed, sticking by her man, despite the world media labelling him a murdering monster. For a man so poorly educated, he obviously had a doctorate in street smarts, yet a misguided prison inmate openly called him a 'bird brain'.[4] Silly inmate!

On one occasion there were whispers of an important Mafia meeting in Palermo, late one night, where matters were to be sorted, and Provenzano, without warning, walked quietly into the meeting room, took a seat and contributed to the agenda. Or, more likely, bellowed his orders, which were never ignored, then calmly exited into the night, the ghost of Corleone. He would then go quiet, as if the tractor's engine had been turned off. By the 1980s, some thought he had moved on to hide elsewhere in Europe. In reality, anyone who offered an idea as to where he went was only guessing.

Provenzano's and Riina's great asset was *omertà*. While the American Mafia had trouble pronouncing the word, the Italians lived by it, and the life and times of these two killers is testament to the importance of keeping your mouth shut. Ernesto Marasà would have smiled. Indeed, Riina ramped up the *omertà* rule during his reign, declaring he would annihilate the entire family of anyone who ratted out the *Cosa Nostra*. Children were not an exemption to his threat.

Meanwhile, he got on with his *capo di tutti capi* role, running it all, literally. His whole life had been devoted to crime; since the age of nineteen, when he was locked away for murder, to be released six years later, he did nothing else. Riina led the realignment, while residents of Palermo, Corleone and Trapani woke to the morning death toll, as those who opposed his changes were disposed of.

Yet death wasn't exclusive to low-level *picciotti* or competing *capi*. Mafia bosses who didn't agree with Riina's or Provenzano's ideology were disposed of, as well as officials of the state; no one was spared. One such luminary was the President of the Sicilian government, Piersanti Mattarella, who came from one of the island's most respected families. His agenda in government was clear: to halt Mafia-owned or affiliated companies from gaining lucrative public works contracts, sources of regular income for the gangsters back in the 1980s, and onwards.

Mattarella wanted to develop a policy of radical moral renewal for all of Sicily, which flew in the face of Shorty and Tractor and their cohorts. The answer was simple: the maverick politician was followed as he walked out of his Via della Libertà apartment to get to his car, to drive his family to Sunday church service, and gunned down. So ended the life of a politician who was described by investigating Judge Giancarlo Caselli as 'an honest and courageous Christian Democrat killed just because he was honest and courageous'. The insult that hovers well above the atrocity of his death – captured in black and white by photographer Letizia Battaglia – was that the execution was done in front of his wife and children, who were following Mattarella, dressed in their Sunday best. As a postscript, Mattarella's younger brother, Sergio, was so shocked by the senseless killing that a few years later he ran for parliament himself, on an anti-Mafia ticket. Today, forty years later, Sergio is President of the Republic of Italy, and a stalwart against the Mafia.

Not long after this killing came the appointment of an investigative judge to focus on all things Mafia in Palermo, Giovanni Falcone. In particular, Falcone examined the maze of criminality behind Totò Riina and Bernardo Provenzano and their broader gang.

In effect, Falcone took on the job no one else wanted, because it came with a certainty of death, so many previous investigating officials having been assassinated in their attempts to slow the Mafia train. Falcone, however, achieved early and extraordinary results. He was the first judge to follow the money, a now well-used method of closing in on the principal players in organised crime. He was also the first to talk openly with law enforcement in other countries, particularly in America, Canada, Australia, Germany and France. Sharing information is the only way to attack international crime syndicates. Falcone was so ahead of his time that he proved that the major European heroin manufacturing and distribution ring that once operated in Marseille, France, had shifted to Sicily. The French Connection had become the Pizza Connection.

By 1982, Falcone was the brains behind a massive prosecutorial attack on the Mafia, heading the biggest investigative task force ever seen in Italy. It was the Pizza Connection that woke politicians up, showing crime, particularly between America and Italy, was worth billions, and the sophistication of the international trade in heroin and cocaine was beyond the scope of Italian law enforcement. Times were a-changing! And joining Falcone was his trusted colleague Judge Paolo Borsellino, two modernists in law enforcement. They became inseparable.

It is worth mentioning the role of the investigative judge in Italy. Most Western countries would be unfamiliar with the power invested in an Italian judge. Part prosecutors, part public advocates, most of all Italian judges are elite detectives, unravelling the complexities of organised crime. They go anywhere, do what's needed and demand answers, in a judicial system that has my envy. They are the key to stopping the Mafia. Nothing in Australia, the UK or United States is as effective.

Falcone believed in a much-needed draft law to make it a serious offence to engage in an act of conspiracy with the Mafia. It was the initiative of politician Pio La Torre, who got his start in politics in Corleone, the same town that bred Shorty and Tractor. The bill bore some traces of what Cesare Mori had attempted, sixty years earlier, using the term 'an associate of the Mafia'. However, the La Torre legislation was safer, well drafted and was, in effect, like the RICO legislation in the United States, which enabled prosecutors and detectives to construct a case against Mafia clans and crush them. The draft law also allowed for the confiscation of property owned by the Mafia, in the event of a successful linkage to crime. Again, following the money was the key.

The national shock and anger at the almost daily bombings and slaughter on the streets enabled La Torre to grab his chance. He pushed the law through the Senate, and suddenly the game against the Cosa Nostra was more evenly pegged. But, as the game between killers and prosecutors intensified, so did Riina, who started to use the Mafia as his personal bloodletting machine. Idle threats, or the traditional Sicilian stare were not part of Riina's manner; he just killed. To aid his thirst for revenge, he enlisted the help of his confidant, Giuseppe Calò. Calò was a good choice: once a Mafia boss, he needed to avoid any trials that might flare up due to the work of people like Falcone and

La Torre. Plus, Calò was an equal to Riina, insofar as he, too, would kill at will. Riina put him to work as he gathered together his revenge gang, who set upon the broader community of Italy. His first target, Pio La Torre. The truly brave politician would go the way of many who challenged the Mafia after his law was passed through parliament. While seated in his car with his bodyguard, in the narrow streets of Palermo on a busy morning, a coward's gun – commissioned by Riina and arranged by Calò – took the life of the dedicated politician. All because of his determination to eradicate the scourge from his island.

Anticipating further strongarm revenge, Rome dispatched General Carlo Alberto dalla Chiesa to Sicily in 1982 to take on the role of Prefect, as head cop, to shut down Riina and Provenzano. Dalla Chiesa had an impressive career from within the Carabinieri tackling serious terrorism, namely the militant Red Brigades, and now – with his new position – he had one aim: to destroy Riina and his *mafiosi* connections (another touch of *déjà vu*, circa 1920s). His public image – he was somewhat of a hero – ensured he would be successful, and the general was more than qualified. Trouble was, he was not supplied with a bulletproof vehicle, nor a security convoy; indeed, all he got was a small secondhand family car.[5]

Soon after moving to Palermo, the general, his wife, Emanuela, and his lone bodyguard were driving along a quiet street when a swarm of motorbikes surrounded their small car, forcing it off the road as the bikers turned into assassins, killing Carlo, his wife and the bodyguard – executed, Mafia style. And, somewhere out in the backblocks of Palermo, Riina sucked in another breath and got back to his gang.

One who was also starting to get nervous was arguably Sicily's most travelled Mafia boss, Tommaso Buscetta, who was staring at the wrath of Shorty. Riina was not getting through to Buscetta, who showed no sign of relinquishing control of his clan, or the purse strings to his riches. And their stalemate was drawing to a close.

Buscetta was the most powerful Mafia honcho in Palermo, with connections around the globe. He was a key part of the Pizza Connection, into New York City. But he was in the way of Riina's takeover plans. Don Tommaso, with his good looks and worldly sophistication – he did business in America, and throughout South

America – was truly international as opposed to his two opposites from the back paddocks of Corleone, Riina and Provenzano, who only ever saw him as an adversary, a man to eliminate. They were too clouded in their judgement to realise that Tommaso was someone they should have embraced. He could have grown Riina and Provenzano's Mafia business internationally.

Don Tommaso, the Mafia pin-up boy, was well liked, the perfect front man for the new Mafia. Trouble was, he disagreed with Riina's ideas and they became enemies. And to be an enemy of Totò Riina was to always be watching over your shoulder. So Tommaso took off to São Paulo, Brazil, where he had fallen madly in love, years earlier, with Cristina, a twenty-year-old Brazilian, who was two decades his junior. As Buscetta had left behind his kids and a wife in Palermo, he intended to flip-flop between the Americas and Sicily. His Mafia business was growing fast – the FBI named him the Godfather of Two Worlds: the Americas and Sicily – and he enjoyed extraordinary profits from scams in New York City, Miami, Canada, São Paulo and Rio de Janeiro.[6]

While Buscetta was cooling his heels, a *mafioso* friend dropped in to try and convince Buscetta to return to Palermo and put a stop to Riina and Provenzano's takeover. He declined, not wanting to be part of a war. His friend went back to Palermo to tell a monumental lie, which spread through the laneways, bars, brothels and cash rooms of the Mafia: that Buscetta was about to return to Sicily to kill Riina. Shorty went into a spin.

Buscetta wasn't home when Riina's men came calling in Palermo.

Before daybreak, Riina's thugs had tortured Tommaso's two teenage sons, murdered them, dismembered their bodies and dissolved their remains in an acid bath. Then left.

Hearing of the atrocities 10 000 kilometres away, Buscetta fell to his knees with remorse and became inconsolable. The message that was behind the killings was simple: Riina was his superior, and Buscetta was now both a Mafia internal fugitive and a marked man, as was his remaining family. It was said that he was unable to communicate with anyone, only Cristina.[7]

Days later, Riina's thugs ran through a pizza shop owned by Buscetta's brother-in-law – carrying handguns. They murdered him, as well as two of Buscetta's nephews as they stood making pizzas. Buscetta's daughter, sitting at the cash register, was spared; she was left as the sole witness of the horror. Left to tell the bloody sordid facts to Buscetta, as Riina wanted his message passed on in all its gory detail. Two days later, Buscetta's cleanskin brother, Vincenzo, a 63-year-old glass fabricator, was paid a visit. He was shot in the face as he sat at his office desk, killed instantly. As he lay dead on the floor, his son raced to his aid and was killed for his efforts.

Each killing further shook the foundations of the Godfather of Two Worlds, until one day he collapsed, ruined by grief. Daily, he picked up the international newspapers to read about his family being annihilated, while he was stuck in Brazil, unable to retaliate. At this point, he questioned the phenomenon of the Mafia and its very existence.[8]

He was locked in his silence, in the deepest of thought on the notion of *omertà*, the duty to remain silent – the only religion in the Sicilian Mafia world. Tommaso kept thinking, kept wrestling with it, thinking back to when he had taken the oath of *omertà* sixteen years earlier.

While trying to make sense of it all, he and Cristina drove his two younger children, now living in Brazil, to school. As they stopped for breakfast at a roadside cafe, the Brazilian authorities were standing behind them, waiting to arrest him. The Brazilians were not going to allow a Sicilian Mafia feud to become a global spectacle. They marched Buscetta off to prison on a trumped-up charge, as the world media converged on São Paulo. The images of a man without hope bounced around the globe as the biggest arrest in criminal history, anywhere, played out.

Little did the aggrieved man know his life would keep changing, in a manner he would never have thought possible. Buscetta was caged in an isolated concrete cell with just his dark memories, and the sound of a clock on the corridor wall, *tick, tick.*

Flying into the airport on a jumbo jet was one Judge Giovanni Falcone, who wanted a sit-down with the devastated *mafioso*.[9] He saw merit in stepping aside from his politically charged prosecutors' office in Sicily to take a side trip to Brazil, to speak to a man with too much on his mind.

The two Sicilians talked, and talked some more. Before long the judge and the crime boss agreed that an extradition to Sicily was Buscetta's only option. Buscetta would face drug charges. However, an odd bond formed between the prosecutor and the criminal, and Buscetta allowed their chat to continue. Waiting in the wings, however, was a team of high-ranking detectives from the FBI, as well as the US Drug Enforcement Administration. They, too, wanted the Mafia honcho, so they joined the queue, biding their time as Falcone kept consoling his opposite number, as hundreds of international journalists competed for a whisper of news.

It didn't take long for the Americans to see there was an instant rapport between Falcone and Buscetta. Both were from Palermo, of similar age, with calm natures, and lovers of Sicilian food and culture. The McDonald's and Coca-Cola culture didn't cut it for the Mafia boss. He knew he had to avenge the death of his family, and to go somewhere, so Sicily it was. He just didn't know how to kill off Riina.

Buscetta was remanded in custody on charges of drug trafficking. A ruse to hold him. Sitting alone in his cell that night, the ticking clock got louder, as he reviewed the demise of almost his entire family.

With his life looking finished, the 'black dog' took hold, and he attempted to kill himself with smuggled strychnine poison. A trip to hospital saved him. As he opened his eyes, strapped to his hospital bed, he saw the kindly face of Judge Falcone, standing nearby in his cheap suit. It was the Mafia boss's epiphany. At that point, he took up Judge Falcone's offer to tell all and become the most important *pentito* in the world of crime. (Tommaso's impact on Mafia crime eclipsed snitch Joe Valachi's, from two decades earlier, by a factor of fifty.) And, all of a sudden, the deafening sound of the ticking clock stopped.

What followed would change the Mafia for all time. In going against the code of *omertà*, Tommaso not only broke it, he smashed it, shattered it and tossed it over the prison fence, into the ether. The two men of different honours formed a bond that would last for years. One that would put them on the same path, a series of trials to bring down the cancer that had permeated the world. And the one target for Buscetta in his redemptive move was none other than Shorty Riina. Buscetta was the man who killed *omertà* in Italy.

Falcone secured Buscetta's release, and the jumbo jet left the Brazilian tarmac.

The two, and an entourage of dozens of security men, arrived in Rome in July 1984 to spend the next five months, each and every day, sitting together in a haze of cigarette smoke to amass a monumental testimonial document.[10] Some reports state the document – outlining hundreds of murders and implicating as many men, as well as detailing the entire criminal background and business dealings of the contemporary Mafia – was thousands of pages long. I have visited the strong room in the town of Corleone that houses the actual document, and inspected the testimony of Buscetta; it is massive, a feat by any measure.

In the TV documentary *Our Godfather* made some years later, in which Cristina cooperated fully with the producers, Buscetta is heard to say his statement was over 400 pages – the largest evidence by a single *mafioso* ever.

Both men, *mafioso* and lawman, were aided by Falcone's most trusted colleague, Judge Paolo Borsellino, and a vast team of the bravest police and prosecutors. Then came the investigators' own form of *omertà* as the team locked themselves away and worked feverishly to organise the evidence. For the next year the Anti Shorty and Tractor task force kept at it, building their mountain of evidence, as Buscetta sat alongside them chain-smoking.

Riina, still out there in hiding, kept the pressure on, and created an act of barbarism in an attempt to scare Buscetta from giving his evidence.

Riina arranged for his henchman Calò to install a massive bomb on the Naples to Milan train in December 1984. It blew a carriage off the tracks, killing sixteen innocents as well as maiming 267 others. It almost worked, as fear ran through parliament and the nation.

It is at this juncture that any normal person might ask the simple question: *where are the cops?* How can these atrocities keep happening? Why is there only a handful of heroes working to catch these killers? It's a question with a simple answer: pay packets. Up until this point, police pay packets were small, compared to what they should have been. I recall my graduation salary, two years before General Chiesa and his wife were executed, less than $15 000 a year. A cop in the NYPD would have been on a similar pittance and someone in Sicily would have been on half that. Pay peanuts and you get monkeys or corruption, and the Mafia.

Amazingly, despite all of Europe being dazed from the horrors that unfolded in Italy, Giovanni Falcone, Paolo Borsellino and their ally Buscetta worked on, seemingly undeterred by the war zone that was now their workplace. For all the efforts of Riina, he could only stay in hiding; his terror would not break Falcone.

By 1986, the evidence against the Sicilian Mafia was overwhelming. It was time to convene a court hearing. The state decided, after encouragement from the pool of prosecutors, to run one massive trial, which would fast become known as the 'Maxi Trial'. To manage the monumental task required a president of the trial – a senior judge – capable of managing the biggest criminal hearing undertaken in Italy, unlike anything since the days of Cesare Mori under Fascism. However, this time around the credentials of the participants were above reproach. Trouble was, no judge seemed to want to take on the role. Twelve declined it, all citing reasons that precluded them from officiating over Falcone and Borsellino's evidence. The legal fraternity was running scared. But not Judge Alfonso Giordano, a 54-year-old veteran of the courts who stepped up to the daunting challenge, alongside his number two, associate judge Pietro Grasso.

In the end, in Palermo alone, 195 arrest warrants were issued. Tough guys were seen running in any direction as they were picked off the dark streets. The two names on top of the pile of warrants were none other than Shorty and Tractor, still missing in action. Undeterred, the plan was simple: Italian law allows for a defendant to be tried *in absentia*, should he fail to surrender. Officially, Riina and Provenzano awaited trial, along with hundreds more. For the first time in Sicilian history, the tables had turned on the *Cosa Nostra* and the bewildered folk of Sicily started to believe in good, instead of evil. Totò Riina, however, was avoiding the spotlight, and Bernardo Provenzano was possibly in Sweden, or Switzerland, or someplace else; again, it was a mere guess.

Judges Falcone and Borsellino kept the pressure up. They were glued to prosecutions for over seven years and countless court cases as Buscetta couldn't shut up. Wouldn't shut up. His reason for telling everything? 'I'm just a tired man who recognizes that all that I once believed in is no more. I want to tell of what I know of this cancer that is the Mafia.' The code of silence was shown to be a sham. The stuff of little boys, inventing silly rules as part of a secret club, all trying to play tough, each trying to outdo each other. *Omertà* was finally buried, laid to rest in July 1984, for all time.

Riina could feel his world caving in. He was rumoured to have run from one fire to the next, trying to keep his band of criminals in line and authorities at bay. The little tough guy had spent years wanting absolute power over his brand of Mafia, and now the authorities and legislators were shadowing him, getting closer to shutting him down. The desire to clean up the Mafia mess became – at last – a national obsession.

Riina reacted by upping the ante. He tried once more to destabilise Buscetta by executing his brother-in-law, a move he felt certain would stop Buscetta and remind him of the sacrament of *omertà*. But, for Buscetta, that door was bolted shut. He suffered his grief, and the murder of another family member only spurred him on.

In fact, he volunteered to visit American courthouses to give evidence against the Mafia thugs he had dealt with over the decades, including the upper echelon of the New York crime families. Nothing Riina did stopped this now-obsessed supergrass. In giving evidence, Buscetta gave prosecutors the meaning of the codes used by Mafia on telephone calls and at meetings – conversations that were recorded by the FBI. Unravelling terms such as 'white shirts' (cocaine), 'chocolate' (money) and so on. A criminal dictionary of more than one hundred coded phrases, now defined. Enough to convince many juries to convict a great many American Mafia honchos.

During this time, it was rumoured that Riina had befriended the Prime Minister of Italy, Giulio Andreotti. They were seen to shake hands before having private discussions. Such a public display of closeness is hard to fathom; it highlights an odd behaviour for a prime minister, to keep company with (by then) one of the worst human beings in modern-day Europe. Much media attention has rightfully focused on this, but in my world of facts, I am uncertain of the veracity of any criminal alignment. Nonetheless, Riina was well connected. Despite his upper-class connections, a purpose-built courthouse awaited him in Palermo, as police set about looking for him. As they would for the next seven years. Meanwhile, Judges Falcone and Borsellino worked on – rolling up their sleeves, loosening their ties and snapping their red braces.

To the panel of judges at his court hearing, which included the now weary presiding head judge Alfonso Giordano, came the 475 accused criminals who stood angrily and listened as Buscetta said: 'I no longer feel part of the organisation I once belonged to. Since the 1970s this organisation known as the *Cosa Nostra* has subverted its ideals. Law-abiding people may have considered them dirty but to us members their [ideals] were once beautiful.' It was all becoming past tense for the *Cosa Nostra*.

Buscetta made it clear that the Mafia itself was responsible for the erosion of its own set of ideals. Its members had become, through men like Provenzano and Riina, killers above all else. They were light years away from the ideals developed and nurtured by the traditional *mafiosi* born in the halcyon days of Garibaldi's *picciotti*.

In among this riot of testimonies, killings and officialdom, Buscetta developed another layer of skin. He too got tougher with every atrocity. He too loosened his tie, snapped his red braces and never went silent again. A rarity for a true-blooded *mafioso* from Sicily. Buscetta no longer had a reason to remain silent, because he was in custody, and safe, as were Cristina and his remaining children. Besides, Riina and Provenzano had already killed off the rest of his family, at least eight of them, so there was no longer anything to fear. And, as *omertà* had ceased to be a religion to Buscetta, there was revenge to be had on the little tough man with too many guns and too many mad friends, hiding out there, somewhere.

CHAPTER **20**

KINGS AND QUEENS

SICILIAN SAYING:

Talìa cu c'é

Look who's here (surprise)

Used when you haven't seen somebody for a long time

It had been another round of fruitless talks in Rome for Judge Giovanni Falcone, another week of banging the table, trying to get the government to tighten laws and broaden their anti-Mafia stance. He didn't care much for the shift in his work, having been in his ministry job since his trial days ended. He preferred the pressure of his seat on the bench, that is, his rickety, torn-leather chair in his office at the end of the corridor, away from the fanfare of politics. But, as a realist, he knew his courtroom fighting days were over; his worth was now in Rome, lobbying for greater powers to keep the Mafia at bay.

On an early summer's day in May 1992, he was on another well-worn leather seat, in his Fiat Croma, his armoured escort car. The car that picked him up at the Palermo airport each time he commuted from his Rome apartment for his week of ministry work. He had travelled many kilometres in that Fiat over the years, over 10 000 escorted trips. At last, he was almost home, just the airport freeway until he was at his apartment front door. His world had become small. Divided between home, his car and his office and, if he was lucky, the occasional meal in a restaurant, where his five-man security team ate alongside him. The life of a judge who had prosecuted hundreds of Mafia over the previous seven years; he had forgotten how many court cases and appeals. Maybe a thousand. Although he always recalled the exact number of acquittals: 114 in all, due to either lack of evidence or the vein of corruption he faced in his courtrooms.

As he sat in his air-conditioned Fiat, with the love of his life – wife Francesca Morvillo – close by him, he soaked up the calm, and reflected on the Mafia wars that almost destroyed his country. He recalled his executed friend, fellow judge Rosario Livatino, who had worked tirelessly in the Agrigento region prosecuting Mafia. Rosario openly refused to have a security detail around him, nor a driver or armoured car, only to be set upon by a fleet of killers on motorcycles who sprayed the lone judge with countless rounds as he travelled to his courthouse. Now, two years later, Giovanni was safe in his usual convoy, surrounded by firepower. Only this day the weary judge did something unusual: he chose to drive the car himself, to enjoy a sense of normality, of freedom, and to take in the harsh beauty of the Sicilian landscape, up front, while his driver enjoyed the privilege of being chauffeured.[1]

There was always a special allure in coming home. The two Palermitans missed their style of cooking and the smell of the ocean along the weekly airport drive. Falcone was born in the oldest part of Palermo, the struggle streets of The Kalsa, and loved to swim the seaside waters of the little town of Capaci, just to his left, off the freeway. A village that sat beside beautiful turquoise waters that lapped burnt-orange rocks, a village where the scourge had taken hold for more than half a century. Growing up in Palermo with a constant sense of illegality and fear drove Falcone to become a judge, a vision from his days studying law at Palermo University. It was the reason he became a law student; law was his escape hatch, his exit from The Kalsa.

As he drove and kept in the centre of the three-car convoy, he reminisced about his student days, when he was a chubby-faced kid with a perpetual smile and a poor excuse for a moustache. He felt ambition returning to his tired 53-year-old body, dressed in a suit that should have found a rag bag by now. It was just a uniform for one half of the famed team that had prosecuted the Maxi Trial a few years earlier. Falcone and Borsellino, etched in legal history, presided over the prosecution of 475 gangsters. The trial that Riina and Provenzano failed to appear at was held inside a vast space, part of a prison. The fugitive murderers at the centre of the prosecution – who hadn't been seen for years – were still out there somewhere, killing. So many accused men, so many death threats, and so many cheap suits. Falcone longed for a glass of his favoured Nero d'Avola wine, and to sit and watch Francesca tossing a pasta. Ten minutes to go, then home.

At the end of the Maxi Trial and most of its concluding statements the world sat up and finally took notice: for once in the life cycle of the Sicilian Mafia there had been a monumental victory. And Falcone and Borsellino and all their staff were supported by jail sentences passed down by the president of the court, Judge Giordano, aided by Judge Grasso. Legally, it was perfect, despite the two ghosts of Corleone killing anyone who posed a threat during the proceedings. Legend has it that Falcone and Borsellino had not exchanged one harsh word between them, testament to their brotherhood.

One of the accused faced sixty-four counts of murder. Another – Giuseppe Calò – for the bombing of the Naples to Milan train and murder of church-going politician Piersanti Mattarella, was sent away for the rest of his life by Judge Giordano. Another hitman confessed to being paid a mere 300 euros a month to murder Riina's victims after first torturing them, then dissolving them in acid. So little for such heartache. Falcone wondered about the madness within Sicily that is Mafia. Atrocity after barbarity, until the newspapers stopped their coverage as people could no longer stomach the horrors. By the end, Falcone and Borsellino were more like auctioneers, hearing judges Giordano and Grasso slamming down their gavels, and the hollering, 'Are you all, are we all, done? All finished? Yes, over!'

Falcone's most treasured memory was of *pentito* Tommaso Buscetta giving evidence of the inner workings of the Mafia, his insights into how *mafiosi* hid their money, and which corrupt police, prosecutors and officials were in bed with the scourge. Falcone knew he wouldn't see anything like it again: three inseparable, committed men – the informer and the informed working for the first time in Italian criminal history to tell the truth, the whole truth and nothing but the Sicilian truth. A total of 2665 years of imprisonment was handed out before their court days were finally over. To place this group achievement in global context, nothing has come near it for its extraordinary assault on organised crime, anywhere. It is legendary.

Did Falcone feel older than his fifty-three years? The 8607-page legal document he and Borsellino had stacked up against the Mafia would make anyone feel aged and weary. Lingering in his mind, however, was Shorty Riina, the little tough guy, ultimately convicted *in absentia* and given twenty-three life sentences. At an impromptu press conference, Falcone said: 'My country has not yet grasped what has happened. This is something historic; this result has shattered the myth that the Mafia cannot be punished.' He and Borsellino had crushed the outside shell of the Mafia.

He was almost home to his glass of vino. Eyes on the freeway, he noticed a number of innocuous roadwork bollards ahead as the front escort car – blue lights strobing – eased off the throttle and slowed down, to navigate the obstruction, at the exit sign to seaside Capaci.

Collectively, the three-car Fiat convoy reduced their speed further. More roadworks. A constant feature on any freeway in Sicily. Giovanni followed the lead and zig-zagged past the bollards. As the front Fiat sped up, so did Falcone, who quickly glanced to his left to the *azzura* blue waters he had swum in as a student. Then he caught the eye of Francesca, his reason for working so hard. She, a fellow judge, admired her husband, but was not naive about his desire to make a difference. The Fiat convoy straightened up then accelerated, as the sun fell behind the rocky massif, introducing dusk and the end of another day.

Boom!

An explosion of massive proportions lifted the tarmac and everything within a twenty-metre radius into the sky. Two of the three Fiats became airborne in deafening slow motion. Falcone's Fiat took the brunt of the blast: 600 kilograms of TNT explosives masquerading as roadworks shook the earth for kilometres, detonated by a coward, hidden behind a concrete structure on the massif side of the road a short stroll away.

Within seconds, the scene looked like something out of Beirut in the same year. Then the twisted wreckage, the bloodied carnage, crashed to earth and started to burn.

By the close of day, Falcone, Francesca and three of their brave bodyguards – a woman and two men – were pronounced dead on hospital gurneys. Victims of the never-ending horror. Falcone's police driver, sitting in the boss's seat, survived.

Riina watched it by way of repeat news stories, on a broken-down TV, while pulling a plastic cork from a bottle of cheap champagne to toast his victory, sharing the celebration with a gang of illiterate thugs, who may well have wondered what on earth they had just done.[2] As Riina brooded over them, one, Santino Di Matteo is said to have uttered this comment about Riina: 'This cuckold will be the ruin of us all.'[3]

Within minutes the news flashed in every coffee shop, bar, street and laneway of every town and city in Italy. Borsellino, for security reasons, was one of the first to be given a formal briefing on the assassination of his dear friend and colleague. He recalled the warning by Tommaso Buscetta: the *Cosa Nostra* will try and destroy the judges physically and professionally. While devastated at the loss of his colleague, Borsellino upgraded his own security; he was now swarmed by bodyguards, weaponry and worry.

Researching inside one of the archives in Palermo, I struck up a rapport with one of the curators, and she gave me a copy of Judge Falcone's personal diary and his running sheet for the daily duties of his security detail, all eighty-eight names. The curator felt privileged to have the documents in her safekeeping. I felt honoured that she shared them.

The running sheet shows the handwriting of Judge Falcone as he selected his team for the convoy on that fateful afternoon. A cross was marked against the individuals chosen. (The judge was known to select his team at the last minute to stop the route being leaked.) Someone, possibly the supervisor of the team, had gently scratched out three names and written 'R.I.P 23/05/92'.[4] To read his diary was achingly sad, a revealing insight into the busy man's life in the lead-up to his death.

Upon a moment of reflection, Paolo Borsellino also recalled the assassination of another work colleague, Judge Rocco Chinnici, nine years earlier, who was blown to smithereens by a car bomb. Again, the work of Riina and his henchmen. The real tragedy in the execution of Judge Chinnici was that he would never see his invention come to fruition; the judge had created the anti-Mafia pool of judges. Indeed, he became a king-maker, recruiting the brave, like judges Falcone and Borsellino.

Cars laden with explosives were now a speciality of the *Cosa Nostra,* and would remain so, from Italy to Australia to America. The murders of Falcone and his wife Francesca, however, were a giant step closer to all-out urban terrorism.

Only a year before Falcone was killed, yet another judge had been chased down and killed, seemingly part of the job description of prosecutors taking on the Mafia. In 1991 alone – the year before the assassination of Falcone – there had been 679 Sicilian Mafia killings. The murder of the Falcones would be the boiling point of a brewing anger that was threatening to overwhelm Italy. The capture or killing of Riina and Provenzano was well overdue.

Soon after the wreckage and bodies were removed, and global sympathies had fallen to a hush, Paolo Borsellino stood and straightened his tired back. He had just stubbed out one of his forty cigarettes for his day. He was known for his handsome face and chain-smoking. He looked into the moist eyes of those gathered in the church, hundreds waiting to hear his words fall from his lips. Words for his friend. Near choking, he said:

> Falcone believed that the fight against the Mafia was the first problem that has to be solved in our beautiful and wretched land. But that fight could not just be a detached, repressive undertaking; it also had to be a cultural, moral and even religious movement. Everyone had to be involved and everyone had to get used to how beautiful the fresh smell of freedom is when compared to the stench of moral compromise, of indifference – of living alongside the Mafia, and therefore being complicit with it. Nobody has lost the right, or rather the sacrosanct duty, to carry on the fight. Falcone may be dead in the flesh, but he is

alive in spirit. If our consciences have not already awoken, then
they must awake. Hope has been given life by his sacrifice, by
his woman's sacrifice, by his bodyguards' sacrifice. They died
for all of us, the unjust.

It was said that Judge Borsellino cut the image of a lonely king, his
champion, Falcone, gone. He struggled with the hope that he spoke
of in the poignant words he offered to the congregation. A eulogy of
harrowing Sicilian sarcasm, underscored by loss:

> There are many dickheads: dickheads who dream of emptying
> the Mediterranean with a bucket . . . those who dream of
> melting the glaciers of the Pole with a match . . . but today,
> ladies and gentlemen, in this very expensive mahogany coffin,
> there is the biggest dickhead of all . . . one who had dreamed
> of nothing less than defeating the Mafia by applying the law.[5]

Not long after, Borsellino left Palermo to visit Rome. Again, I was
offered a copy of his diary for that time, and he marked 7 July 1992
as his arrival in the capital. As was often the case, he was on a secret
mission to visit a witness, this time the young, extraordinarily brave
Rita Atria, who wanted to give evidence against the Mafia. She was
just a seventeen-year-old kid, who was forced to become a wise woman,
as she readied herself to embrace the role of *pentito* and snitch on her
Mafia family. Six years earlier she had seen her father, a useless cattle
thief and Mafia tough guy, murdered. Soon after, her older brother
was standing inside his pizzeria with his wife, Piera Aiello, when he
too was shot in the face, killed.

These deaths were just a sprinkling of what Rita and Piera had seen
all their lives; indeed, as a teenager, Piera had been told who and when
she would marry: the son of a Mafia boss. Days after her miserable
wedding, gangland murders unfolded. Their home town was in the
midst of a gang war and a realignment of power. The only 'romance'
in Piera's marriage was having forced sex with her husband, until
someone killed him.

Huddled together during this period of bloodshed, Rita and her
petrified sister-in-law went on the run, escaping the Mafia stronghold

village on the southeast of the island. Exhausted by their escape, they both fell into the caring arms of Borsellino, who hid the star witnesses, promising them safety. Promising security. This relationship was the saviour for both women; at long last they were able to trust an adult male. Borsellino split the girls up; Rita went to Rome, hence his need to visit her.

Despite the deep sorrow the judge felt, he kept his appointment with Rita, secreted away in a sixth-floor apartment with a security door. All Rita wanted to do was remove the scourge from her life, so she sat, waiting nervously, for her day in court, and her judge's visit. She adored the 'uncle' persona of her judge.

Honest to the bone, Borsellino listed his meagre expenses for accommodation and modest amounts for food and refreshments in his diary.[6] After their meeting, it was time to take his return flight to Punta Raisi Airport, Sicily. Inside his diary, Borsellino drew a tiny sketch of a two-winged aircraft above the word 'Punta Raisi'. He then jotted 'Bellevie' – the name of his summer house outside Palermo where he spent time with his family.

Borsellino had a newspaper clipping tucked away inside his diary that caught my eye. It was the story of a fellow investigative judge, Luigi Russo, who stated that the Mafia asking for *pizzo* – extortion – was not a crime.[7] The case centred around a businessman who bravely refused to pay the *pizzo*. Ludicrously, Judge Russo highlighted examples of other business owners being stood over and said it was understandable that they paid the *pizzo* when the Mafia came calling! Borsellino had marked up his quotes and written notes alongside.

In context it was clear Borsellino was annoyed with Russo and his lenient approach to extortion. Was he wanting to challenge Russo as a soft judge? We will never know. Soon after the court case, the businessman was murdered by the Mafia, who then went on to their next target, their *pizzo* tactics seemingly acquiesced to by Judge Russo. To me, Judge Russo's words are repugnant.

Once back in Sicily, Borsellino went to his Bellevie for a break. On 19 July, he returned to Palermo. His security detail weaved its way through the outskirts of Palermo, towards his mother's house. The afternoon was well advanced, and the heat hung heavy; Borsellino's shirt stuck to his back. Double parked, he stepped out of his armoured car, stubbed out his cigarette and . . . *boom!* Another massive explosion. Another almighty car bomb. And another Fiat sedan jammed full of explosives, blowing the judge and all around him into next week.

Apart from Borsellino, his five bodyguards were also murdered, and twelve neighbourhood cars were reduced to blackened scrap metal. It was the same bombmaker at work, the same close associate of Riina delivering the same vendetta.

Palermo residents erupted.

What Riina never anticipated was the rage of the people from the street. Mobsters never do. They are too busy stuffing riches into their pockets and killing to think about popular sentiment and the impact of their crimes.

Televisions across Palermo and Italy broadcast images of angry people and vivid footage of death. Wild street scenes of locals demanding an end to violence resulted. Not only because two judges had been murdered, but because five ordinary cops in the security details had been sacrificed, killed in the name of a vendetta.

The common folk were no longer buying into it. The five were part of suburban Palermo, men and women who experienced the daily issues and struggles of regular citizens. Cops with kids, school fees, mortgages, and the omnipresent stresses of surviving on meagre wages at a time when fear dominated their lives. That the Mafia could blow up, kill and maim anyone on its march for vengeance was now, suddenly, intolerable. The anger turned to riots, which shook the foundations of parliament in Palermo and Rome. As the voice of the people only got louder and more unwavering, forty million Italians tuned their televisions on to station Mafia Central, Palermo city, and watched all the gore in colour.

As the media kept spreading the bad news, protestors kept walking the streets and boulevards demanding an end to the Mafia. All politicians could do was to peep from behind windows in offices that had their doors bolted shut in fear of more bombs. Then came the spirit of the common person. Women from poor suburbs pulled in the bedsheets they usually pegged out to dry across the laneways. They then took to the streets, raising the sheets skywards, demanding change as they walked the maze of alleyways. Wives and mothers who had remained dutiful and silent for decades had had enough of the horrors and violence. They chanted for the end of the madness, the end of the Mafia. Their collective protests shocked and inspired Sicily, and the global media reported it all.

But how did this women-led movement start? Who birthed it?

Just hours after the massacre of Judge Falcone and his wife and staff, one tenacious woman, Marta Cimino, stepped out of the shadows and into the men's domain – the streets – needing to do something, anything.[8] With a group of friends, she decided it was time to let their dissent be heard. As one of the co-founders of the now famed 'Bedsheets Committee', university professor Giovanna Fiume, explains, the bedsheets hanging from the balconies of the houses showed that, 'I live right here, my name is on the bell, and I'm not on your side. Don't count on me. I belong to another Palermo.'[9] Fiume adds:

> We tried to invent a symbol. The bedsheet that the newspapers always reported as stained with blood of the lifeless bodies – a veil to the decomposition of a violent death – was now washed and bleached and hung on the balconies of our houses. Palermo is known for the bedsheets adorning our narrow laneways, a signal of cleanliness, a striking self-denunciation inside the most at-risk areas of the city.[10]

When I interviewed the professor, she recalled a time she had sat with Judge Falcone. They were alone in his office, the door was closed and his large desk was covered in cash seized from the Mafia.[11] Falcone had drawn the short straw to count the cash (an exhibit) for the court. She was there to interview the man she so respected and midway through their chat he needed a toilet break, leaving Giovanna in charge of millions. It was the longest ten minutes of her professional career, and when the judge returned, he asked if she was okay; she seemed anxious. Giovanna explained that she had never been with such money, to which Falcone instantly corrected her: 'You have never been with such dirty money.' The emphasis was on the word dirty, as they went on with the interview and the count. She also asked, in reference to the fight against the Mafia, if he felt 'alone'. He answered in the negative, that 'I am with young judges who are engaged with me'. And that was possibly the key to his success, a new young front was attacking the Mafia from all directions. Professor Fiume also recalled a comment by Falcone that he was at odds with Sicilian academics' approach to the Mafia.[12] He challenged their narrative whenever he could. He referred to fellow professors in Fiume's broader world, whose works were widely published. In short, Falcone disagreed with some of the academic thinking on his island. (I agree with Falcone – academics have too big a role in unravelling crime and its origins. And some can claim ownership on history. I was a practitioner, inside and around the Mafia for decades, as was Giovanni Falcone. We came face to face with the scourge, in our different capacities. Our perceptions would, naturally, be vastly different to those who spend their careers in classrooms.)

The Bedsheets Committee was about ordinary people speaking to ordinary people and asking them to take responsibility; even those who could do very little had to do something. The movement, in various incarnations, has kept growing ever since.

Giovanna Saladino, once journalist for the now defunct newspaper *L'Ora* and Marta Cimino's mother, describes the object that would become the symbol of dissent:

> The white bedsheet, an intimate object that presides over birth, sex, death, so mundane, is loaded with other symbols, it marks the will to expose and recognize oneself. Those bedsheets were our answer to the Mafia and said: 'We don't belong to these bloodthirsty, blood-stained, uncivilized bloodsuckers.'[13]

In this way, the testimonies of every woman in Palermo who had scalded her bare hands washing bedsheets now represented the need to shake the indifferent ones – those who looked the other way, remaining silent – into a movement against Mafia crime. The committee members got on their phones and lobbied a vast network of women. Within three days of the killing, the committee managed to encourage once-fearful housewives to hang their sheets on their balconies with slogans such as 'Don't count me in!' and 'No more Mafia'.[14]

In the beginning, the balconies of apartments owned by the well-to-do folk along Via della Libertà kept their linen indoors. The gentry were afraid to join the movement. But change was coming. Within a week, Palermo was flapping under the gusts of white cotton.

However, there was still resistance. The Archbishop of Palermo, Cardinal Pappalardo, was asked to sound the church bells exactly one month after the massacre of Judge Falcone, his wife and staff, but he chose to keep them silent.[15] Eventually, due to lobbying by women, the bells of all fifty-three of Palermo's churches would ring in remembrance of the dead. Not since the crazed days of Garibaldi, when all church bells clanged, had the noise of change rung so loudly in Palermo. They kept the pressure up, the Bedsheets Committee, instigating a hunger strike in Piazza Castelnuovo to demand the removal of those responsible for the insufficient protection of Judge Borsellino. The strike lasted weeks and ensured Piazza Castelnuovo became a landmark for the resistance against the Mafia. It remains so today.

The media, by contrast, were as quiet as a church mouse about the emerging movement. That is, until a fundraiser was set up to pay for commercials to be broadcast on national television. Within a week, all of Sicily had embraced the sentiment, including politicians and, most importantly, Italian women.

Within a month, the Bedsheets Committee had managed their most ambitious task: to string together a human chain. They held hands as they marched the streets, starting from the Palace of Justice and finishing at the former home of Giovanni and Francesca Falcone. All along the streets, their signature bedsheets hung from the balconies, adorned with anti-Mafia sentiments. That human chain became a symbol for so many who had suffered decades of intimidation.[16]

At last, the streets belonged to the citizens again, thanks to a league of women – the queens of the bedsheets – who brought about change in a world of bad men. Women across Italy joined in, carrying bedsheets and telling nervous politicians what they wanted, what they expected. The message was clear: women were not putting down their linen for anyone! Italian democracy, finally, at work.

The summer of 1992 brought many small yet significant changes in civil consciousness, and women were the protagonists of this uniquely powerful revolution, a manifesto for an extraordinary anti-Mafia movement, which has grown, year by year.

Broader initiatives of the movement include teaching school children about the shame of the Mafia and educating in ways to avoid crime. In a short time the queens of Palermo achieved more than most men, who'd wasted decades fighting the Mafia or taking their penny.

But the gains achieved by the Bedsheets Committee must be balanced against the utter sadness that also prevailed at that time. Horror stories really. Best told by the story of Rita Atria, the seventeen-year-old hidden away in Rome. A week after the assassination of Paolo Borsellino, the brave young *pentito* the judge had visited days earlier sat totally alone inside her apartment. She was lost. She adored her compassionate judge and all the encouragement he had offered. Her week had been a dark shade of nightmare as she thought of nothing but the death of a good man. Saddened by the assassination of Borsellino, she penned a note in her diary: 'Borsellino, you died for what you believed in, but without you I am dead.'[17] Then she closed her diary and jumped to her death from the sixth-floor window of her apartment.

And her sister-in-law Piera Aiello was so grief stricken she walked into a convent with her young daughter, locked the doors and stayed.

CHAPTER 21

HELL ARRIVED

By the start of the new year – 1993 – the achievements of the Bedsheets Committee were impressive. Legislators were racing around the corridors of power drafting innovative laws, and prosecutors had an extra spring in their step as, possibly for the first time in its chequered history, the country seemed united. Or at least on the same path of reform.

The assassination of the two judges was both the high and low point, of the Mafia in Italy. The scourge could never have orchestrated a more shocking assault on society; however, that same society bit back – like a cowering canine that's been kicked once too often.

As if Saint Nicholas was gifting an entire nation, and all of central Europe, one massive *Natale* present came the way of prosecutors. Thanks to pressure by the women of Sicily, law enforcement upped its resources, making extra funds available to capture Riina and Provenzano. A massive surveillance effort blanketed Sicily. Everyone knew the Corleone ghosts were out there somewhere, hiding after the attack on justice.

Miraculously, in January, the monster Totò 'Shorty' Riina was followed into a maze of back streets in Palermo. A police surveillance crew saw an opportunity and used their covert cars and nondescript motorcycles to follow behind, careful not to overuse their police radios. Riina was known to listen in on police activities with his scanner. Each city block, set of traffic lights, slow truck and pedestrian crossing gave Riina a chance to slow down, stop, glance around, check his rear-view mirror and run his counter-surveillance moves to ensure he wasn't being followed. Then off he'd go again, into the labyrinth.

The dogs – as surveillance cops are called – waited patiently for their chance to pounce. They could smell a victory, and felt a massive pressure not to lose Shorty again. At one point, due to a festive crowd on the streets, the team of dogs lost sight of their target, up ahead somewhere, around the corner, over there, hopefully. Then came the break many had waited decades for – it was as if Moses had cast his hand over the Red Sea of traffic, and the cars parted from the roadway, and the cobblestones became clear. Just Riina's car up ahead; they had an uninterrupted run at him. Then he pulled to the side of the street, as if he was looking for a shop, and the little man with a killer reputation stepped out.

Coming from all sides the posse of dogs and detectives descended on the lone car and a brazen mass murderer. No one was going to allow Europe's most wanted man to get away!

Riina was finally under arrest, and, just as quickly, rushed away to maximum security to face a wall of judges and police, each with a folder of facts to put to the Ghost of Corleone. The churches of Palermo did not ring their bells that day, as they had for Falcone and Borsellino. Instead, the common folk of the back streets and laneways of the bruised city, who had suffered so much from the death march of Totò Riina, rang their urban bells – thousands of car horns tooted in celebration well into the night.

One embarrassing fact about the final days of Riina was hushed up straight after his arrest, to hide red faces. Apparently the most dangerous man in the history of the Mafia had been living in a luxurious gated community in Palermo all along.[1] And, for reasons that defy transparency, his house went unsearched for more than two days.

Regardless, for all the post-arrest excitement, police had no idea of the plan Riina had put in place should he be arrested. The year before, he had galvanised a small but powerful team of killers, the same team who had planted the TNT that destroyed Falcone and Borsellino, and who vowed to deliver urban terrorism to all of Italy. First choice on Riina's list of madmen was Leoluca Bagarella, his trusted brother-in-law. Bagarella had the provenance of murdering a journalist and assassinating the Chief of the Police Flying Squad, Giorgio Giuliano, more than a decade earlier. Giuliano was the top cop of his era, having kick-started the famous Pizza Connection investigation after stumbling over a suitcase crammed full of US currency at the Palermo airport, wrapped in pizza shop aprons, hence the name given to the task force. The investigation would forever link the NYC Gambino Mafia family to their home-bred cousins. Bagarella's brazen killing showed he had no respect for police nor freedom of speech.

Then came Salvatore Cancemi, who had amassed a fortune in cash over many years. He too happily went along with the elaborate bomb-making strategy that had slaughtered Falcone, his wife and guards. And he was aching for more of the same. Next was Santino Di Matteo, who, as a principal player in the Capaci bombing, was the man who lugged the TNT to the freeway and gave the signal to detonate.

Also finding a place on the list was Giovanni Brusca. A butcher by trade, he was known as 'the swine', mostly due to his putrid body odour and the way he lived, in huts and hovels. His speciality, along with his brother, was to make smart work of his victims with his cleavers and boning knives.

There were over twenty killers in Riina's vendetta gang of terrorists. Suffice to say, prosecutors had a hard time trying to piece together connections – the nexus between one crime and another – their job made even more difficult by the fact that most of the gang lived separately, in hiding, and police had no idea where to look. (And before 1993, I believe some police were too afraid to look.)

Then came the terror, designed to deter future prosecutions. Their strategy was simple: urban terrorism, in the same fashion as Christmas nine years earlier when they blew up the Naples to Milan train. In May, the famed Uffizi Gallery, on Via dei Georgofili in beautiful Florence, suffered an almighty explosion. A Fiat full of TNT was detonated, destroying and damaging many priceless artworks, as well as killing five people, including (shockingly) a child and a two-month-old baby. Rome would not be spared, either: over the next four months, four car bombs ripped through the ancient streets, killing and maiming. The imperial city was tasting urban warfare with an unseen enemy, and the anti-Mafia police headquarters was in overdrive.

In July, another Fiat car bomb killed five at the Gallery of Modern Art in Milan. Even the Olympic Stadium in Rome was targeted. As football fans left the ground, the detonator for a bomb that would have killed hundreds malfunctioned, and the crowd was spared. The leaning tower of Pisa, only a few degrees off tumbling, had 200 kilos of plastic explosives earmarked for its toppling, only to be discovered by the investigative skills of the anti-Mafia team, who neutralised the threat. And on it went, under the directive of Riina and command of his brother-in-law; they chose to wage war on the country first, so as to mould the peace afterwards. Then, by the end of the year, all went silent. Perhaps Bagarella's madmen ran out of dynamite, perhaps they realised that the Italian spirit – after 3000 years of adversity – would never be broken.

Yet for every bomb there was another march of the Bedsheets – *brava* to the queens, *brava*! As the women stirred, so did the police and prosecutors, who took up the fight and worked at creating *pentiti*, snitches to help stop the mayhem.

Joining the fight came the youngest ever investigative judge to the anti-Mafia pool, 28-year-old Alfonso Sabella, a native Sicilian who knew the cultural nuances. He carried one asset into the fight that few had: he was a protégé of Judge Falcone, and hoped one day to emulate his hero. He also carried a bitter-sweet personal memory of Falcone. Both men chain-smoked Dunhill cigarettes, of which Falcone was always on the borrow from him. Alfonso, being the junior, reckoned the tally in cigarettes owed was far in favour of the seasoned judge.[2] He wished he could enlarge that tally far more. As the kid judge to the team, he had much to gain in correcting the mess that Sicily found itself in. And, equally, much to lose.

The new terrorist Mafia would see Sabella as easy prey, from the moment he opened his briefcase for the first time, and went looking for a rickety chair at one of the many now empty desks in the anti-Mafia pool. Sabella's bravery, in my view – over the next nine years – would be something rarely seen in judicial circles, akin to the bravest deeds of any decorated soldier. Equal to the bravery of all the judges who had fallen before his arrival.

Quickly, Sabella sensed an opening and rolled over the thug Santino Di Matteo. Strategically chosen, Di Matteo became the first weak link, the first to discard *omertà* and help make inroads into the Mafia bombings.[3] This move would open the door to solving dozens of murders. Di Matteo went into witness protection and, like Tommaso Buscetta nine years earlier, sat down and unburdened himself of horror stories that would make their way onto the pages of the morning newspapers, implicating many. And sitting opposite him was Alfonso Sabella with his full notebook.

One of Sabella's first challenges was that Bagarella and Brusca threatened to harm Di Matteo's family, to deter him from giving evidence. But Di Matteo was undeterred; he thought it a joke. Sabella was not so light-hearted, and it would be a day he has never forgotten.[4] In fact, the Mafia kidnapped Di Matteo's son, twelve-year-old Giuseppe, and Brusca took on the task no one wanted: to hold the boy in a shed, hoping his father would see the light. Di Matteo toughed it out, believing his boy would be okay. After all, his old Mafia mates were the kidnappers, and surely they would let the boy go free. The stalemate held for two agonising years, and acted as an alarm clock for Judge Sabella, waking him each morning before the sun rose, worrying about how to find the boy.

Meanwhile, the terror campaign continued. Riina's brother-in-law took on the mantle of caretaker boss, mostly because Provenzano considered it too harsh to kill innocent civilians or involve children in Mafia politics, and so decided to stay clear of terrorist tactics.

With Tractor in hiding, Bagarella and Brusca took the Italian Mafia into the festering bowels of humanity. Together, they set about killing anyone who dared question their authority. And any of their gang who failed to kill on their orders. In a final abhorrent act, victims were chopped up and stuffed into drums of acid, to be dissolved into a thick caramel-coloured liquid, which was then emptied into waste waterways across Sicily.[5]

Everyday Italians, learning of the descent of their society through revelations in their morning newspapers, put down their coffee cups, pushed back their chairs, and stared out their windows, wondering what the fuck had happened to the beauty and culture of their beloved Italy.

On the 779th day of the kidnapping, Giuseppe – who had been shifted around farms in the interior of Sicily, sleeping on straw, chained to fence railings or kept in an underground cellar, or a pig pen, by Giovanni Brusca – met his fate at the hands of the butcher. With the police closing in on the gang, Brusca strangled Giuseppe, who was said to be in an advanced state of mental decline, and then dissolved his tiny malnourished body in acid. Leaving nothing for his mother to mourn.

Vincenzina Marchese, the wife of Leoluca Bagarella, was so distraught knowing her husband had ordered the kidnapping, she was unable to conceive. She mounted her own private vigil – to have the boy freed – a protest that went unknown as she rarely left her home. Bagarella, arguably the most rabid murderer of that period, ignored her pleas and went on with his atrocities, so Vincenzina, unable to stomach any more, released herself of her overwhelming shame and hanged herself. And Judge Sabella slumped at his desk, his morale near destroyed by his inability to find the boy, alive or dead.

For the first time in history, the Vatican got involved in Mafia business. Pope John Paul II was so disturbed by the degeneration of southern Italian society and the callous murder of young Giuseppe that he decided to act. His Holiness visited Agrigento, from where the deceased boy had been snatched, and stood in a stadium, speaking to local folk. He denounced the Mafia, warning that unless its members repented, they would all go to Hell. In a raised voice he said to any Mafia connections that might have been nearby, 'Convert, the judgement of God is coming.'

Italy went numb. The media crept away. The mourners sobbed. But nothing changed.

To get closer to the reasons behind this madness I would sit with Judge Sabella on a cold day in Rome in March 2021 (and many days after) and talk over his tenure, and his exhaustive attempts to pull down the Mafia. He was quick to point out that he was part of a team, a young dynamic group of judges. He felt the acid bath chapter was the lowest point in the Mafia's long history, to which nothing compared.[6] He called the *Cosa Nostra* of the 1990s 'the most dangerous criminal organisation in the world'.[7] The judge was as relentless in his hunt for *mafiosi* murderers as they were in killing. In all, Sabella and his team reined in a hundred fugitives, including Brusca, to face justice. Sabella considers that period one of the darkest in his country's long history.

Sabella sat in front of Brusca for two days, questioning him over the number of notches on his belt. To help, the judge offered the *mafioso* hundreds of photographs of thugs who were known to have disappeared. Brusca pointed to sixty images, and stated that he had probably killed upwards of 200; he had lost count.[8] One image stood out: that of a thug who was due to be married. Brusca related how he went into a tizz, trying to locate the mobster before his wedding day, and kill him. The reason for the urgency was simple: he did not want the young bride to suffer as a widow. Best to kill her intended before the church bells rang.

The judge estimated that possibly 200 victims of the madness of Riina's gang were dissolved in acid, this method of disposal making it impossible to give an accurate figure.[9] The big twist in it all, as far as tough-guy *mafiosi* were concerned, centred around the killer Brusca. After three days on remand, in a cold cell in May, the prison governor rang Sabella and simply said, 'The baby needs some love.'[10] Meaning, Brusca was struggling as an inmate, unable to handle solitary, and wanted to see the judge to broker a deal as a *pentito* and tell all on his Mafia colleagues and crimes. He talked and didn't shut up, and the raids continued.

Judge Sabella's most troubling find was not the drugs, nor the stashes of cash, but a secret, massive underground tunnel connected to where young Giuseppe spent his last months chained up. At the end of the tunnel was a huge subterranean vault, which contained the largest cache of weaponry ever uncovered in Italy, enough to arm an African junta.[11]

On 31 May 2021, Brusca was paroled and released back into society, having served twenty-six years as a *pentito*. Italy erupted in disbelief. Using the numbers Brusca spoke to Judge Sabella about – up to 200 killed – his sentence bore no relation to his atrocities. But he was not convicted of that number; in fact, far fewer. He was sentenced for detonating the bomb that killed Judge Falcone and his entourage, and a handful of other murders. It was said that Giuseppe Di Matteo's father, assassin Santino Di Matteo, also out of prison, was bent on revenge once he heard of Brusca's release.

Judge Falcone's sister reminded the world that it was her brother who had advocated early release sentencing for potential *pentiti*, as a reward for their assistance in helping shut down the Mafia. Little did Falcone know that his killer would be his law's greatest beneficiary, receiving the gift of freedom rather than life in prison.

I contacted Judge Alfonso Sabella about that extraordinary day in Italian judicial history. He confided that he had been inundated for comment from the global media about the release of Brusca, but had refused each request. He made an exception for me, which I appreciate deeply. He then suggested I insert the following quote in my book, and hopefully readers will understand.[12] He said, '. . . when I questioned him [Brusca] for the first time, the man Alfonso would never have squeezed his hand, but the magistrate Sabella squeezed that hand. And we have erased the *Corleonesi* massacres from history . . .'. Of course, he is referring to a deal, to tell all, an agreement (handshake) between the killer and the chief investigator, to explain the facts and close many chapters in the Mafia book that was written by a ruthless gang with its roots in Corleone. What happened after Sabella closed that book and sent the gang to prison is not his concern. That's an issue for political Italy. I get it. Sabella's work was behind him, over. Latter-day outcomes cannot be his concern. Ask the law-makers!

The day after Brusca walked to freedom, a video interview with the killer surfaced. It had been made five years earlier, in prison. In the interview Brusca is heard to say, '. . . working with justice . . . is right because it serves to put an end to the factory of death called *Cosa Nostra*.'[13] Flash words from an evil man. I'm a sceptic.

•

As a detective in Australia, back in Sabella's time, I too was sensitive to the urban warfare in Italy. Not just from the media, but from the morning chatter in police muster rooms, as we, figuratively, ducked for cover every time we received an internal bulletin of another explosion in Italy. The 1990s were the days of my infiltration into the 'Ndrangheta Mafia. I recall sitting nervously in my sports car, driving to a night club with an extraordinarily brave female undercover operative, who was acting as my girlfriend. We were about to dine with the head of the Australian Mafia, the leader of a broader gang of thugs getting away with everything – drugs, murders, bombings – just like their Italian cousins. An anti-drugs campaigner named Donald Mackay had been murdered two decades earlier, in 1977, by the Mafia for his courageous anti-drugs stance and I was asked to gain admissions of the execution, by way of a covert recording device. I will never forget Donald's wife, in tears, pleading for me to obtain answers, as her husband's body had never been found, but his bloodstained car had. All my Mafia 'friends' would tell me, captured on my tape, was to stay out of 'our business'.

Our strain of the Mafia was nowhere near the mad-dog types in Italy; however, in proportion to our population, through this 1970s to 2000 period just as concerning. In any case, there is no scale to measure rotten, it's just rotten. The second year of my covert sting, our premier law enforcement agency, the National Crime Authority, suffered a bomb planted by the Mafia, killing Detective Geoffrey Bowen and maiming many others. The entire 13th floor was tossed into the street below and engulfed in flames.

While undercover, I asked my Mafia 'friends', why was the building bombed? They answered that it was merely revenge, a vendetta against the detective for arresting one of the *cosche*. I was on a small jet aeroplane – flying over a jungle – with those Mafia men arranging a drug importation and wanted to throw them out of the plane when they said that, but of course I couldn't; I had a bigger job to do. I had to suck it up and keep infiltrating.

Two years later, I had gathered enough evidence on that fateful bombing, only to have the evidence denied, the court process blocked by a public prosecutor with a dubious character.

I have no doubt that the bombing of the NCA was inspired by what was happening in Italy. Over the years – even after I'd resigned from the police – I kept a tight grip on my documents, transcripts and notes of my covert investigation into the execution of Detective Bowen, unwilling to surrender them to the same dubious prosecutor. And waited for his death. After sixteen years the moment arrived. A new regime of prosecutors – supremely dedicated to justice, supported by honest detectives – had taken his place, and my *mafioso* suspect was finally prosecuted for murder and attempted murders. I and my fellow undercover operatives gave our evidence during the nine-month trial. In late 2021, at the time of writing this book, the trial had come to an end. All that remained was for the judge to deliver his finding and a verdict. A task that was expected in the new year.

•

As the new century approached, the floodgates in Italy opened – for the good guys. There were more than 4000 Mafia arrests as anti-Mafia police raided countless homes and hideouts, and all *mafiosi* named in this chapter were jailed for life. Extraordinarily, each of the acid killers and bombers begged prosecutors to be a *pentito*. They snitched on their mates, their gang, and showed *omertà* to be the laughing stock of the Mafia. All except Bagarella, who held firm to the ideals of Ernesto Marasà. And one other, a criminal by the name of Matteo Messina Denaro, born in 1962 – he too was recruited into Leoluca Bagarella's gang and took part in the atrocities, but slipped the net in 1993. He has not been seen since.

Provenzano was the only other one remaining out there, somewhere, on the loose in the interior of Sicily. He had picked up the fallen reins and was running the Mafia in his own ghostly way. He abandoned bombings. Then, one day, the life of the fugitive Bernardo 'Tractor' Provenzano also changed.

In 2006, fourteen years after he and Riina killed the kings of Palermo, the police finally caught up with the other Ghost of Corleone. Since the deaths of Falcone and Borsellino, a newer, stronger, more educated and determined police regime had emerged, prompted by the queens of Palermo and all of Italy. These honest cops undertook a surveillance operation on Provenzano's wife, Saveria. For more than a year, the cops hid in long grass, up trees and in creek beds as they watched her from a distance with long-range binoculars. They had a hunch that the wife would lead them to the treasure they had failed to find for forty-three years.

Just as the trail on Provenzano had almost gone cold, the weary cops had a breakthrough. Saveria was on the move and they followed her out of town. She took a bundle of washed clothing and a block of cheese for a drive around a network of country laneways, carefully weaving through the hills and fields of Corleone. Way off, through the flickering lens of the field glasses, the police spotted her walking across a sheep paddock to a hut, three kilometres from town. Then came the moment the surveillance cops had waited a year for. The door was opened from the inside, and the relief parcel was given over to a lone hand that protruded from the doorway. Provenzano's wife then stepped inside. At last, police could arrest the Ghost of Corleone, the mad Mafia killer.

Provenzano had survived most of his life running the Mafia living as a humble shepherd, moving from hut to hut – a discovery that shocked police with its simplicity. He looked weathered and worn, like a broken-down tractor in a field. He rarely showered, ate poorly and walked the paddocks at midnight to meet his crew; he looked nothing like his legend suggested. He received twelve life sentences for a string of murders, as well as for conspiring with Riina to kill Falcone and Borsellino. He died in prison nine years later of complications related to bladder cancer, a frail version of his former murderous self. Even so, before his arrest, the specialist doctor who had treated Provenzano for prostate cancer had been murdered under his instructions, to ensure he never told anyone of his fugitive patient's whereabouts. Provenzano's fellow ghost, Riina, went about serving his twenty-three life sentences and died of old age in 2017. A hero to the Mafia of Corleone.

Through these years, Sicily (and all of Italy) grappled – it always will grapple – with the social cancer that is the Mafia. From the deaths of Mafia hierarchy came the beginning of a movement to halt the scourge, and, perhaps, limit the disease that had spread after a red-shirted general stepped onto the timber jetty at Marsala harbour back in 1860. Yet for all the heroics of the judges and cops, there's no marble allocated to their memory. Not like Crispi, King Vittorio

Emanuele and Giuseppe Garibaldi, whose statues clutter up the country. Strange sentiment in Italy.

The Punta Raisi Airport of Palermo, from where Falcone and Borsellino travelled almost weekly, is the main airport on the island. The people of Sicily decided to honour the legacy of Giovanni Falcone and Paolo Borsellino by renaming the airport after them, dropping the Punta Raisi tag.

Fitting in another way too: the Mafia were instrumental in the building of the airport on Mafia-owned land.

CHAPTER 22

MAFIA POSH

SICILIAN SAYING:

Un lu vulissi mancu pì cumpagnu di prucissìoni
I would not even be seen with them at a procession

Meaning, you don't like a person at all

In trying to understand how the Mafia became so powerful, so swollen – like a massive pimple on the chin of society – you only have to look at law enforcement globally. Wherever the Mafia has burst onto the streets and interfered with communities, there, in parallel, will be a police department with pockets of corruption. The two are mutually linked: Mafia and police corruption. There is always a smell of cash in the air, of money that invariably finds its way into the bottom drawer of a public official. The more cash in the game, the faster the wheels on the Mafia wagon spin.

This is the enigma of policing organised crime. Ideally, what is needed is the cleanest squad room, a police station full of honest cops. Law enforcement utopia. In a police department the size of, say, the New York Police Department there are 36 000 cops. It is lunacy to think all of them will be honest. Likewise, Victoria Police in Australia – which sees a lot of Mafia crime – is made up of 22 000 cops; I was one of them. In Italy there are more than 324 000 police, across their six agencies, an amazing number of uniforms. Which raises a question. With so many cops, how can the Mafia problem be so bad? Basically,

268

corruption and resources, or lack thereof. The problem is, with police numbers that high, you cannot vet each cop, so the utopian desire for an entire force of honest cops is mere fantasy. But you can create a group of elite cops, highly trained and educated men and women – well paid – to take on the dangers of fighting the worst gang on the planet. Enter the anti-Mafia units of Italy. That country's only hope.

Since the Mafia wars of the 1980s, when Italians saw their streets covered in bodies, there has been a demand for better resources. Enough is enough, came the call from Sicilians. It is the same in and around Naples, with the Mafia gangs under the *Camorra* banner. These tribes of (mostly) vicious young punks – a modern-day version of *picciotti* – rule the streets of this once-cultured European mecca, dealing in street-level drugs, under a haze of bullets fired from the most devastating weaponry. The *Camorra* Mafia has devastated the great city to such an extent that it is hard to see it ever returning to its former glory. Naples' favourite son, Pino Daniele, a singer of international fame, wrote many of his lyrics about the impact the *Camorra* has had on his town, his home. His song 'Napule E'' is one of my all-time best odes: 'Naples is a thousand fears . . . a bitter sun . . . a dirty waste paper and nobody cares.'

Likewise, its southern neighbour is in fast decline. The 'Ndrangheta-infested towns of Calabria – where tourists dare not venture – are hideouts for vast illicit drug shipments that are dispatched around the world, from the closest dock, the massive Gioia Tauro seaport, which is near impossible to surveil or control.

Today's Mafia members are mostly young, dangerous and everywhere, pulling any scam they can to gain cash, while their elders hide behind the very best lawyers and investment bankers, and watch their wealth multiply.

During the time of the Mafia wars in Sicily, when the *Cosa Nostra* wrought havoc on the people of Italy, bombing and killing at will, the 'Ndrangheta slowly took over the distribution of white-powder drugs across Europe and – in time – around the globe. Leaving their island criminal cohorts to waste away in prisons and, eventually, to go through the pains of regrouping, which has taken time. Meanwhile, the stocks of the 'Ndrangheta have seen a continual rise. The 'Ndrangheta would become the most violent of all Mafia cartels, and the most capable on the world stage. Their ruthlessness shocks even the hardest lawmen. Today, they are the Mafia to watch and, in my opinion, they will not be quashed, because they are simply too dominant and must never be underestimated. However, to the credit of the Italian authorities, the anti-Mafia pool of judges and investigators have themselves been regrouping, and their fight is impressive.

But I cannot help believing the Mafia story suffers from cycles of *déjà vu*. The best example is the fugitive Matteo Messina Denaro, who avoided apprehension after the Bagarella bombings in 1993. No one has seen a whisker of him since he headed for the hills of Sicily; he has become like Shorty and Tractor, another ghost with almost 30 years on the run. Despite being convicted of murders *in absentia*, and with a life sentence hanging over him – and suspected of being complicit in dozens of other slayings in recent years – he has made fools of police who say they are on his trail. He is known to be the *capo di tutti capi*, the supreme authority in the *Cosa Nostra*, and the anti-Mafia unit has seized hundreds of millions worth of his assets – cash, olive groves, real estate and a supermarket chain. Yet, no Matteo. It's a case of history repeating itself. This clever criminal must be caught! And this maddening cycle of spending decades chasing a lone man must change.

As I write – in December 2021 – the Calabrese Mafia are embroiled in the biggest criminal trial in the world, in the 'largest courthouse' in the world: 355 mobsters, mostly murderers and drug traffickers of the extended Mancuso 'family' – a powerful clan based around Catanzaro, but, in actuality, spread across the foot of Italy and further afield – are standing trial together. To accommodate the number of people involved in this Maxi Trial, proceedings are underway in a purpose-built courtroom, measuring an incredible hundred metres long.[1] Copious CCTV screens observe the work of hundreds of lawyers, an equal number of police and as many as a thousand witnesses.

This prosecutorial feat is the brainchild of head investigative judge Nicola Gratteri, who has worked tirelessly against the Mafia for decades. To get to this point in proceedings the gentlemanly, quiet Gratteri and his talented team first had to find many of the accused in many of the member countries of the European Union. The 'Ndrangheta operates all over. In some ways this monumental battle to uphold justice in the south of Italy could also be narrowed down to a fight between two men. A judge with an extraordinary desire to clean up Calabria and Luigi Mancuso, the supreme boss of the Mancuso clan. The 66-year-old – who spent half of his life in prison – has become (allegedly) the crime bunion on the toe of Italy. However, Gratteri has an ace card to play, sixty *pentiti* have agreed to tell all on the *mafioso*.

The courthouse, built in the record time of four months during the COVID-19 pandemic, will, in the future, be able to connect to 150 prisons across Italy simultaneously with its network of sixty-four cameras to allow video prosecutions from jail cells.[2] Inside the fortress-like facility is a medical station, doctors and nurses and full emergency equipment, to cater for the slightest pre-court nerves. There is even a year-round no-fly zone above, for tens of kilometres in all directions, ensuring a Mafia vendetta attack is unlikely. And, just in case, a full Army unit and specialist Carabinieri assault team are on standby 24/7, with Judge Gratteri's safety their first priority.

This is now the way of justice in Italy, where Gratteri can glimpse a future in southern Italy in which the Mafia has been suppressed and where young people can grow up without being forced into crime. But that's a long way off. For now, Judge Gratteri aches for a stronger commitment from international law enforcement, to dig for evidence, to undertake wiretaps, surveillance and discover the links between countries with an 'Ndrangheta presence.[3] So far, the cooperation is limp.

'Ndrangheta crime is having an extraordinary impact on the world, and the Italians are now meeting the demands head-on, having licked their wounds after the death of judges Falcone and Borsellino and many before them. However, as the people of Italy know only too well, their country's political climate can change any minute: today a well-funded anti-Mafia regime, tomorrow a return to shoestring funding and the bad old days of the Falcone era when prime ministers were seen shaking hands with monsters.

With an anti-Mafia concentration of manpower and resources in the regions of Sicily, Calabria and Campagna – once the battlegrounds of Garibaldi – the fight shows no sign of a winner yet. While this new style of cop is the most proactive approach to dealing with the Mafia, it's still not enough. There needs to be a doubling of resources to allow the state to beat the 'Ndrangheta.

Yet, in this toxic environment, you hear of the most heroic men and women who are fighting the scourge. Like prosecutor Alessandra Cerreti – stylishly attired, highly intelligent and hugely focused – who took the job no one else wanted, working in the anti-Mafia prosecuting team in Calabria for ten years. It was a time when anyone falling foul of the 'Ndrangheta simply disappeared – no body, no forensics, no hope of finding facts. Fingerprint dust, luminol lamps or blood spatter analysis are pointless. Southern Italy is unlike anywhere else. Crime scene principles and procedures have little prospect of success; such skills might work on the streets of Los Angeles, Toronto or Sydney, but the main hope in Italy is to keep finding *pentiti*. And follow the money. Prosecutor Alessandra Cerreti jailed many, before taking her skills to northern Italy. In so doing, she left behind a conviction rate the envy of contemporaries in New York City or Amsterdam.

A crusty old police sergeant once told me, when I was wet behind the ears as a rookie cop, that a community gets the police department it deserves. I witnessed this truism in my career, when the public showed their contrariness. On one hand, they expected crime fighters – like Alessandra – to instantly remove organised crime. Yet the same public are the first to criticise should a defence lawyer claim a denial of the civil rights of their client. The public are good at flip-flopping, especially now with so much social media at their fingertips.

At the time of writing, I was advised that the anti-Mafia cops had just arrested a cunning criminal who was part of the *Cosa Nostra* Riina/Provenzano crew thirty years earlier and had amassed extraordinary wealth, including 2700 properties. Try getting your investigative head around that puzzle. Then in late May 2021, Rocco Morabito, a 'Ndrangheta boss – dubbed the 'King of Cocaine' by the media – was arrested in Brazil, after being on the run for decades from a thirty-year jail sentence in Italy. He literally travelled the world with a box of false passports and identities, hiding in plain sight, running his empire from South America to who-knows-where. Due to sheer luck, he was captured and locked away in a Uruguayan prison, only to escape once more. He has been suspected of shipping tonnes of white powder drugs as a fugitive. Then he was recaptured when enjoying time at the beach, and law enforcement wonders what the outcome will be as – cashed up – he fights his extradition to Italy to serve his original sentence. The man at the helm of his arrest, Calabria's chief prosecutor Giovanni Bombardieri of the Reggio region, considers Morabito 'one of the most important brokers in narco-trafficking', the movement of drugs into the United States and Europe.

Morabito's arrest, again, is an example of contemporary anti-Mafia success, and there are many more cases just like his. Each convoluted, each requiring hundreds of international police from different time zones all working in sync like a Swiss watch. But they don't! And anyone who says they do is delusional. At best, they do what they can with the resources they are given.

Yet the number of anti-Mafia cops compared to others in Italy is minuscule. Most of the Italian police resources are focused on municipal issues, guarding state buildings, revenue raising by giving out traffic fines, or standing around in beautifully tailored uniforms looking dapper as tourists take their picture. A professor teaching public administration in Rome told me recently that Italy has 44 000 state-owned cars, each with a full-time chauffeur, one allocated to each member of parliament or high-ranking official. The cost to the public purse is astronomical, yet the same politicians cry poor when crime fighters put their hands out. With that sort of waste the government doesn't stand a snowflake's chance in Hell of crushing the scourge. The Italian government must make the decision: revenue raising, squandering funds and further Mafia crimes or breaking the back of the Mafia.

The problem is only slightly better in the United States, where there are fewer specialist Mafia investigators now than at any time in the past forty years. Although when US authorities do act they are very impressive and use the full force of their laws. At times they are magnificent. But on a day-to-day basis they face overwhelming numbers of transnational crime gangs from myriad ethnicities that operate by countless illegal means, irrespective of the geography and size of the country. The sheer number of gangs is mind-boggling, the land of liberty suffers them all. Yet Italian organised crime is still up there, alongside (and in bed with) the South American drug cartels, the biggest problem that the American premier law enforcement agency, the FBI, must combat. Regardless, in a country obsessed with anti-terrorism pro-activity, and collecting, listening to and linking personal, digital and telephone data, there will still always be a need to investigate the traditional crime activities of the Mafia, and support Italian anti-Mafia authorities.

In Australia, there are no specialist task forces tackling Italian organised crime – zero. It's not trendy in a time of terrorism. Additionally, Australia has succumbed to social correctness, that we shouldn't marginalise ethnic groups. Australian police – except for the wonderful efforts of a handful of dedicated Federal police and Customs officers – prefer to take a reactive approach to the Mafia, pulling together a team of investigators once a series of crimes or an atrocity has taken place. I cannot agree with this limp approach to the global problem of the Mafia.

Let's not forget, in 2007 the largest haul of ecstasy (MDMA) pills the world has ever seen – 4.4 tonnes – was shipped from the Aspromonte mountains in Calabria, then secreted in a forty-tonne container of jumbo-sized tins of juicy Calabrian tomatoes, before being shipped to Melbourne, Australia. Half a billion dollars' worth! While a dozen *mafiosi* were prosecuted – some killed each other over the loss – and jailed, others took their place (which is always the case). It was believed to be only one of possibly a dozen shipments. And cocaine, heroin, vast marijuana crops and other illicit drugs are just as worrisome. The dynamic commissioner of the Australian Federal Police at the time, Mick Keelty, said, 'It's classic organised crime, we are part of a European and Australian attempt to shut this syndicate down. This is part of a global international syndicate, a major disruption to transnational organised crime both in this country and abroad.'

What happened next? Nothing, really. Keelty retired. And the effort against that same international syndicate has since dried up.

Judge Gratteri acknowledges the competence of police in Australia; however, he also recalls the death of Australian police, murdered by the Mafia, for their brave fight against Italian organised crime.[4] Gratteri remembers how the criminal genius of the ecstasy shipment – who

I can't name for legal reasons – was a wanted man in Calabria, and how Gratteri applied for his extradition long before the tinned-tomato scam. Only to have Australian politicians deny the extradition. Preferring to support the mastermind's request to remain in Australia. A real controversy, as the same politicians were linked to a $100 000 political donation from connections of the mastermind, today considered the most powerful *mafioso* in Australia. It erupted into global news for the better part of a year, yet the politicians held firm, until it blew away. Actually, what really blew away was Australia's international credibility in fighting the growing threat of the 'Ndrangheta. Prosecutor Bombardieri also has a clipboard full of extradition requests for other *mafiosi* hiding away in Australia, with little hope of any of them being granted. It's as if no one in the federal Attorney-General's office in Australia has any interest in the big-picture fight against global narcotics. The current Australian Liberal government's track record on making extradition easier is abysmal, as are the nation's relations with the international law enforcement community.

It is political arrogance like this that has allowed the 'Ndrangheta to eventually take over the world's major drug routes. I was particularly annoyed, as I once met the same mastermind in the tomato tin importation at a Mafia dinner table when I was undercover, way back when.

Judge Gratteri considers the Australian legal system to be below what is needed in a united front against the Mafia, and easily corruptible.[5]

Perhaps Gratteri is right. In the two-party political arena of Australia, the National Crime Authority, a Labor Party initiative, was formed in 1984 to attack nationally significant crime, at a time when the Mafia was known to kill their opponents and had corrupted many of the police squads around the country. The NCA was the new broom that swept through the Mafia with its highly secretive investigative regimes and undercover operations. I worked within this regime for more than three years, and the effect we had on Mafia crime (collectively) was impressive. However, the fortunes of government changed and the Liberal Party government was voted in for three terms. Trouble was, the NCA was embroiled in a sensational investigation into the federal President of the Liberal Party, a controversial businessman (nothing to do with the Mafia investigations). A decade later, with the Liberal government still in power, the investigation into the Liberal Party luminary John Elliott had ended with the loss of his personal fortune.

Immediately afterwards the NCA was closed down, to the shock of law enforcement officials. Don't tell me that wasn't political meddling!

Shortly after, the same government allowed the mastermind of the ecstasy importation to remain in Australia, denying extradition. Added to this sorry tale, the agency that replaced the NCA only gathers data, and has no strategic investigative or arrest powers – about as useful as a wet bus ticket in a blizzard!

Disturbingly, the man who blew up the NCA head office in Adelaide, killing Detective Bowen, was a 'Ndrangheta thug, born in the miserable town of Plati, in the Aspromonte mountains. I have visited Plati twice. It is arguably Calabria's ugliest town. A town that sent hundreds of hard-nosed Mafia criminals to Australia under a generous post-war immigration treaty. But, as reality in crime often dictates, one of Plati's sons would go on to cause a chain reaction – of murder and mayhem – that ended up shutting down the only agency dedicated to investigating him and his Mafia cohorts. In the history of the Australian Mafia, Plati will always be known as the seed town of the scourge, like Castellammare in Sicily is to the New York crime families.

I would just add another factor in the recent good fortunes of the Australian 'Ndrangheta. Today – an era when police commissioners stand in front of media microphones as often as flip-flopping politicians – the police have cleverly learnt to proffer rosy figures on easy-to-solve crimes, against going after entrenched criminals of Italian ethnicity. Those who speak a difficult-to-translate dialect. Those who are running the world of drugs – hence, global drug addiction and widespread corruption, and all the deaths that follow from that.

The status quo will only keep the Mafia growing internationally, with pockets where the Mafia controls entire towns or cities. That has happened already – think of the social decay in parts of Naples, where the Mafia has had a devastating effect on communities.[6] Their influence has had Mafia-friendly, Mafia-funded candidates elected to public office, who then meticulously dismantle the institutions and processes that were designed to pull apart organised crime.

Naples is not alone in this conundrum. There are many towns in Sicily that have suffered the same virus, likewise in Calabria. The towns of Locri and Siderno (and Plati) in southern Calabria, for example, have become a hive of imported prostitution and nasty two-star accommodation for working-class Russians with too much duty-free vodka.[7] I have been there many times, watching the crass goings-on, witnessing the sleaze. It stands in stark contrast to the idyllic tourist places the rest of the region has to offer.

Politicians in all countries where the Mafia has a presence are the key to smashing the Mafia; have no doubt of that. Throughout history, however, politicians have been constant cowards in the face of the Mafia. Too many have affiliations with unions, commercial operators and working-class groups that – once you lift the veil of business names and public entities – are merely affiliates of the wider Mafia community. Like dodgy detectives who salivate at the fat wad of cash in the *mafioso*'s pocket, politicians are equally tainted the second they accept campaign funds from the Mafia. Even more so when campaign funds are listed on electorate funding records as coming from an 'anonymous' or ambiguous source, as happens in Australia.

Politics must be transparent. Like the crusty old police sergeant said, a community gets the police department – and politicians – it deserves! Under the rule that we all deserve better, we also deserve better politicians.

I would argue that while terrorism is abhorrent, and the life of an innocent victim lost to a terrorist bomb is heart-wrenchingly shocking, it is no more troubling than what parents face daily, when confronted with the loss of life of their teenage offspring taken by drugs peddled by the Mafia. Loss should not be measured by the sound of a bomb over an anguished silent death in a squat house from a dirty syringe filled with Mafia junk.

I recall a short passage written by the collective of Carabinieri police eighty-three years ago, found in the red report:

> The mafia must be fought with fire and iron, without mercy
> or hesitation, both above and below, all the way, with precise

and decisive strokes, cutting down every one; including the intellectuals and titled staff of the voracious octopus which has polluted and paralysed every activity of public and private life . . .[8]

If there is any doubt about effecting change – that is, people power, through politics – then the story of the brave bedsheet women of Palermo must be remembered.

At this juncture, it is worth mentioning a comment by Elena, my main translator in my search for the inception of the Mafia. She and I not only spent too much time eating from the best *pasticceria* in Palermo, but we would wax lyrical about the anti-Mafia, the movement that is causing change for the good. The anti-Mafia vibe in Italy is here to stay. Newspaper editors are more vigilant in exposing Mafia schemes, authors are naming names, and even schools are teaching the anti-Mafia message.

But Elena has also noticed some false aficionados among the devotees of the anti-Mafia movement. People who appear at the rallies, raise their hands, tick the right boxes but in reality do little. In other words, those full of brimstone and fire but low on action. Elena calls them part of the new Mafia Posh movement. A subgroup, telling their friends about all the good work they are doing. But, as Elena knows, they take little action. For some, it suits their community profile; it pays to be Mafia Posh. Many of them are seen taking selfies at rallies, their heads nodding as speakers tell their sad tales. But their charity is exaggerated.

Elena is of an age that she recalls the Mafia wars on the streets of her city, stepping over the bloodstains on the way to university, reading the newspaper and seeing names she knew. She remembers judges Falcone and Borsellino. She almost heard the bombs; she certainly heard shots fired in the night. Palermo is her town, and the changes it has suffered are her changes. She owns part of the collective sorrow, as well as the collective hope. Indeed, all Palermo people own optimism, or else all hope would fade. All she wants is for the Mafia to go away, and the Posh people too.

I have observed another oddity during my research for this book. A number of people I spoke to – albeit a smallish number – were unfairly critical of the extraordinary efforts of the champions against the Mafia. Names like Gratteri and Sabella and even Falcone and Borsellino were scoffed at. A reaction that offended me, but, then again, the same critics probably spend their time putting a dent into a sofa cushion in front of their television, such are the ways of armchair critics.

Regardless, I understand Elena's sentiment, and a thought must be spared for the man who inspired the anti-Mafia movement: Giuseppe Impastato. The anti-Mafia light started to shine because of the sheer bravery of Impastato.[9] He was born into the Mafia, in 1948, and would just see his thirtieth birthday before he was executed in 1978. What made him stand out as a Palermitan was his stance against the scourge; he was the very definition of defiant, and his only hope of effecting change in a corrupt 1970s Sicily was to stay defiant. That's why Mafia-Posh is an insult to his memory.

Impastato's father was immersed in the Mafia as was his father's brother-in-law, a Mafia boss in the seaside town of Cinisi, on the way from Palermo to the airport, not far from where the roadworks bomb exploded and killed Judge Falcone. Back in the 1970s, it was Mafia business as usual. Impastato had a harrowing upbringing; he was against anything to do with crime, and his own uncle – the head of the notorious Cinisi Mafia – was murdered by a car bomb. Shocked as much by the devastation of the car bomb as the death of his uncle and the horror of what bombs can do to a tiny community – the fear, the anxiety – he vowed to fight the Mafia for the rest of his life. Before he was twenty, Impastato was already a veteran radio journalist, voicing his views against the Mafia, to the point that he was becoming a local annoyance. He also wrote press articles. There was always lots to talk about during the time of Provenzano and Riina, and mobsters such as Gaetano Badalamenti, a man who could be best described as perfectly embodying the worst attributes of the Mafia. His life was dedicated to a lust for money and bloodstained power. He once tried his luck at thuggery in the United States, and made a feast of it, only to be 'exported' back to Italy as an undesirable.

While this might have slowed any normal thug down, Badalamenti turned it to his advantage, telling wild stories of how successful he had been in America. He impressed so many fellow *mafiosi* that he had a chair at the infamous dinner and meeting in the Grand Hotel et des Palmes in Palermo in 1957, alongside Vito Genovese, Lucky Luciano and others. The Board of the modern Mafia. 'Timing is everything' proved to be correct for Badalamenti. Soon after, a new airport was on the drawing board and Badalamenti bribed officials to build the airport on his land, on the water's edge, next to a huge rock massif. The location is unsuitable for an airport as the cliffs produce adverse bounce-off winds for aircraft wanting to land, but, hey, he was Mafia, and the airport *would* be built on his land! And Impastato told the story – in retrospect – to his listeners and readers each day. In summary, Badalamenti made a fortune.

The airport not only needed land, but crushed rock and gravel, and, yes, Badalamenti had an earth-moving business that supplied all the construction needs. Concrete? He had one of those companies too, so the airport was built. True to the adage that money makes money, Badalamenti became famously rich, and his grip on Cinisi due to shady business ventures was frightening. Badalamenti was said to have the local Carabinieri in his employ, slipping them bribes in return for their ignorance. He was seen walking the piazza at night with senior cops, at times arm in arm. After Lucky Luciano lent his hand to getting heroin onto the Mafia hit list, Palermo's Punta Raisi Airport was used by Badalamenti to move tons of the narcotic in and out of Sicily – billions of dollars' worth over the decade from the mid-1970s – as well as planeloads of illegal cigarettes.[10] This elaborate smuggling operation – the Pizza Connection – would involve many of the New York crime families.

The Mafia boss rose to dizzying heights. Investigating magistrates even alleged the prime minister contracted Badalamenti to kill a journalist who was writing unfavourable articles about his politics. Strange place, Italy!

It is no surprise that Impastato's radio news bulletins became the thing to listen to throughout the mid-1970s. Badalamenti was also in bed with Tommaso Buscetta, the former Mafia boss who would turn snitch for Judge Falcone; both Mafia bosses lived temporarily in São Paulo, Brazil. It is worth noting that these two men were on the very top of the highest tree in the world of the Mafia. They, in a fashion, set the path for all other families under them. Even though Tractor and Shorty were dominating Sicily at that time, and the likes of Gotti, Gigante, Sammy Gravano and others ruled in the United States, they were not global in their reach, not like Gaetano Badalamenti and Tommaso Buscetta. None had the bold gumption to spend their weeks jumping on jumbo jets and sewing up lucrative drug deals between the new worldwide web of Mafia.

Yet brave Impastato made sure his radio show went to air each day, as he tried to enlighten an Italy that was becoming blasé about the Mafia. Impastato was only doing what the police should have done, as well as the courts and the prosecutors: he was informing the public. It wasn't long before Impastato's insightful voice was being heard by too many influential people – so he had to be removed, permanently. In 1978, his body was found on a railway track, blown up by explosives. The police who investigated the death – an obvious murder – stated that Impastato had suicided while undertaking an attempt to blow up a railway line in an act of urban terrorism.

Appalled by the police corruption, Impastato's brother and mother broke all ties with the Mafia and worked for twenty years to prove Badalamenti had ordered the execution.

Given enough time, justice often prevails, even with the worst criminals. The US Department of Justice mounted a massive investigation through the 1980s into the importation of Sicilian heroin. The Pizza Connection would soak up years of inquiries by the FBI and the New York Police Department, as they played catch-up. A new breed of investigative prosecutor was born, men and women who became household names as they chased down mobsters, aided by a team of maverick top cops. Collectively, and incorruptibly, they unravelled the international network that had lined the pockets of the New York crime families, resulting in the biggest criminal trial in US history. And the first man that would feel the isolated chill of a remand cell in New York was Gaetano Badalamenti, who had been in hiding in Spain.

Seventeen New York mobsters were jailed, along with Badalamenti, thanks to the crucial evidence of Tommaso Buscetta, now a *pentito*, and the magnificently brave Joe Pistone, aka Donnie Brasco, who helped decode the many words used by the Pizza Connection to arrange the distribution of the narcotics.

In 2002, twenty-four years after Impastato's murder, Badalamenti – who (by then) was serving a forty-five-year sentence for his role in the Pizza Connection – was finally prosecuted and convicted of Impastato's death, receiving a life sentence. He died two years later of old age.

The legacy of Giuseppe Impastato is the anti-Mafia movement, which has made wonderful inroads in battling the Mafia and educating against the scourge. The only people who can sit alongside Impastato in inspiring a change of attitude against the Mafia are the kings and queens of Palermo. For me, in closing this book, there is no finer example of single-minded determination than Giuseppe Impastato.

Across Sicily there are anti-Mafia banners that catch the breeze and show off its motto: *Centopassi*. The word translates as 'One Hundred Steps' and holds great sentiment among Sicily's young, better-educated people, in particular the various student movements: the island's future. It has become a slogan for change. Impastato lived exactly one hundred steps from the front door of the Mafia boss Badalamenti, the bastard who silenced him.

MY LAST BULLETS

SICILIAN SAYING:

Tu scurdasti quannu l'acqua du puzzu ti parìa sciampagna?
Have you forgotten when the water from the well seemed to
taste like champagne?

Said to people who no longer remember their humble origins

With Italian organised crime bolted down in this new millennium, it's a fitting time to walk away from our story on the birth, rise and spread of the Mafia. This book was never meant to be an anthology of the Mafia – it cannot name all the names nor all the twists and turns – it's just a story on how and when, and perhaps why the slimy octopus engulfed the world. I hope it can correct the record, as far as the back story of the Mafia is concerned. More than 160 years after the Mafia's birth, the tentacles have spread to every corner of the planet; almost no major city or country is without the scourge.

Wherever there's a buck, a quid, a euro, a peso or a yen to be made, the men of the hardest club in the world to become a member of will be there to ensure they snatch as much as they can. And it's their diversity that stuns. Not only do they – collectively – have their fingers on the majority of illicit drugs globally, and continue to stand over small businesses and individuals across Italy. They have also camouflaged their ownership in casinos, five-star resorts, main-street hotels, high-end and low-end restaurants, wineries, fashion houses, shipping and road transport, the toxic waste disposal industry, passenger ferries, domestic garbage collection, bridge building, hospitals, freeway construction, and on it goes. The FBI and anti-Mafia teams in Italy have even discovered the Mafia is actively involved in trafficking military weapons, human trafficking, and fashion and currency counterfeiting. They are so entrenched in Italian society that major civil engineering projects are often undertaken by Mafia-affiliated companies, in which the quality of workmanship and materials is highly questionable. Likewise, many labour unions are either controlled by Mafia influence or suffer the weekly demands for cash handouts in return for calm. (It's the same in parts of America.) And if I were to touch on Mafia involvement in money laundering, I'd need another chapter; suffice to say, their rackets in cleaning ill-gotten cash are massive. Many of us have our ticket clipped directly or indirectly by one of the Mafia strains weekly, from Italy to the United States, France to Germany, Canada to Australia, Hong Kong to Luxembourg. For years, the Mafia have been shovelling mountains of cash into tax haven banks (and many other banks around the world) with funds that could equal the GDP of smaller countries in the European Union.

The Mafia is the epitome of a black market. Everything its members do is clandestine, cash is king and despite the will of police and prosecutors it's impossible to track the truckloads of money that change hands weekly between the families. Internationally, nationally, locally or under the bed. Besides, the rarest professional on the Mafia payroll is an accountant, so how can anyone quote the yearly turnover of many hundred Mafia *cosche*? For God's sake, *mafiosi* even own supermarket chains, and most recently came to the notice of the head of the Italian Anti-Mafia Investigation Directorate, Maurizio Vallone, for putting their hands out for part of the €2 trillion coronavirus subsidies the EU is doling out to struggling companies.[1] The trick in this particular Mafia scam is to buy up fledgling companies then suck in the subsidies. If that doesn't sound abhorrent enough, Judge Alessandra Cerreti, now based in Milan, is hunting dodgy Mafia-owned companies for distributing (with standover tactics) questionable-quality face masks and sanitiser used to combat COVID-19.

Analysing the strategies of today's Mafia is a mind-boggling task. The number of deaths attributed to the Mafia is incalculable. Yet the Italians are a forgiving, or perhaps forgetful, race, particularly those in Sicily. Evidenced by a line out of a Roberto Benigni film called *Johnny Stecchino*, released in 1991 – the middle of the mass murders era – a story about a *mafioso* with a split persona.[2] With mayhem all around, he is asked what is the worst thing about Palermo, to which he replies, 'The traffic jams'! Such is the resilience of the Italians, and New Yorkers too.

In my covert days, it took me three years to bag enough evidence to bury my twenty *mafiosi* in jail time and shut down two clans, before I could walk away. But in the end, it was only temporary; others stepped forward to take over the scams, and on the game went. That's how it works, it's a hamster wheel.

During the time of the COVID global lockdown, the Mafia were not at home working 'smart'. They were out there smartly changing their *modus operandi* in an effort to keep a few steps ahead of the various law enforcement agencies on their tail. Statistics from the Polizia di Stato (a premier law enforcement agency in Italy that works alongside anti-Mafia police) showed a 130 per cent increase (13.4 tonnes) in the amount of cocaine seized in the first COVID year (2020), compared to the previous year. It also showed that the traditional transport route to get the drugs to Calabria, via West Africa and the Netherlands, had shifted. The contraband is now moving across the oceans, through the Dardanelles on to the Black Sea before unloading in Bulgaria, Romania or Ukraine, from where it is taken by road down to Calabria in readiness for onward passage. This could mean Albanian criminals will help push the narcotics into Italy, which means the docile east coast of Italy may play a bigger role for the global Mafia. This area, known as Puglia, is considered the market garden of Europe, responsible for the magnificent *gusto* flavours that tourists flock to Italy to enjoy: the tomatoes, nectarines, wine grapes and the liquid gold of olive oil. It's also the home to the little brother *mafiosi* in the league of Mafia, the lessor known *Sacra Corona Unita cosca*. Highly capable and often flying under the radar of law enforcement, due to the activities of their southern neighbours, the *Sacra Corona Unita* are more than capable of partnering with their bigger brothers in trafficking the shipments of narcotics as they arrive. And opening the ports to more Albanian crime than is currently the case.

Just as worrying, the three main Mafia sects – the *'Ndrangheta*, the *Camorra* and the *Cosa Nostra* – appear to have developed a closer working relationship, assisting each other in their criminality. No doubt to confuse the police and ensure the multi-billion-dollar business of narcotic trafficking is even harder to detect. In fact, intelligence suggests the *Cosa Nostra* are getting back into the game in a major way, which will only mean a return to horrific deaths and more drugs available globally. On top of this, the drug cartels feeding the Mafia are now using submarines to transport the drugs. The Spanish authorities, in conjunction with the Italians, seized two submarines in 2019, one with 3000 kilograms of pure cocaine on board. Any wonder the war on drugs shows no sign of abating.

It's when one digests data like this that I often ask myself some difficult questions. Did I make a difference going undercover? Did my crew of skilled detectives change anything when we took on the Mafia? Likewise, in years past, did Detective Joe Pistone tilt the Mafia off its game? Did the legal smarts of all the investigators and prosecutors like Alfonso Sabella across Italy and the United States slow down the scourge? When you hear stories like that of young Giuseppe Di Matteo, ones that rip your heart out, it's difficult to know if any of our efforts have helped. We can only pray that we have put a few grains of sand on the scales of justice.

It's at this juncture that it is worth looking at the story arc of a Mafia killer. Roberto Cannavò is a fair, but rare, example. He had his heyday as a murderer around the time of Falcone and Borsellino and was convicted of killing thirteen people. We might ask why, what makes him want to destroy another human, in the name of the Mafia? Cannavò was born into poverty in Catania, on the east coast of Sicily. As an adolescent, he suffered the collapse of his parents' marriage, as well as schoolyard bullying – some might say nothing remarkable at that point – before his father was mistakenly murdered by the Mafia. By early adulthood, he displayed deep scars. By the time he was inducted into the *Cosa Nostra*, he had killed many times. Apparently, it was easy. His initiation gave him a sense of empowerment, to have been welcomed into a club, a fraternity, something lacking in his formative years.

His killing continued, only because he believed he was immune from remorse; after all, he was only killing criminals, he thought. Then his world stopped the day he murdered the wrong person, an eighteen-year-old baker on his way to work. All of a sudden, he saw his father's accidental killing as a stain on himself, and remorse finally came knocking. It was that wrongful taking of life that ate at him, chewed him up and spat him back to reality, ending his Mafia career. He admitted his sins and served twenty-seven years in the hardest prison in Italy.

Cannavò, who has only recently been given parole, carries an overwhelming need to redeem himself in the eyes of his remaining family and for himself. Shame had been his bedfellow in his concrete cell for all those twenty-seven wasted years. He is now on a solid path of helping young criminals, teaching them that Mafia life has no silver lining, just fool's gold. Society needs more Robertos, to change the mindset of vulnerable wannabe thugs. It's just that we don't need his credentials – the killings that he undertook so easily – to ultimately change, and do good. We need better qualified do-gooders. People who don't cause rivers of tears from grief-stricken mothers and shattered fathers.

And we need governments – especially in the United States and Europe – to undertake social reforms to sway our young from a life in crime. But most of all, we need people of Judge Nicola Gratteri's ilk, with his pure-hearted dedication, in heading up the Maxi Trial against 355 accused to ensure justice is delivered to the 'Ndrangheta Mafia.

Gratteri has also served a 'sentence' of sorts for twenty-seven years: his career as a prosecutor. He cut his teeth on investigations into the Trimboli–Sergi–Perre mafia clans (the same clans I infiltrated in my covert years), which had textbook outcomes. His 'prison cell' has been his concrete bomb-proof courthouse – cut off from family and surrounded by guards – where he methodically constructs the complex evidence needed to bring down the 'Ndrangheta. The name Nicola Gratteri is now a powerful brand in the world of prosecutions globally.

Piera Aiello is another of pure heart. The young bride forced to marry the son of a Mafia boss only to see both murdered in front of her, Piera went on the run with her baby daughter and her seventeen-year-old friend Rita, who later suicided. Broken, not beaten, Piera battled on, moving from her convent hiding place after many years to a house, to a couch, to a spare bedroom, across the country for her twenty-seven years, too afraid to look back. While not technically confined, she still lived the life of a trapped victim of the Mafia process, with a vendetta hanging over her head. Her evidence jailed many, including the mayor of her town, ensuring the vendetta will always be with her.

Throughout her time in exile, Piera kept her face covered, and changed her name often, fearful of reprisals. But she and her daughter survived. Eventually, her (now) grown daughter and honest police encouraged her to turn her defiance into political power, so she put her name down for an upcoming election in the region she grew up in. As she campaigned, she moved quickly, shielding her face with a veil, which gave rise to the nickname 'ghost lady', until finally, in 2018, she won a seat in parliament. That night she took off her veil, and got down to work. No prizes for guessing, her mandate is to reform Italy from the Mafia. The next year she was recognised by BBC television as one of the Top 100 women of the world.

It's Gratteri's and Piera's stories that reinforce my faith in Italy and its people.

•

I adore the Sicilian people; I have nothing but the highest regard for the ordinary man and woman. They are such stoic, sometimes humorous and kindly people, who have treated me with nothing but the warmest hospitality. But they also carry a tribal burden, and it is written all over their faces; you see it in their eyes, on their foreheads. They hurt. There is a shade to some of their men – albeit a minority – that is not consistent with a contented community. They are angry and, like Mount Etna, explosive at times.

These men are capable of the most shocking crimes, and the island's people ache because of it. I firmly believe it's in the breeding of these men, perhaps a violent inheritance of too many invasions. Certainly, the same can be said for men of the 'Ndrangheta Mafia and the Camorra Mafia. They all seem to find it easy work to kill, like Roberto Cannavò once did. Few are able to truly repent.

Never lose sight of the fact that the Mafia is composed of individual men. Men who dissolve the bodies of people, including children, in acid. Men who chop up their fellow citizens into butcher-size pieces, bomb innocent passers-by, burn people alive, and drive into crowded marketplaces on the back of a motorcycle, to shoot their intended victims in the head. In recent times the 'Ndrangheta Mafia have been known to force their victims to drink hydrochloric acid – a more agonising death cannot be imagined. Or feeding a suspected woman *pentito* to the pigs. It's sociopathic men. The Mafia is nothing without sociopathic men. It cannot exist without these killer soldiers, for the head honchos are too weak to confront another man, to stand alone without a gun.

Confusingly, perhaps, Mafia violence sometimes seems to have no rhyme or reason to it. Perhaps it's just the luck of the draw, or someone being in the wrong place at the wrong time, or maybe just simple opportunity. The most shocking death can come upon someone for the most innocuous reason, yet other people who have had a real impact on the Mafia can go unscathed. Like the stoic Judge Alfonso Giordano, who handed out life sentences to the nineteen most senior Mafia heavyweights in all Sicily in the Maxi Trial of the 1980s, along-side Judge Pietro Grasso. Both spared. There is little doubt the twelve judges who originally refused the job of president of the court – before Giordano took it on – were of the belief that it would be a death sentence. Not so. Judge Giordano, who once said that he was 'only doing my duty', would go on to live a long life, dying 'serenely' in July 2021 at the ripe old age of ninety-two. Likewise, Judge Grasso is enjoying old age after an impressive post-judiciary career in politics. I think it's more a game of chance, call it Italian Roulette, where the odds are undefined, where winners become losers dependent only on the number of bullets in the chamber, balanced against the number of police bodyguards Mafia targets have access to. That seems to be the case with the tenacious young journalist Roberto Saviano, who, in 2006, published *Gomorrah*, a ground-breaking book on the *Camorra*

Mafia. A latter-day Giuseppe Impastato type, he was whisked away from Main Street, Italy, and encased in a police bodyguard cocoon, as his story sounded bells around the world on the ways of the contemporary Mafia.

None of the Mafia's abhorrent disregard for human life can be excused under the cheap plastic cover of loyalty to a club of men, delusional in their belief they are men of honour. Their dishonourable ways are no less than the behaviour of monsters, worthy of being hunted until captured, then jailed for the terms of their natural lives.

I also know that Italian women are not of the same ilk. They don't harbour this trait of violence; they are wonderful people who, until recently, stood by and suffered the ways of their men, or men they knew of, men down the street, around the corner. Too scared to lift their eyes from their worn shoes, they shuffled back into the workplace, their kitchens and laundries, taking their dismay with them, twisting their handkerchiefs into knots. But these same women are now in the forefront of confronting the Mafia problem. As the Bedsheets Committee showed, they have been able to effect change, and their efforts must be promoted at all costs.

Judge Giovanni Falcone once wrote that the Mafia would evolve and, ultimately, its run would end. The way I see it, the Mafia is still evolving, as it has done since 1860, and its end seems inconceivable. Especially if the 'Ndrangheta continue to take over most of the global rackets, as they are doing!

Have any of us made a difference? All I know is that we must keep trying to. The sum of deaths and barbarity at the hands of the Mafia, mentioned in this book, would only account for ten per cent of the overall total, a few grains in the hourglass of the Mafia. I cannot help wonder, as I approach this last page, what the Italian organised crime landscape might look like today had Francesco Crispi not donned a set of disguises – back in the days of unification – and run around the interior of Sicily stirring up headstrong low-lifes on a promise of land for their muscle.

While the atrocities of 9/11 in America saw a shift in policing budgets, intelligence and security priorities, moving resources and activity away from the fight against global *mafiosi*, we must, in memory of so many wretched souls, keep attacking them.

I liken it to coming home to your house to find that someone has left all the windows open, and the place is full of mosquitoes. Do you just drop your bag, slump in a chair and look at the cloud of mosquitoes, wondering how they got in? No, you get up, take preventative measures, do something: shut the windows, spray the rooms and make sure you eradicate them all, as soon as you can. One by one.

It's that simple! The fight must always go on.

ACKNOWLEDGEMENTS

Just thinking about undertaking a history of the Mafia is enough to give a writer nausea. I am grateful to my archival researchers, curators and translators who pushed through their endless red tape: Elena, Agata, Nicolo, Gabriella, Daniele, Anna-Lisa, Cinzia, and others. In particular, Enza, who, in my early days of writing produced a spark of information that set my curiosity alight.

And the alluring Anna of Luxembourg for translating very old text, over my most miserable winter – 2019.

I am indebted to my 'readers' who suffered my early drafts; Jeni, Margie, Mouse. And mostly to Melanie Myers, who gave me her blood, sweat and tears, to make my story more approachable.

I owe a gratitude to Hachette. To Fiona, Vanessa, Sophie and the always sympathetic Karen for the load you carried in getting my book to the public, and copyeditor John. And my literary lawyer, Shaun, and ex-manager Daniel for their welfare calls during my European COVID isolation, making sure I punched out the one hundred and twelve thousand words. And, my dedicated writers' agents, Gabriella and Diletta in Milan, for their great ideas.

Thanks to Dr Anna Sergi, Professor of Criminology at the University of Essex, for her preface. And to the supremely heroic investigative

Judges Alfonso Sabella and Nicola Gratteri, and the supremely charming Professor Giovanna Fiume. Also, the obliging Foreign Press Club members Josephine McKenna and Ron Fangel, and European correspondent Sarah Greenhalgh. And of course the encyclopedic – Sicilian based – historian Louis Mendola. Also, to Francesca Di Pasquale, for allowing me to infiltrate her extraordinary Gancia vaults to find much of my story.

Also, the Sicilian film director Salvo Cuccia, for his enthusiasm proffered over copious home-cooked meals and fine wine, and for convincing the Marasà family to trust me. And to the Marasà family themselves for bravely letting go of their secret and allowing me to publish their pictures, thereby placing the last missing piece in the vast Sicilian Mafia jigsaw puzzle, *Grazie mille*!

But most of all to the supremely dedicated Elena Stella and her culinary driven husband-come-tailor, Angelo.

Lastly, I recall the words of the wise Irish writer Edna O'Brien: 'When a writer wants to go away there are two reasons attached to it. One is adventure, danger, whatever. The other is to escape his own family. Writers do. They have to.' Thanks to gorgeous Chelsea (my only child) who has learnt to silently acquiesce to her sons' grandfather constantly running off on obsessive whims, in search of a truth to write about. The fact is I've been on the run since my nineteenth birthday. It's my own upbringing that I'm still running from, as well as my desire to find unblemished truth.

Colin McLaren
Mafiosothebook@protonmail.com

ENDNOTES

CHAPTER 3

1 President's speech of 20 June 2010 quoted in *dell'Unità d'Italia*. Held in the Istituto Gramsci, Palermo.
2 Michele Pantaleone, *Mafia and Drugs* (New York: Coward-McCann, 1966).

CHAPTER 4

1 Charles Stuart Forbes, *The Campaign of Garibaldi in the Two Sicilies* (Cambridge: Cambridge Library Collection, 2013; originally published 1861).
2 Don H. Doyle, *The Cause of All Nations* (New York: Basic Books, 2014), p. 113.
3 Paul Moses, *An Unlikely Union: The Love-Hate Story of New York's Irish and Italians* (New York: NYU Press, 2017), p. 20.
4 Ibid.
5 Walter Laqueur, *Guerrilla Warfare: The Historical and Critical Study* (New York: Little, Brown and Company, 1998).
6 Louis Mendola, *The Kingdom of Sicily 1130–1860* (New York: Trinacria Editions, 2015).
7 John A Garraty and Mark Carnes (eds), *American National Biography* (New York: Oxford University Press, 1999), p. 427.
8 Paul Moses, *An Unlikely Union: The Love-Hate Story of New York's Irish and Italians* (New York: NYU Press, 2017), pp. 14–16.
9 Louis Mendola, *The Kingdom of Sicily 1130–1860* (New York: Trinacria Editions, 2015).
10 Alberto Mario Banti, *il Risorgimento Italiano* (Rome: Editori Laterza, 1990).
11 Ibid.
12 Ibid.

13 George Macaulay Trevelyan, *Garibaldi: and the Thousand* (London: Longmans, Green, and Co., 1909), pp. 166–68. Held in Biblioteca dell'Archivio Centrale dello Stato, Rome.

14 Ibid.

15 Ibid.

16 Lucy Riall, *Garibaldi: Invention of a Hero* (London: Yale University Press, 2007).

17 George Macaulay Trevelyan, *Garibaldi: and the Thousand* (London: Longmans, Green, and Co., 1909), pp. 166–69.

18 Bert Casey, *The Double Life of Laurence Oliphant* (New York: Post Hill Press, 2015).

19 Erminio De Biase, *Britain against the Kingdom of the Two Sicilies* (Rome: Controcorrente, 2002).

20 Ibid.

21 Lucy Riall, *Garibaldi: Invention of a Hero* (London: Yale University Press, 2007).

22 Denis Mack Smith, *Victor Emanuel, Cavour and the Risorgimento* (London: Oxford University Press, 1971), pp. 175–76.

23 Ibid., p. 222.

24 *Garibaldi e la Sicilia Collezione Romeo* (Italy: Federico 11 Foundation, 1989).

25 Denis Mack Smith, *Victor Emanuel, Cavour and the Risorgimento* (London: Oxford University Press, 1971), citing letter to Nigra, 12 May 1860.

26 George Macaulay Trevelyan, *Garibaldi and the Thousand* (London: Longmans, Green, and Co., 1909).

27 Cavour telegram to Governor of Cagliari in Sardinia, 7–8 May 1860. Cited in D Mack Smith, 'Cavour's Attitude towards Garibaldi's Expedition to Sicily', *Cambridge Historical Journal*, Vol. 9, No. 3, 1949.

28 D Mack Smith, 'Cavour's Attitude towards Garibaldi's Expedition to Sicily', *Cambridge Historical Journal*, Vol. 9, No. 3, 1949, p. 369.

29 Admiral Persano Diary 1860, published 1869, pp. 14–15.

CHAPTER 5

1 *London Encyclopaedia, Universal Dictionary of Science, Art and Literature*, 1845.

2 Daniele Fiorentino, *Gli Stati Uniti e il Risorgimento d'Italia*, 1848–1901 (Italy: Gangemi Editore, 2014), pp. 165–67.

3 George Macaulay Trevelyan, *Garibaldi and the Thousand* (London: Longmans, Green, and Co., 1909), p. 245.

4 James Fentress, *Rebels and Mafiosi: Death in the Sicilian Landscape* (Ithaca: Cornell University Press, 2000), p. 129.

5 Opuscolo Bertani, Notes from interview in 1860. 'Risposta del Generale Turr all'' (Milan, 1874), pp. 8–12.

6 Denis Mack Smith, *Victor Emanuel, Cavour and the Risorgimento* (London: Oxford University Press, 1971), p. 202.

7 G. Oppo, *Garibaldi's Thousand*, p. 217.

8 Giovanni Fasanella and Antonella Grippo, *1861* (Rome: Sperling & Kupfer, 2011), p. 82.

9 Carlo Corsi, *Sicilia* (Milan: Kessinger Publishing, 1894), Chapter XIV.

10 Account cited from Denis Mack Smith, *Victor Emanuel, Cavour and the Risorgimento* (London: Oxford University Press, 1971), p. 199.

11 Ibid., p. 194.

12 Ibid., p. 255.

13 G Cesare Abba, *The Diary of a Garibaldi Thousand* (London: Oxford University Press, 1962), pp. 30–37.

14 Denis Mack Smith, *Victor Emanuel, Cavour and the Risorgimento* (London: Oxford University Press, 1971); widely reported in newspapers around the world and in many books.

15 Carlo Corsi, *Sicilia* (Milan: Kessinger Publishing, 1894), pp. 206–11.

16 Letter written to King Francesco of Naples, held in the archives, Istituto Gramsci, Palermo.

17 Carlo Corsi, *Sicilia* (Milan: Kessinger Publishing, 1894), pp. 210–14.

18 Letter from Massimo d'Azeglio to his colleague Michelangelo Castelli, 17 September 1860. Held in Archivio di Stato, Palermo.

19 Interview by author with Louis Mendola in Palermo, 5 March 2021.

20 Denis Mack Smith, *Victor Emanuel, Cavour and the Risorgimento* (London: Oxford University Press, 1971), p. 202.

21 Ibid.

22 Tommaso Palamenghi-Crispi, *Memoir of Francesco Crispi* (London: Nebu Press, 2010).

CHAPTER 6

1 'Italian Statesmen – Francesco Crispi', *Encyclopaedia Britannica* (London: 20 July 1998).

2 Christopher Duggan, *Francesco Crispi 1818–1901* (Oxford: Oxford University Press, 2002).

3 Ibid.

4 Packe, Michael St John, *Orsini, The Story of a Conspirator* (Boston, Toronto: Little Brown and Company, 1957), p. 282.

5 Raffaella Bonsignori, University of Rome Law Faculty, 'Happy Orsini and the Attack on Napoleon III', In *Libertà* newspaper, 2017.

6 Karl Marx, *New York Daily Tribune*, 8 August 1860, p. 6.

7 George Macaulay Trevelyan, *Garibaldi and the Thousand* (London: Longmans, Green, and Co., 1909), p. 152.

8 Ibid.

9 Luigi Genuardi, *Palermo* (Rome: Edizioni Tiber, 1929), pp. 196–99.

10 Nicola Giordano, 'An interesting unpublished letter from G. La Masa to G. Garibaldi (against Crispi and his coterie)', Palermo: Sicilian Society for Homeland History, 1970.

11 Held in Library of the Società Siciliana per la Storia Patria, created 1873, Piazza San Domenico 1, Palermo. In the files of the Risorgimento Collection.

12 Luigi Genuardi, *Palermo* (Rome: Edizioni Tiber, 1929), pp. 194–99.

13 Ibid.

14 Giovanni Fasanella and Antonella Grippo, *1861* (Rome: Sperling & Kupler, 2011), p. 82; Carlo Corsi, *Sicilia* (Milan: Kessinger Publishing, 1894).

15 Ibid.

16 Nisio Palmieri, *La Mafia fece l'Italia* (Italy: self-published, 2017).

17 George Macaulay Trevelyan, *Garibaldi and the Thousand* (London: Longmans, Green, and Co., 1909), pp. 152–54.

18 Ibid., pp. 148–54.

19 Giovanni Fasanella and Antonella Grippo, *1861* (Rome: Sperling & Kupler, 2011), p. 82; Carlo Corsi, *Sicilia* (Milan: Kessinger Publishing, 1894), p. 77.

20 Giuseppe Quatriglio, *A Thousand Years in Sicily: From the Arabs to the Bourbons* (Canada: Legas Publishing, 1922).

21 Lucy Riall, Garibaldi and the South (thesis, Yale University, 1990).

22 Giovanni Fasanella and Antonella Grippo, *1861* (Rome: Sperling & Kupler, 2011), pp. 55–56.

23 George Macaulay Trevelyan, *Garibaldi and the Thousand* (London: Longmans, Green, and Co., 1909), pp. 152–54.

24 Ibid., p. 154.

25 Ibid., p. 157.

26 Ibid.

27 Lucy Riall, *Garibaldi: Invention of a Hero* (London: Yale University Press, 2007), p. 210.

28 George Macaulay Trevelyan, *Garibaldi and the Thousand* (London: Longmans, Green, and Co., 1909), pp. 158–59.

29 Dr Christopher Duggan, *Francesco Crispi 1818–1901* (Oxford: Oxford University Press, 1988).

30 Lucy Riall, *Garibaldi: Invention of a Hero* (London: Yale University Press, 2007), p. 212.

31 George Macaulay Trevelyan, *Garibaldi and the Thousand* (London: Longmans, Green, and Co., 1909), pp. 160–61.

32 Lucy Riall, *Garibaldi: Invention of a Hero* (London: Yale University Press, 2007), p. 212.

33 Bert Casey, *The Double Life of Laurence Oliphant* (New York: Post Hill Press, 2015).

34 Palermo Security Reports: Filippo Antonio Gualterio, Sicily 1865. Archivio di Stato, Palermo.

35 Giuseppe Marino, *Storia della Mafia* (Rome: Newton Compton, 2006).

36 Palermo Security Reports: Filippo Antonio Gualterio, Sicily 1864. Held in Archivio di Stato, Palermo.

37 Maria Attanasio, *The Girl from Marseille* (Palermo: Sellerio Editore, 2018).

38 Ibid.

39 Letter by Cavour to Nigra, 12 July 1860, quoted in Denis Mack Smith, *The Making of Italy* (London: Palgrave Macmillan, 1988), p. 325.

40 Ibid., letter by Cavour to Nigra, 12 May 1860 (just before the Calatafimi attack).

CHAPTER 7

1 Antonio Traina, author of *Sicilian-Italian Dictionary* published in Palermo, 1868.

2 Carlo Gemelli, *Histoire de la Revolution Belge de 1830* (Nabu Press, 2012).

3 Giuseppe Petrai, *Novel of a Bandit* (Edoardo Perino, 1899).

4 Reported interview with nineteenth-century historian and professor Pasquale Villari.

5 Prefect's report, by Filippo Antonio Gualterio dated 25 April 1865, sent to Minister of Interior, p. 60. Archivio di Stato, Palermo.

6 Report by Magistrate Pietro Calà Ulloa of Trapani, 3 August 1838. Archivio di Stato, Palermo.

7 Professor Giuseppe Marino, University of Palermo, *Storia della Mafia* (Rome: Newton Compton, 2006).

8 Harry Hearder, *Italy in the Age of the Risorgimento, 1790–1870* (London: Routledge, 1983). Comment by Lord Brancaccio di Carpino in 1860, Palermo.

9 Giuseppe Cesare Abba, *Noterelle di uno dei Mille edite dopo vent'anni* (original edn, 1880; English translation, Oxford University Press, 1962).

10 Giuseppe Guerzoni, *Garibaldi: Volume 2* (Wentworth Press, 1882).

11 Ibid.

12 Professor Giuseppe Marino, University of Palermo, *Storia della Mafia* (Rome: Newton Compton, 2006).

13 Magistrate Diego Tajani, Palermo, 1865 (published in Francesco Benigno, 'Rethinking the origins of the Sicilian Mafia', *Crime, History and Societies*, Vol. 22, No. 1, 2018), pp. 107–30. And Michele Pantaleone, *Mafia, Yesterday and Today* (Turin: Giulio Einaudi Editore, 1966).

14 Comment by Minister of the Interior Giovanni Giolitti, late nineteenth century.

15 Report by the Parliamentary Commission of Inquiry of 1875. Authored by Duke Cesaro Colonna. Held in Archivio di Stato, Palerm .

16 Robert Holland, *Blue Water Empire* (New York: Penguin, 2012).

17 Comment made by Mayor of Palermo, Lucio Tasca.

18 Gaetano Falzone, *History of the Mafia*, (Italy: SF Flaccovio Editore).

19 Michele Pantaleone, *Mafia and Drugs* (New York: Coward-McCann, 1966).

20 Ignazio Coppola, 'I Vespri Siciliani', 31 May 2017. Online journal. www. inuovespri.it

21 Luigi Genaurdi, *Palermo* (Rome: Edizioni Tiber, 1929), p. 198.

22 Luigi Genuardi, *Palermo* (Rome: Edizioni Tiber, 1929), pp. 198–99.

23 Francesco Renda, *Storia Della Mafia [History of the Mafia]* (Palermo: Pietro Vittorietti, 1998), Chapters 1 & 2.

24 Giuseppe Rizzotto and Gaspare Mosca, *I Mafiusi de la Vicaria*, stage play, Palermo, 1863.

25 Interview by author with Pasquale Hamel, Historian and Director of Museo del Risorgimento Vittorio Emanuele, Palermo, 26 February 2021.

26 Baron Turrisi Colonna, Prefect of Palermo, 1861. Archivio di Stato, Palermo.

27 Ibid.

28 Ibid.

29 Prefect's 63-page report, *Public Security in Sicily*, for period 1863, printed in 1864, by Nicolo Colonna. Istituto Gramsci, Palermo.

30 Ibid.

CHAPTER 8

1 Denis Mack Smith, *Victor Emanuel, Cavour and the Risorgimento* (London: Oxford University Press, 1971), pp. 205–12.

2 Lucy Riall, *Sicily and the Unification of Italy* (Oxford: Clarendon Press, 1988), p. 71.

3 Luigi Genuardi, *Palermo* (Rome: Edizioni Tiber, 1929), p. 201.

4 Lucy Riall, *Garibaldi: Invention of a Hero* (London: Yale University Press, 2007), p. 213.

5 Charles Stuart Forbes, *The Campaign of Garibaldi in the Two Sicilies* (Cambridge: Cambridge University Press, 2013, first published 1861).

6 Henry Adams, *The Education of Henry Adams, an Autobiography* (New York: The Modern Library, 1909), pp. 82–94.

7 Ibid. p. 95.

8 Ibid. p. 94.

9 Ibid. p. 95

10 Ibid.

11 Luigi Genuardi, *Palermo* (Rome: Edizioni Tiber, 1929), pp. 199 and 201.

12 Raffaele D'Amato, *Roman Centurions* (Oxford: Osprey Publishing, 2012).

13 Giuseppe Marino, *Storia della Mafia* (Rome: Newton Compton, 2006).

14 Interview with Palermo historian and lawyer Luigi Mendola (Palermo, 5 January 2020).

15 Lucy Riall, *Sicily and the Unification of Italy* (Oxford: Clarendon Press, 1988).

16 Luigi Genuardi, *Palermo* (Italy Edizioni Tiber Rome, 1929), p. 199.

17 Giuseppe Marino, *Storia della Mafia* (Rome: Newton Compton, 2006).

18 Lucy Riall, *Garibaldi: Invention of a Hero* (London: Yale University Press, 2007), p. 213.

19 Denis Mack Smith, *Victor Emanuel, Cavour and the Risorgimento* (London: Oxford University Press, 1971), pp. 212–14.

20 Lucy Riall, *Garibaldi: Invention of a Hero* (London: Yale University Press, 2007), p. 214.

21 Denis Mack Smith, *Victor Emanuel, Cavour and the Risorgimento* (London: Oxford University Press, 1971), pp. 214–16.

22 Governor's reports from Termini and Corleone (Polizia), 19 June and 16 September 1860. Held in Stato Archivio di Palermo.

23 Denis Mack Smith, *Victor Emanuel, Cavour and the Risorgimento* (London: Oxford University Press, 1971), pp. 214–15.

24 Governor's reports, 20 July and 25 August 1860. Held in Stato Archivio di Palermo, Gangia.

25 Denis Mack Smith, *Victor Emanuel, Cavour and the Risorgimento* (London: Oxford University Press, 1971), pp. 214–16.

26 Luigi Genuardi, *Palermo* (Rome: Edizioni Tiber, 1929), 200.

27 Harry Hearder, *Italy in the Age of the Risorgimento, 1790–1870* (London: Routledge, 1983), Chapter 10.

28 Article in *Otago Witness* (New Zealand), 28 November 1862, p. 2. General Garibaldi is quoted throughout and his name is signed at the bottom of a short essay referenced in the article, titled 'Italy and Garibaldi'.

CHAPTER 9

1 *Il Trovatore*, 31 October 1860.

2 *Cronaca Contemporanea* in *Civilta Cattolicà*, October 1861.

3 Axel Korner, *America in Italy* (Oxford: Oxford University Press, 2017).

4 Alexandre Dumas, *The Memoirs of Garibaldi* (Livorno, Italy: L'Editore Santi Serraglini, 1860), Chapter 10.

5 Lucy Riall, *Garibaldi: Invention of a Hero* (London: Yale University Press, 2007), p. 246.

6 Ibid.

7 Alexandre Dumas, *The Memoirs of Garibaldi*, (Livorno, Italy: L'Editore Santi Serraglini, 1860), Chapter 10.

8 *London Illustrated News* quoted in Lucy Riall, *Garibaldi: Invention of a Hero* (London: Yale University Press, 2007), p. 246.

9 Charles Stuart Forbes, *The Campaign of Garibaldi in the Two Sicilies* (Cambridge: Cambridge University Press, 1861).

10 Ibid., p. 22.

11 Ibid., p. 28.

12 Ibid., p. 30.

13 'General Francesco Landi: a Neapolitan officer from Napoleonic times to the Risorgimento', published in Charles Stuart Forbes, *The Campaign of Garibaldi in the Two Sicilies* (Cambridge: Cambridge University Press, 1861), pp. 33–35.

14 Giuseppe Guerzoni, *Garibaldi: Volume 2* (Wentworth Press, 2017).

15 Louis Mendola, *The Kingdom of Sicily 1130–1860* (New York: Trinacria Editions, 2015).

16 Charles Stuart Forbes, *The Campaign of Garibaldi in the Two Sicilies* (Cambridge: Cambridge University Press, 1861), pp. 40–45.

17 Lucy Riall, *Garibaldi: Invention of a Hero* (London: Yale University Press, 2007), p. 254.

18 Ibid.

CHAPTER 10

1 Erminio De Biase, *Britain against the Kingdoms of the Two Sicilies* (Rome: Controcorrente, 2002).

2 Eugenio Di Rienzo, *The Kingdom of the Two Sicilies* (Rome: Rome University Essay, 2017).

3 Erminio De Biase, *Britain against the Kingdoms of the Two Sicilies* (Rome: Controcorrente, 2002).

4 Louis Mendola, *The Kingdom of Sicily 1130–1860* (New York: Trinacria Editions, 2015); reiterated in interview with Mendola in Palermo, January 2020.

5 Ibid.

6 Ibid.

7 Francesco Saverio Nitti, *Principi di Scienze delle Finanze*, (Pierro, 1903); Anteo d'Angio, 'La Situazione Italiana dal 1796–1870', published 1912; interview with Mendola in Palermo, January 2020.

8 Ibid.

9 Louis Mendola, *The Kingdom of Sicily 1130–1860* (New York: Trinacria Editions), 2015.

10 Ibid.

11 Ibid.

12 *Gazzetta Del Popolo*, published 1860.

13 Louis Mendola, *The Kingdom of Sicily 1130–1860* (New York: Trinacria Editions, 2015); reiterated in interview with Mendola in Palermo, January 2020.

14 Ibid., p. 290; reiterated in interview with Mendola in Palermo, January 2020.

15 Ibid., pp. 287–95; Reiterated in interview with Mendola in Palermo, January 2020.

16 Joseph T. Durkin, *Catholic Historical Review* (USA: American Catholic Historical Association, 1946).

17 Henry Nelson Gay, archived essay materials, Harvard University, pp. 352–55.

18 Louis Mendola, *The Kingdom of Sicily 1130–1860* (New York: Trinacria Editions, 2015).

19 Diary Note, *La Fine delle Due Sicilie e la Marina Britannica – Diario di un Ammiraglio 1859–61* by Admiral Sir George Rodney Mundy, British Fleet shadowing Garibaldi, May 1860, republished by Berisio Arturo, Napoli, 1966.

20 Ibid.

21 Ignazio Coppola, 'I Vespri Siciliani', 31 May 2017. Online journal. www.inuovespri.it

22 Ibid.; George Macaulay Trevelyan, *Garibaldi: and the Thousand* (London: Longmans, Green and Co., 1909), p. 311.

23 Erminio De Biase, *Britain against the Kingdoms of the Two Sicilies* (Rome: Controcorrente, 2002), pp. 129–30.

24 Ibid.

25 Henry Adams, *The Education of Henry Adams, an Autobiography* (New York: Modern Library, 1909).

26 George Macaulay Trevelyan, *Garibaldi: and the Thousand* (London: Longmans, Green and Co., 1909), p. 322.

27 'Cronache degli avvenimenti di Sicilia dal 4 aprile ai principi dell'agosto 1860 – la spedizione garibaldina e la rivoluzione siciliana vista dalla parte dei borboni,' Palermo 1863 – Reprint – *Editoriale Insubria*, pp. 143–44.

28 Internal Administration of Bourbonic Times, Folder 2318, sub folder 35.

29 Louis Mendola, *The Kingdom of Sicily 1130–1860* (New York: Trinacria Editions, 2015), p. 285.

30 Ibid.

31 'Italian Revolutionary La Farina,' *Encyclopaedia Britannica*. Also from letters of La Farina to Cavour published by Ausonio Franchi, titled *Epistolano di Giuseppe La Farina*, 1869.

32 Il Carteggio: private letters between Prime Minister Cavour and Nigra (1858–61) Held in Archivio di Stato, Genoa.

33 Chronicles, 'Conaca degli avvenimenti di Sicilia, da Aprile 1860–Marzo 1861' and 'Estratta da documenti, Italia, 1863'. Contains an official document by the Neapolitan army never published elsewhere or reported as cited in George Macaulay Trevelyan, *Garibaldi, and Cavour and the Risorgimento* (London: Longmans, Green and Co., 1909).

34 Karl Marx, *New York Daily Tribune,* 23 July 1860, p. 5.

35 *New York Times,* 31 July 1860, p. 1.

36 *Opinione National,* Turin, 31 July 1860, p. 3.

37 Interview with Louis Mendola in Palermo, January 2020.

38 Lucy Riall, *Garibaldi: Invention of a Hero* (London: Yale University Press, 2007), pp. 218–22.

39 George Macaulay Trevelyan, *Garibaldi and the Thousand* (London: Longmans, Green & Co., 1909).

40 Riall, p. 222.

41 Quoted in Lucy Riall, *Garibaldi: Invention of a Hero* (London: Yale University Press, 2007), p. 222.

42 Professor Lorenzo Nigro, *I Geni di Mozia* (Rome: il Vomere, 2020).

43 Maria Attanasio-Sellerio, *La Ragazza di Marsiglia [The Girl from Marseilles]* (Palermo: Sellerio, 2018).

44 Lucio Zinna, *Come un Sogno Incredible [Like an Incredible Dream]* (self-published, 2019).

45 Ibid.

46 Stanislao Nievo, *Il Prato in Fondo al Mare [A Meadow at the Bottom of the Sea]* (Rome: Newton & Compton, 1974).

47 Ibid.

48 Denis Mack Smith, 'Documentary Falsification and Italian Biography' in *History and Biography*, T.C.W. Blanning and David Cannadine (eds), (Cambridge: Cambridge University Press, 1996).

49 Lucy Riall, *Garibaldi: Invention of a Hero* (London: Yale University Press, 2007), p. 248.

50 Don Doyle, *The Cause of all Nations* (New York: Basic Books, 2015).

51 Ibid.

52 Ibid, p. 266.

53 Paul Moses, *An Unlikely Union: The Love-Hate Story of New York's Irish and Italians* (New York: NYU Press, 2017), pp. 20–22.

54 Ibid., p. 26.

55 Ibid., pp. 241–43.

56 Antonio Ciano, *Southern Italy 1830–1946* (Milan: Ali Ribelli Editore. 2019).

CHAPTER 12

1 James Fentress, *Rebels and Mafiosi: Death in the Sicilian Landscape* (Ithaca: Cornell University Press, 2000).

2 Michele Pantaleone, *Mafia, Yesterday and Today,* (Turin: Giulio Einardi Editore. 1966).

3 Prefecture Report of 1866, held in the Gancia Archivio Palermo.

4 Pantaleone, *Mafia, Yesterday and Today.*

5 Giuseppe Di Felice Giuffrida, *Mafia and Criminality in Sicily* (Palermo: Edizione History and Social Studies, 2014 (1900)).

6 Ibid.

7 Leopoldo Franchetti and Sidney Sonnino, *Political and Administrative Conditions of Sicily* (Florence: Vallecchi, 1925).

8 Michele Pantaleone, *Mafia and Drugs* (New York: Coward-McCann, 1966).

9 Ibid.

10 Thomas Monroe Pitkin and Francesco Cordasco, *The Black Hand* (Totowa, NJ: Littlefield, Adams, 1977).

11 Ibid.

CHAPTER 13

1 Michele Pantaleone, *Mafia and Drugs* (New York: Coward-McCann, 1966).

2 Giuseppe De Felice Giuffrida, *Maffia e Delinquenza in Sicilia* (Ragusa: Edizioni di Storia e Studi Sociali, 2014 (1900)).

3 Ibid., pp. 26–31.

4 David Critchley, *The Origins of Organized Crime in America* (New York: Routledge, 2008).

5 Thomas Monroe Pitkin and Francesco Cordasco, *The Black Hand* (Totowa, NJ: Littlefield, Adams, 1977).

6 Ibid.

7 Michele Pantaleone, *Mafia and Drugs* (New York: Coward-McCann, 1966).

8 Thomas Monroe Pitkin and Francesco Cordasco, *The Black Hand* (Totowa, NJ: Littlefield, Adams, 1977).

9 Ibid.

10 Michele Pantaleone, *Mafia and Drugs* (New York: Coward-McCann, 1966).

11 Thomas Monroe Pitkin and Francesco Cordasco, *The Black Hand* (Totowa, NJ: Littlefield, Adams, 1977).

12 Ibid.

13 Ibid, pp. 118–35.

14 Michele Pantaleone, *Mafia and Drugs* (New York: Coward-McCann, 1966).

15 NYPD Officer Down Memorial internet site, by NYPD in NYC. www.odmp. org

16 Metal plate in the Marina Gardens in Palermo, with details of where Joseph Petrosino died.

CHAPTER 14

1 Arrigo Petacco, *L'uomo della Provvidenza* (Turin: UTET Publishing), p. 190.

2 Gaetano Zingali, 'Liberalismo e Fascismo nel Mezzorgiorno d'Italia,' *International Affairs*, Volume 13, Issue 4, July–August 1934, pp. 593–94, doi. org/10.2307/2603447.

3 G. Barone, S. Lupo, R. Pallida and M. Saija, *Power and Society in Sicily in the Crisis of the Liberal State* (Rome: Pellicano Libri, 1999), pp. 101–109.

4 *Il Giornale Fascista* and *Il Corriere Italiano*, 5 May 1924.

5 Arrigo Petacco, *Il Prefect di Ferro [Story of the Iron Prefect]* (Milan: Mondadori, 1978).

6 Alfredo Cucco (politician who recruited Mori), quoted in article, *Il Mio Rogo*.

7 *D'Ora*, Sicilian newspaper printed in Palermo, article from 1928.

8 Extract by Cesare Mori, *Con la Mafia ai Ferri Corti* (Milan: Mondadori Press, 1932), p. 23.

9 G. Ingrasci and V. Sansone, *Sei Anni di Banditismo in Sicilia* (Milan: The Social Editions, 1950), pp. 36–9.

10 Cesare Mori, *Con la Mafia ai Ferri Corti* (Milan: Mondadori Press, 1932); in addition to countless police reports and media stories of that time.

11 Christopher Duggan, *Fascism and the Mafia* (New Haven: Yale University Press, 1985), pp. 106–15.

12 *Il Giornale di Sicilia*, Avvisatore article, 29 October 1925.

13 Il Salso report, *Il Giornale di Sicilia*, 26 January 1926, p. 5.

14 Salvatore Porto, *Mafia e Fascismo* (Sicily: Messina Armando Siciliano Editore, 2001).

15 Cesare Mori, *Con la Mafia ai Ferri Corti* (Milan: Mondadori Press, 1932), pp. 242–45, 292–94.

16 Richard Washburn Child, 'How Mussolini Smashed the Mafia', February 1926. Notes from research whilst ghost writing *My Biography* for Benito Mussolini, published 1928.

17 Newspaper reports, including *Il Giornale di Sicilia*, 1 May 1926.

18 Politician Alfredo Cucco, quoted in an article in *Il Mio Rogo,* 1926.

19 *Corriere della Sera*, 27 February 1926, p. 3.

20 Administrative report: Processo di Corleone, Verbali di Polizia. Held in Archivio di Stato di Palermo, pp. 10–14.

21 Ibid.

22 Newspaper report, *Il Giornale di Sicilia*, December 1926.

23 Processo di Corleone, Verbali di Polizia. Dibattimento and Istruttoria, Testi.

24 Charlotte Gower Chapman, *Storico di Milocca* (Cambridge, MA: Schenkman Pub., 1971).

25 Cesare Mori, *Con la Mafia ai Ferri Corti* (Milan: Mondadori Press, 1932), p. 367.

26 Ibid., pp. 39–47.

27 Benito Mussolini, *My Biography,* foreword by Richard Child (New York: Charles Scribner's Sons, 1928).

28 Cesare Mori, *Con la Mafia ai Ferri Corti* (Milan: Mondadori Press, 1932), p. 320.

29 *London Times*, January 1928, p. 3.

30 *Il Giornale di Sicilia*, October 1927.

31 Ibid. (throughout 1927).

32 *Il Giornale di Siciliana*, October 1927–June 1928.

33 Numerous letters of complaint to the Minister of the Interior alleging torture in February 1927, cited and quoted by Michele Pantaleone, *Mafia e Politica* (Turin: Einaudi, 1962), pp. 56–8.

34 Report by Ambassador Sir Ronald Graham to A. Chamberlain, 1 August 1928.

35 Cesare Mori, *The Last Struggle With the Mafia* (Black House, 1933), p. 210.

36 Diary by Tina Whitaker, April 1928. Original held in Whitaker Family Trust. Quoted in Raleigh Trevelyan, *Princes Under the Volcano* (London: Faber & Faber, 2012), p. 410.

37 *Il Giornale di Sicilia*, March 1929, p. 3.

38 Telegram from Mussolini to Mori, 23 June 1929. Made public. Cited in Christopher Duggan, *Fascism and the Mafia* (New Haven: Yale University Press, 1985), p. 160.

CHAPTER 15

1 *Associazione per Delinquere* document, written by head of Carabinieri and forty-six officers, 1938, detailing Mafia activity from 1926 to 1938; 180 pages, with signatures. Locked in vault at Gancia Archivio di Stato, Palermo.

2 *Associazione per Delinquere* document, p. 70.

3 Ibid., p. 13.

4 Ibid., p. 14.

5 Prosecutors' report on investigation into Marasà and gang, marked as 4135, pp. 360–64, of 1942, held in Gancia Archivio di Stato, Palermo.

6   *Associazione per Delinquere* document, written by head of Carabinieri and forty-six officers, 1938, detailing Mafia activity from 1926 to 1938; 180 pages, with signatures. Locked in vault at Gancia Archivio di Stato, Palermo, pp. 16–18.

7   Prosecutors' report on investigation into Marasà and gang, marked as 4135, pp. 360–64, of 1942, held in Gancia Archivio di Stato, Palermo. Also *Associazione per Delinquere* document, p. 16.

8   Ibid., p. 80.

9   Ibid., pp. 81–2.

10 Ibid.

CHAPTER 16

1   Aristide Spanò, *Faccia a Faccia con la Mafia [Face to Face with the Mafia]* (Milan: Arnoldo, Mondadore Editore, 1978), p. 29.

2   Three-page Essay, 'L'Unita', *Sicilia Rossa*, 30 December 1937, held in Istituto Gramsci, Palermo.

3   Ibid.

4   Procedimenti Penali Anno 1942, folder 4135, Allegata 115, pp. 421–23. Held in Gancia Archivio di Stato, Palermo.

5   Ibid.

6   Ibid.

7   Ibid., Folder 620–27, pp. 1–175 report of Arrest Strategy.

8   Ibid., pp. 817–18.

9   Ibid., document No. 1029, Order by the Court to not seek Ernesto Marasà'.

10 Essay, *La voce della Sicilia: quotidiano del popolo siciliano* on 28 February 1946, held in the Istituto Gramsci, Palermo.

11 Commissioner Cosenza, Questure of Palermo, report 35538–2, 8 May 1947.

12 Ibid.

CHAPTER 17

1   David Critchley, *The Origins of Organised Crime in America* (New York: Routledge, 2008), Chapter 7.

2   *Associazione per Delinquere* document, written by head of Carabinieri and forty-six officers, 1938, detailing Mafia activity from 1926 to 1938, 180 pages, with signatures. Locked in vault at Gancia Archivio in Palermo.

3   Francesco Renda, *Storia Della Mafia [History of the Mafia]* (Palermo: Pietro Vittorietti, 1998).

4   Michele Pantaleone, *Mafia and Drugs* (New York: Coward-McCann, 1966).

5   Raymond Chandler, notes of meeting with 'Lucky' Luciano, copy held by film producer Weiland Shutz-Keil, in Marsala, Sicily. Also notes published in *The London Magazine*.

6   Michele Pantaleone, *Mafia and Drugs* (New York: Coward-McCann, 1966).

7   *Daily Mail* (UK), 5 November 2010.

8   Francesco Forgione, *Mafia Export* (Milan: Dalai Editore, 2009).

9   Michele Pantaleone, *Mafia and Drugs* (New York: Coward-McCann, 1966).

10 The US Senate Special Committee to Investigate Organized Crime in Interstate Commerce, also known as the Kefauver Committtee report, final outcome, S.Res.202, 1951, Palala Press, USA.

11 Michele Pantaleone, *Mafia and Drugs* (New York: Coward-McCann, 1966).

CHAPTER 18

1 Interview with friend of Gotti and author Andrea Giovino (2018). Recorded on film by Colin McLaren in February 2018, in New Jersey, USA.

CHAPTER 19

1 *Le Monde*, 13 July 2016.
2 Article in *La Repubblica*, 4 January 2010.
3 Ibid.
4 *The Guardian*, 24 April 2001.
5 Interview with correspondent Ronald Fangel, who worked on Mafia stories in Rome from the 1980s for thirty years with press Agenzia ANSA. From his notes made after discussions with his confidential police contacts.
6 *Our Godfather*, directed by Mark Franchetti and Andrew Meier (London: Black Earth Films and Phenomena Films, 2019), DVD (interview with Tommaso Buscetta).
7 Ibid.
8 Ibid.
9 Ibid.
10 Ibid.

CHAPTER 20

1 Interview with Ronald Fangel of Agenzia ANSA and his notes.
2 *The Guardian*, 27 May 2017, p. 4.
3 Alexander Stille, *Excellent Cadavers* (New York: Vintage, 1995), p. 404.
4 Running sheet of Falcone security crew the day he died, held in the National Archive in Palermo.
5 Borsellino's speech at Falcone's funeral was widely reported on and quoted in newspapers across Italy at the time.
6 Work diary of Judge Borsellino held in the National Archive of Palermo.
7 Ibid.
8 Roberto Alajmo, *Un Lenzuolo Contro la Mafia [A Sheet Against the Mafia]* (Gelke, 1992).
9 Ibid.
10 Professor Giovanna Fiume. Interview in Palermo on 2 March 2021. A recollection of her time with the Bedsheets Committee
11 Professor Giovanna Fiume. Interview in Palermo on 2 March 2021. A recollection of her time with Judge Falcone and the Bedsheets Committee.
12 Ibid.
13 Roberto Alajmo, *Un Lenzuolo Contro la Mafia [A Sheet Against the Mafia]* (Gelke, 1992). Confirmed by interview with Professor Fiume.
14 Ibid.
15 Ibid.
16 Ibid.
17 Robin Pickering-Iazzi, *Dead Silent: Life Stories of Girls and Women Killed by the Italian Mafias, 1878–2018* (Milwaukee: University of Wisconsin, 2019), p. 147.

CHAPTER 21

1 Interview by author with correspondent Ronald Fangel, who worked on Mafia stories in Rome from the 1980s for thirty years with press Agenzia ANSA. From his notes made after discussions with his confidential police contacts.
2 Interview by author with Judge Sabella in Rome on 11 March 2021.
3 Ibid.
4 Ibid.
5 Ibid.
6 Ibid.
7 Ibid. Plus narrative in documentary, by Judge Sabella, with Michele Fiascaris, 2014.
8 Interview by author with Judge Sabella in Rome, 11 March 2021.
9 Ibid.
10 Ibid.
11 Ibid.
12 Interview by author with Judge Alfonso Sabella, 2 June 2021.
13 Interview of Giovanni Brusca on tape, by filmmaker Mosco Levi Bocault, first aired on Italian TV on 2 June 2021.

CHAPTER 22

1 Interview by author with Australian senior journalist Sarah Greenhalgh, who attended the facility to interview Judge Nicola Gratteri on 2 July 2021, and filmed his courthouse. Interview transcription supplied to me in part along with vision of the courthouse.
2 Ibid.
3 Ibid.
4 Ibid.
5 Ibid.
6 Roberto Saviano, *Gomorrah* (London: Macmillan, 2007).
7 Colin McLaren, *Infiltration* (Carlton: Melbourne University Press, 2008).
8 The red report, *Associazione per Delinquere*, final pages, outcome. Only copy held in Archivio di Gancia, di Palermo.
9 Umberto Santino, *Mafia and Antimafia: A Brief History* (Palermo: Bloomsbury, 2008).
10 Ibid.

MY LAST BULLETS

1 Maurizio Vallone, quote to Bloomberg News, 8 March 2021, from article emanating from *Washington Post* story of 6 March 2021.
2 From the screenplay by Roberto Benigni, *Johnny Stecchino*, which premiered in Rome in 1991.

INDEX

Colin McLaren was one of Australia's finest detectives; he travelled the world on high-end investigations during the 1980s and 1990s. He faced down the underbelly of Australian crime and his work has been the subject of many police genre documentaries and television series. A film of his own life, based on his hugely successful first book *Infiltration*, the true story of his efforts as an undercover cop, was made in 2011. Colin writes constantly and is a regular advisor to TV and film productions. His book on John F. Kennedy's death, *JFK: The Smoking Gun*, was a bestseller. He is a judge on the US Emmy Awards and highly respected in the US as well as Australia for his investigative journalism. His style of writing is to burrow down in archives and hidden sources to find the indisputable facts to tell the undeniable truth.